Country Locator for Volume 9

MALAYSIA, SINGAPORE, BRUNEI, AND THE PHILIPPINES

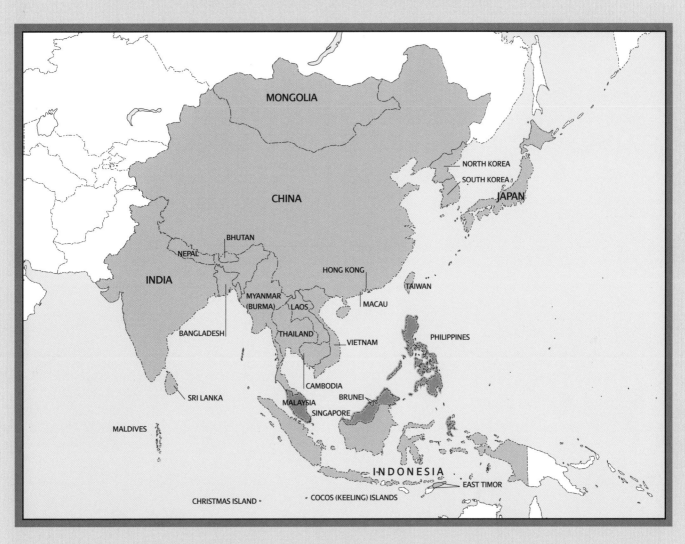

The following countries and political regions are covered in the eleven-volume encyclopedia *World and Its Peoples: Eastern and Southern Asia*. Detailed discussion of the following can be found in the volumes indicated in parentheses.

Bangladesh (3,4)
Bhutan (3,4)
Brunei (9)
Cambodia (6)
China (1,2)
Christmas Island (10)
Cocos (Keeling)
   Islands (10)

East Timor (10)
Hong Kong (1,2)
India (3,4)
Indonesia (10)
Japan (8)
Laos (6)
Macau (1,2)
Malaysia (9)

Maldives (3,4)
Mongolia (1,2)
Myanmar (Burma) (5)
Nepal (3,4)
North Korea (7)
Philippines (9)
Singapore (9)
South Korea (7)

Sri Lanka (3,4)
Taiwan (1,2)
Thailand (5)
Vietnam (6)

EASTERN and SOUTHERN ASIA

9

MALAYSIA, SINGAPORE, BRUNEI, AND THE PHILIPPINES

Marshall Cavendish
Reference
New York

SET CONSULTANTS

Anne Blackburn, Department of Asian Studies, Cornell University, Ithaca, New York

Ellen Fuller, Department of Sociology, University of Virginia, Charlottesville

Jeffrey E. Hanes, Center for Asian and Pacific Studies, University of Oregon, Eugene

Suvir Kaul, Department of South Asian Studies, University of Pennsylvania, Philadelphia

Philip Kelly, York Centre for Asian Research, York University, Toronto

Mike Parnwell, Department of East Asian Studies, University of Leeds, England

Ronald Skeldon, Department of Geography, University of Sussex, Brighton, England

VOLUME CONSULTANTS

Alfred McCoy, Department of History, University of Wisconsin-Madison

Andrew Ng, School of Arts and Sciences, Monash University Malaysia, Petaling Jaya, Selangor. Malaysia

Aihwa Ong, Department of Anthropology, University of California, Berkeley

Anthony Reid, Asia Research Institute, National University of Singapore

Thomas Leinbach, Department of Geography, University of Kentucky, Lexington

WRITERS

Michael Barr, School of History, Philosophy, Religion, and Classics, University of Queensland, Brisbane, Australia

Rachel Bean, Church Stretton, England

Mark T. Berger, History Department, University of British Columbia, Vancouver, Canada

Chang Chiou Yi, Institute of Southeast Asian Studies, Singapore

Terence Chong, Institute of Southeast Asian Studies, Singapore

Christopher Dent, Department of East Asian Studies, University of Leeds, England

Lawrence Douglas, London, England

Michelle Felton, School of the Environment, University of Leeds, England

Luisa Igloria, Department of English, Old Dominion University, Norfolk, Virginia

Chris McNab, Swansea, Wales

James Martin, London, England

Emmanuel K. Mbobi, Department of Geography, Kent State University, Canton, Ohio

Terry E. Miller, The Hugh A. Glausner School of Music, Kent State University, Ohio

Jürgen Neuberg, School of Earth and Environment, University of Leeds, England

Ian Proudfoot, Faculty of Asian Studies, Australian National University, Canberra

Mina Roces, School of History, University of New South Wales, Sydney, Australia

Karen Romano-Young, Bethel, Connecticut

Henry Russell, London, England

Andrew J. Wood, Sandbach, England

Marshall Cavendish Corporation
99 White Plains Road
Tarrytown, New York 10591-9001

www.marshallcavendish.us

© 2008 Marshall Cavendish Corporation

Created by **The Brown Reference Group plc**

Library of Congress Cataloging-in-Publication Data

World and its peoples : Eastern and southern Asia.
    p. cm.
    Includes bibliographical references and indexes.
    ISBN 978-0-7614-7631-3 (set) -- ISBN 978-0-7614-7632-0 (v. 1) -- ISBN 978-0-7614-7633-7 (v. 2) -- ISBN 978-0-7614-7635-1 (v.3) -- ISBN 978-0-7614-7637-5 (v. 4) -- ISBN 978-0-7614-7638-2 (v. 5) -- ISBN 978-0-7614-7639-9 (v. 6) -- ISBN 978-0-7614-7640-5 (v. 7) -- ISBN 978-0-7614-7641-2 (v. 8) -- ISBN 978-0-7614-7642-9 (v. 9) -- ISBN 978-0-7614-7643-6 (v. 10) -- ISBN 978-0-7614-7645-0 (v. 11)
    1. East Asia. 2. Southeast Asia. 3. South Asia.

    DS504.5.W67 2007
    950--dc22
                                                            2007060865

Printed in China

12 11 10 09 08 07 1 2 3 4 5

PHOTOGRAPHIC CREDITS
Front Cover: **Alamy:** Tibor Bognar (main image); **Tourism Malaysia 2004:** (right and left).
Alamy: Tibor Bognar 1218, 1230, Jon Bower 1231; Jenny Matthews 1286; **Brown Reference Group:** Alastair Gourlay 1287; **Corbis:** 1180, Paul Almasy 1179, 1249, 1258, Dave Bartruff 1265, Ciaro Cortes IV/Reuters 1244, Erik De Castro /Reuters 1254, Ho/Reuters 1198, Catherine Karnow 1257, Earl & Nazima Kowall 1284, Bob Krist 1283, Kevin R. Morris 1282, Carl & Ann Purcell 1280, Steve Raymer 1279, Reuters 1232, 1233, 1281, Kevin Schafer 1172, Greg Smith 1246, Stapleton Collection 1176, Nik Wheeler 1264, Michael S Yamashita 1201, 1202, 1205, 1206, 1260; **Eye Ubiquitous/Hutchison:** Derek Cattani 1194/1195, T. E. Clark 1163, Robert Francis 1160/1161, 1166, 1199, 1206, 1268, Dr Jon Fuller 1253, Jon Hicks 1285, Hilly Jakes 1239, Michael Macintyre 1270, Jeffrey A Paul 1175, Paul Seheult 1222; **Getty Images:** Time Life Pictures 1278; **Image State:** Anup et Manoj Shah/Jacana/Hoa-Qui 1173; **Mary Evans Picture Library:** 1183; **Photos.com:** 1288; **Robert Hunt Picture Library:** 1186, 1189, 1191, 1245; **Superstock:** 1227, Age Fotostock 1237, 1252; **Sylvia Cordaiy Picture Library:** K Harrison 1225, Carola Holmberg 1274, Hilary Scudder 1168, Julian Worker 1276; **Topham:** Michael J Doolittle/The Image Works 1158, Boyd Norton/The Image Works 1238, Photri 1165, Charles Steiner/The Image Works 1271; **Tourism Malaysia 2004:** 1153, 1212, 1214, 1216, 1219, 1220, 1221, 1229, 1236; **Travel Ink:** Abbie Enock 1262, 1263, David Guyler 1255.

For **MARSHALL CAVENDISH**
Publisher: Paul Bernabeo
Project Editor: Stephanie Driver
Production Manager: Alan Tsai

For **THE BROWN REFERENCE GROUP**
Project Editor: Clive Carpenter
Deputy Editors: Felicity Crowe, Paul Thompson, Aruna Vasudevan
Design: Focus Publishing
Cartography: Encompass Graphics Ltd
Picture Research: Clare Newman
Art Editor: Lynne Ross
Senior Managing Editor: Tim Cooke
Indexer: Kay Ollerenshaw

CONTENTS

Geography and Climate

Malaysia, Singapore, Brunei, and the Philippines are four very different nations. The Philippines is an archipelago of more than 7,000 islands that contains a considerable variety of landscape. Malaysia is a developing nation that has two separate "wings:" the southern part of the Malay Peninsula on the mainland of Southeast Asia and the northern sector of the island of Borneo. Singapore is a developed city-state, while Brunei is an oil-rich sultanate.

THE SULU SEA

The Sulu Sea, which lies between the Philippines and Malaysia, has an area of around 100,000 square miles (250,000 sq. km). Bordered by the Malaysian state of Sabah in the south, the Philippine island of Mindanao and the Sulu Archipelago in the east, Palawan in the northwest, and the Visayan Islands in the north, the Sulu Sea is characterized by steep coasts. The sea formed when a large block of land dropped along a line of faults that are now marked by cliffs along the coastlines. Apart from the small coral Cagayan Islands and the volcanic Cagayan Sulu group, the sea contains very few islands. In modern times, the Sulu Sea is an important fishing ground.

THE MULU CAVES

The Mulu Caves, in Gunung Mulu National Park in the interior of Eastern Malaysia between the Penambo Range and Brunei, are the largest caves in the world. Water has eroded limestone to form huge chambers and passages that stretch for more than 188 miles (300 km). The vast Sarawak Chamber, the world's largest cave chamber, is 2,300 feet (700 m) long and 230 feet (70 m) high and it has a ground area greater than 16 football fields. Deer Cave, a cave passage. is 1 mile (1.6 km) long and is partly lit by natural light from above; it is a routeway for hundreds of thousands of bats every evening as they emerge at dusk to feed. It is often claimed that the corridor of Deer Cave could house five rows of eight Boeing 747 airplanes parked nose to tail. Lang's Cave, the third-largest cave in the system, is famous for its spectacular stalactites and stalagmites. The Mulu Caves are a major tourist attraction.

MOUNT APO

At 9,692 feet (2,954 m) above sea level, Mount Apo in the island of Mindanao is the highest peak in the Philippines. Mount Apo, which overlooks Davao City, is an inactive volcano; there have been no eruptions in historical times. Apo means "the grandfather," a reference to its white peak. From a distance it appears to be snowcapped, but the color derives from a crust of sulfur around the summit. The mountain is sacred to local people who follow traditional religions. At the center of a national park, Mount Apo is an important reserve for fauna and is the only remaining home of the Philippine eagle.

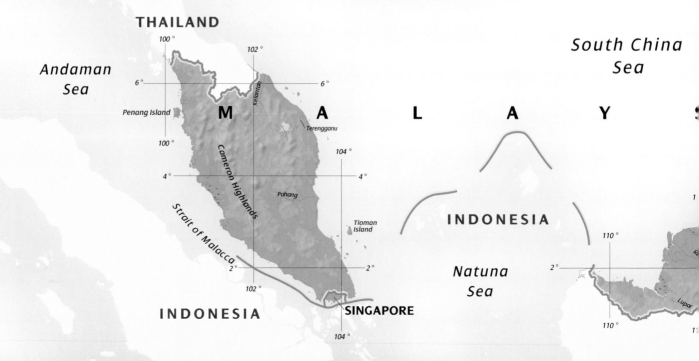

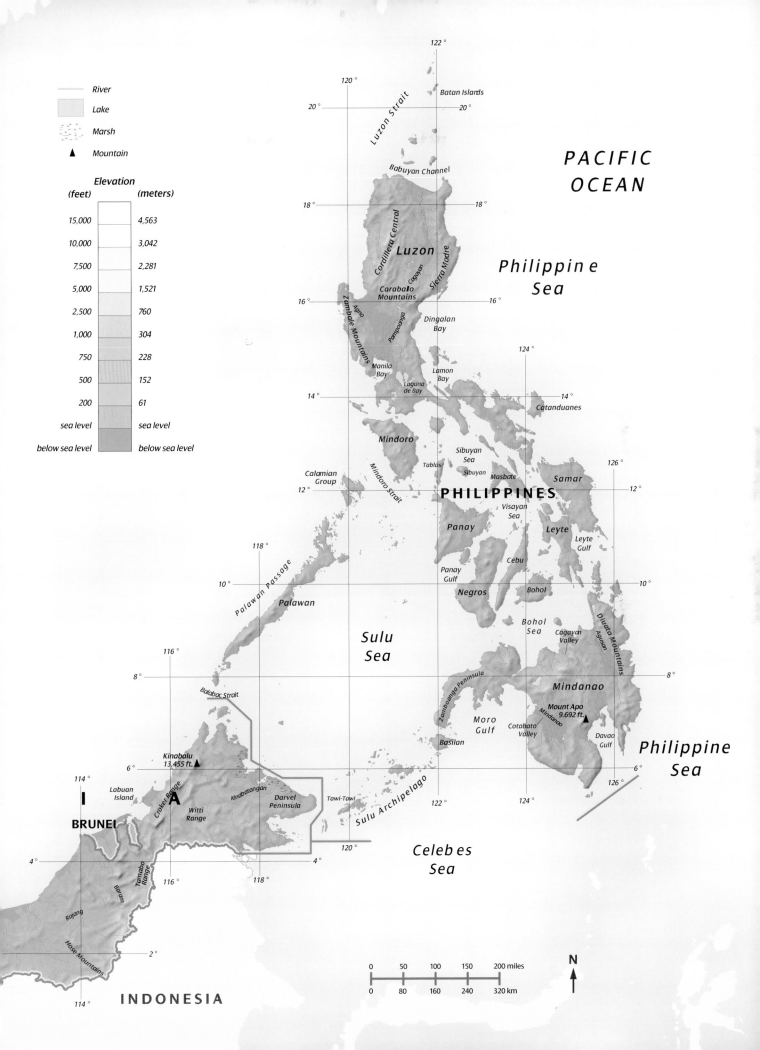

The Land of Malaysia, Singapore, Brunei, and the Philippines

Malaysia, Singapore, Brunei, and the Philippines are disparate nations beside the South China Sea in Southeast Asia. The sea is important throughout the region as a means of transportation, a source of fish and other resources, and as a moderating influence upon temperature. The four countries of the region experience a similar hot and humid tropical climate.

Malaysia comprises two major physical regions: Peninsular Malaysia and Eastern Malaysia. Together they form a nation about the same size as the state of New Mexico. The two broad regions contain some diversity of landscape, with coastal plains and interior highlands. Physically, the island of Singapore may be treated as an extension of Peninsular Malaysia, while Brunei is part of the same physical region as Eastern Malaysia. Many more distinct physical regions are generally identified in the Philippines than in Malaysia, although three major

regions are often delineated: Luzon and the northern islands, the Visayan Islands in the center of the archipelago, and Mindanao and the southern islands.

MALAYSIA

Malaysia is the only country that includes territory both on the mainland of Southeast Asia and in the islands that stretch between the Asian continental mass and Oceania. Mainland Malaysia is commonly referred to as Peninsular Malaysia or, less often, as West Malaysia. Mainland Malaysia occupies the

Granite on the top of Mount Kinabalu, Malaysia's highest peak, is marked with deep scratches eroded by glaciers.

southern half of the Malay Peninsula—the northern part comprises Myanmar (Burma) and Thailand. The peninsula accounts for 40 percent of Malaysia's landmass. Peninsular Malaysia is bordered by Thailand to the north and the island-nation of Singapore (to which it is connected by a causeway) to the south, the Strait of Malacca to the west, and the South China Sea to the east. The other wing of Malaysia, known as Eastern Malaysia, comprises the states of Sabah and Sarawak along the northern coast of the island of Borneo, which Malaysia shares with Indonesia and Brunei.

PENINSULAR MALAYSIA

Peninsular Malaysia is about 500 miles (800 km) from north to south and, at its widest, around 200 miles (320 km) from east to west. The peninsula, which has a tropical climate, is largely mountainous, with more than one-half of the total area over 500 feet (about 150 m) above sea level.

Several rugged ranges with elevations rising to over 7,000 feet (about 2,130 m) run more or less parallel from north to south through the peninsula, forming a mountainous core that is cooler than the lowlands. The central ranges include the 300-mile (480 km) long Main Range, the highest ground in Peninsular Malaysia. The range is largely granite and other igneous rocks (rocks formed when magma and volcanic lava cools). The Cameron Highlands, part of the Main Range, is a popular hill resort whose cooler temperatures attracted British residents in the colonial era (before 1957). In modern times, the Cameron Highlands grow tea, flowers, salad vegetables, and orchard fruits.

In parts of central and northern Peninsular Malaysia, deposits of limestone have been eroded to form caves, underground passages, and steep-sided narrow valleys. These landforms are all features of a karst landscape (a characteristic eroded limestone region). The karst regions typically have stunted trees and bushes and are sparsely populated.

Alluvial plains border the uplands to the east and the west. To the east, the lowlands are discontinuous, and higher ground reaches the South China Sea in the northern and southern districts of the state of Terengganu. The greatest extent of fertile plains occurs where river valleys reach the sea; lowlands extend around the mouths of the Kelantan, Terengganu, and Pahang rivers, forming the most populated regions of the three states of the same name. The main cities along or near the east coast are, from north to south, Kota Baharu, Kuala Terengganu, and Kuantan, all of which are state capitals.

The coastal plain along the Strait of Malacca in the west is wider, in places up to 50 miles (80 km) across. The western coastal lowland is the most densely populated region of Malaysia. Ports developed beside the Strait of Malacca, one of the busiest shipping lanes in the world, and in the nineteenth century deposits of tin were mined and rubber plantations were worked. In modern times, all of Malaysia's major cities are in the region, including Kuala Lumpur, the legislative capital and the

Singapore

Singapore is an island located at the narrowest point of the Strait of Malacca at the tip of the Malay Peninsula. The Singapore Channel forms the shortest sea route between India and China, and a strategic position, with a natural deep-water harbor, helped Singapore to develop as one of the world's major ports. The city-state of Singapore includes a number of smaller islands, but Singapore Island itself comprises more than 90 percent of the national territory. The tropical island has a varied topography, and its high temperatures are moderated by its proximity to the sea. Rainfall is heavy, and the greatest natural hazard is local flash flooding, the threat of which has increased as buildings and paved roads have replaced natural vegetation; large areas of the island are now covered with concrete. Despite heavy precipitation, Singapore still imports water from reservoirs in upland Johor state in Malaysia; the water comes through a canal under the causeway that links Singapore with the Malaysian city of Johor Baharu.

The center of Singapore Island contains a number of rounded granitic hills, including the city-state's highest point, Bukit Timah (545 feet or 166 m). In the western and southwestern parts of the island, a series of ridges that are low but steep-sided in places trend northwest to southeast. The eastern part of the island is flat, with alluvial soils into which streams have cut steep-sided gullies. The island is drained by a large number of short waterways, some of which flow through mangrove swamps, lagoons, or broad estuaries to the sea. Singapore was originally covered by tropical rain forest and mangrove swamps, but most of the island is now covered by urban development and only around 2.5 percent of the area is countryside. The immediate catchment areas of three large reservoirs in the center of the island preserve a portion of the original tropical forest. Since the mid-1960s, the size of the island has increased by 44.7 square miles (115.7 sq. km) through reclamation projects. At the same time, hills have been flattened, wetlands drained and filled, and many of the neighboring islets and reefs enlarged and joined to form new, larger islands in an effort to increase the land available for development.

nation's main industrial and commercial center; the Kuala Lumpur metropolitan area was home to 2,220,000 people at the 2000 Malaysian census. Kuala Lumpur's central position in the peninsula led to its choice as capital. Today, the city has engineering industries (including railroad engineering), cement and building construction industries, sawmills, and iron foundries, as well as a range of modern high-tech industries (including electrical and electronic engineering and computer assembly) and banking and finance. Other large cities in the region include the port of Kelang (Malaysia's principal port), the industrial city of Shah Alam (the home of automobile manufacture in Malaysia), the former mining center of Ipoh, and the port of George Town, which is sited on the island of Penang off the northwestern coast of Peninsular Malaysia. The rapidly expanding city of Johor Baharu lies at the southern tip of the peninsula, facing Singapore.

Brunei

Brunei lies on the northwest coast of Borneo, facing the South China Sea. It has a land area of 2,226 square miles (5,765 sq. km) and had a population of 333,000 at the 2001 Bruneian national census. Sarawak, in Eastern Malaysia, divides Brunei into two; the small eastern part is Temburong District, which is home to fewer than 9,000 people. The larger western sector of Brunei contains the national capital, Bandar Seri Begawan (whose metropolitan area was home to 230,000 people in 2001), and the offshore oil and natural gas fields that are the principal source of the sultanate's revenue. Oil wealth transformed the nation's economy in the second half of the twentieth century.

Forested, inland western Brunei is home to indigenous groups such as the Iban, Tutong, Kedayan, and Dusun. Most of western Brunei has swampy mangrove-covered coastal plains that are divided by alluvial valleys. Hilly regions cover much of the interior, which rise to about 900 feet (275 m). Behind a broad coastal plain, eastern Brunei is mountainous, reaching 6,070 feet (1,850 m) at Bukit Pagon, the country's highest peak. The Belait, Tutong, and Brunei-Muara rivers drain western Brunei, while most of eastern Brunei drains toward the Temburong River. Primary tropical jungle covers about 75 percent of the country, which contains some of the best preserved mangroves in the region.

EASTERN MALAYSIA

Eastern Malaysia—the large states of Sabah and Sarawak in northern Borneo, plus the small island of Labuan—has three broad physical regions: coastal plains adjoin a region of hills and valleys, inland from which rises a rugged mountainous core with elevations averaging 4,000 and 7,000 feet (around 1,220 to over 2,130 m) above sea level.

Sarawak, a larger southern state that is about the same size as the U.S. state of Alabama, is mainly lowland in the south around the estuary of the Rajang River, where mangrove swamps stretch some 150 miles (240 km) along the coast. Kuching, the capital and only large city in Sarawak, lies in the far southwestern part of the state. Farther north, the coastal lowlands are restricted by a region of plateaus that are dissected by river valleys. Inland, mountains rise in a series of ranges that trend either north-south or southwest-northeast. The ranges include the Boven Kapuas Mountains in the south, the Hose Mountains in the center, and the Tamabo and Penambo ranges in the north. The highest ranges form the border between Sarawak and Kalimantan, the Indonesian part of Borneo. Many of the mountains of Sarawak are jagged, heavily eroded limestone peaks, the most spectacular of which are the serrated Pinnacles in Gunung Mulu National Park in northern Sarawak. The park also contains the Mulu Caves, the world's largest cave chambers.

Northern Sarawak divides the nation of Brunei, which is physically part of Eastern Malaysia, into two unequal parts. The Crocker Range runs parallel to the coast through northern

Sarawak and Brunei into the Malaysian state of Sabah in north Borneo. Sabah has three indented coasts: a west coast along the South China Sea, a northeast coast along the Sulu Sea, and a southeast coast along the Celebes Sea. There is little lowland along the coasts of Sabah. In the extreme northeast, a mountainous core contains Mount Kinabalu (13,455 feet or 4,101 m), the highest peak in Malaysia. Sabah's inland mountainous region is formed of plateaus and ranges that are deeply cut by ravines. The only major city in Sabah, Kota Kinabalu (the state capital), lies along the west coast, where a narrow swampy zone runs south toward Brunei.

Most of Sabah and Sarawak were formerly forested; the rain forest contained around 2,000 tree species including stands of ebony, sandalwood, teak, and palms. Hot and humid, the forests of the two states remain home to many endangered species. Sabah was once swathed in a nearly continuous blanket of rain forest but, particularly since the 1960s, loggers have destroyed stands of trees, while shifting cultivators have removed much of the rest of the tree cover. In Sarawak, around 80 percent of the forest has been felled. Although conservation measures restrict timber companies to taking a small number of designated tree species, surrounding forest is often felled in order to gain access. Logging has had a serious environmental effect on Sabah and Sarawak. Much of the region has been reduced to scrubland, where occasional clumps of trees punctuate deeply eroded hills.

The activities of the timber industry, formerly the principal industry in Sarawak, have polluted the state's waterways and silted the lower reaches of some of Sarawak's main rivers. The reduction of the tree cover has exposed a greater area of the land to erosion and has damaged local agriculture.

The island of Labuan, off the southwestern coast of Sabah, is a Malaysian federal territory. Labuan, which has an area of 36 square miles (92 sq. km), had a population of 78,000 at the 2000 Malaysian census. The island is a tourist destination for people from nearby Brunei and an offshore banking center that caters to Bruneians.

THE PHILIPPINES

The 7,107 Philippine Islands are mountainous and were once covered by stands of tropical rain forest. The two main islands, Luzon and Mindanao, cover around 66 percent of the total land area of the Philippines and are also home to nearly two-thirds of the nation's population. The 11 largest islands in the archipelago account for 94 percent of the land area of the Philippines, and only 350 of the islands have an area that is greater than 1 square mile (2.6 sq. km). Around 2,000 of the Philippine Islands are inhabited, and one-third of the islands in the archipelago are unnamed.

The Philippine Archipelago adjoins some of the deepest regions of the world's oceans. The Philippine Trench (sometimes called the Philippine Trough), off the coast of eastern Mindanao, descends to a depth of 34,219 feet (10,430 m). The archipelago is part of a western Pacific arc system of active volcanoes that is popularly known as the "Ring of Fire." Physically, the islands divide into three main regions: Luzon and its neighbors in the north, the Visayan Islands in the center, and Mindanao and neighboring islands in the south.

LUZON AND THE NORTHERN ISLANDS

Luzon, with an area of 40,420 square miles (104,688 sq. km), is the largest, most important, and most populated Philippine island. Luzon is also home to the national capital, Manila, whose metropolitan area contained 9,933,000 people at the 2000 national census. The physical region is usually taken to include the Batanes and Babuyan islands to the north, as well as the islands of Catanduanes, Marinduque, Masbate, Mindoro, Palawan, and Romblon, along with smaller islets to the south.

The so-called "chocolate hills" of the Philippine island of Bohol are named for the parched brown grass that covers them during the dry season.

Luzon is mountainous and contains Mount Pulag, which at 9,587 feet (2,922 m) is the nation's second-highest peak. The island's northern rectangular-shaped section includes the Cordillera Central, one of the highest mountain chains in the Philippines, to the east of which is the north-south Cagayan Valley through which flows the Cagayan River, the second-longest Philippine waterway. East of the Cagayan Valley rises the Sierra Madre Range, which extends into the southern half of the island, making it the nation's longest mountain chain.

The narrow, mountainous Bicol Peninsula, which has an indented coast, forms the southeastern part of Luzon. The peninsula contains several volcanoes, including Mayon, which is 8,071 feet (2,460 m) high. Mayon is famous for its symmetrical shape. The islands of Burias, Masbate, and Ticao lie off the southwestern coast of the Bicol Peninsula.

Central Luzon, the area between northern Luzon and the Bicol Peninsula, contains the Zambales Mountains and the nation's main lowland, the Central Luzon Plain. The Zambales Mountains include Mount Pinatubo, an active volcano, and stretch southward to form the Bataan Peninsula. The rocky peninsula that separates Manila Bay, one of the finest natural harbors in Southeast Asia, from the South China Sea rises 4,111 feet (1,253 m) to Mount Natib in the north. The Mariveles Mountains occupy the southern part of the Bataan Peninsula.

The Central Luzon Plain is the principal Philippine farming region, growing rice, vegetables, and a wide variety of other crops. The lowland region contains Laguna de Bay, the nation's largest lake, which is drained by the Pasig River. The national capital, Manila, is sited where the Pasig River reaches the sea, flowing into a large natural harbor. The Manila agglomeration contains a number of cities, including Quezon City, which is more populous than Manila itself. The urban area's industries include textiles and garments, furniture making, electrical and electronic engineering, optical goods, printing, pharmaceuticals, metalworking, and a number of industries that are based on processing the region's agricultural produce (including coconut oil and soap, food processing, and making rope from Manila hemp), as well as banking, finance, and other commercial interests and government employment.

RIVERS OF MALAYSIA, SINGAPORE, BRUNEI, AND THE PHILIPPINES

River	Country	Length in miles	Length in km
Kinabatangan	Malaysia	350	563
Rajang	Malaysia	350	563
Pahang	Malaysia	271	436
Baram	Malaysia/Brunei	250	400
Agusan	Philippines	240	390
Cagayan	Philippines	220	350
Mindanao	Philippines	200	320

The other main islands within the Luzon group are Mindoro and Palawan. Mindoro, which lies southwest of Luzon, covers an area of 3,759 square miles (9,735 sq. km). The largely agricultural island rises to a mountainous core. Many small islands fringe Palawan, which is southwest of Mindoro. Palawan is a long narrow island that covers 4,550 square miles (11,785 sq. km). The island, which has an indented coast and a high mountainous spine along its entire length, has much in common with Borneo in terms of its flora and fauna. Logging was the island's principal industry until it was banned in 1992. Tourism is now a major industry, largely catering to visitors from Germany and other countries of northern Europe.

THE VISAYAN ISLANDS

The central Philippines is formed by the Visayan Islands, the smallest of three major island groups into which the nation is customarily divided. There are hundreds of Visayan Islands, but the major islands are Bohol, Cebu, Leyte, Negros, Panay, and Samar. Samar, the large Visayan Island near Luzon, lies southeast of the Bicol Peninsula. With an area of 5,050 square miles (13,080 sq. km), Samar is the third-largest island in the Philippines. The island has restricted coastal lowlands, and although it is much lower than most other major Visayan Islands, rising to only 2,776 feet (846 m), the sparsely populated interior of Samar is characterized by steep slopes.

Leyte, southwest from Samar, is joined to its larger neighbor by a bridge. The island has a high rugged mountain ridge running through the center. A single low gap through the mountains forms a natural routeway across the island. Discontinuous plains stretch along the jagged coastline. Bohol, an oval-shaped island southwest of Leyte, is famous for its "chocolate hills," low, symmetrical, cone-shaped hills that turn brown in the dry season. Most of the settlement in the island, which is largely volcanic with a central plateau, is confined to the coasts.

Cebu, west of Bohol, lies at the center of the Visayan region. The island is long, narrow, and at its widest is 20 miles (32 km) across. The Bogo Plain in the north, a sugarcane-growing region, is the only significant lowland on a hilly island that is overpopulated. Many Cebuanos, the people of Cebu, have migrated to other parts of the Philippines and abroad. Cebu City, on the eastern coast, is the third-largest metropolitan area in the Philippines, with a population of 1,080,000 in 2000.

Negros, west of Cebu, is an irregularly shaped island with an active volcano, Mount Canlaon (8,071 feet or 2,460 m) at its center. The island is rugged and heavily dissected by ravines. The southwest part of the island, the Tablas, is a plateau that supports little farming and has few people. Negros was once the region's main exporter of sugar, and the island still produces around one-half of Philippine sugar. However, since demand for sugar from the Philippines decreased toward the end of the twentieth century, sugar from Negros is now almost entirely consumed within the Philippines. Bacolod in the northwest is

Taal Lake on the Philippine island of Luzon is a former volcano crater that has filled with water. The island that is formed by the crater of a small volcano within the lake (left center) also contains a small lake. Taal Lake is a popular tourist destination.

the largest city in Negros. Panay, which is west of Negros, is the most westerly of the larger Visayan Islands. The island's central plain, which runs from north to south, is flanked on the west by steep unpopulated mountains and on the east by hills. The plain, which is densely populated, is an important agricultural region. The city of Iloilo grew where the central plain reaches Panay's southern coast. The deltas of several rivers form another lowland in southeastern Panay.

MINDANAO AND THE SOUTHERN ISLANDS

Mindanao, the second-largest island in the Philippines, lies in the southern part of the archipelago. Toward the southwest a chain of islands, the Sulu Archipelago, extends toward Borneo and includes the islands of Basilan, Jolo, and Tawi-Tawi.

Mindanao is mountainous, rising to Mount Apo, a volcano which at 9,692 feet (2,954 m) above sea level is the highest peak in the Philippines. The island has three major peninsulas: the long Zamboanga Peninsula in the southwest, the Cotabato Peninsula in the south, and the Surigao Peninsula in the north.

The wide Moro Gulf forms a large indent on the southwestern coast of the island. Narrow coastal plains surround Mindanao; wider regions of swamps and fertile basins provide the principal areas of lowland, but the interior of the rugged island is sparsely populated. The Agusan River, the longest waterway in the Philippines, drains a substantial basin in northeastern Mindanao. The island has three major cities: Zamboanga in the southwest, Davao in the southeast, and Cagayan de Oro in the north. With a population of 1.2 million in 2000, Davao is the second-largest metropolitan area in the Philippines.

Mindanao is home to the greater part of the Philippine Muslim minority, and there has long been a separatist movement in the island. However, due to waves of migrants from other Philippine islands to Mindanao—particularly when the island came under Spanish rule from the sixteenth century until the end of the nineteenth century and then under U.S. administration until 1946—the island's Muslims are now a minority. A region with limited self-government, the Autonomous Region in Muslim Mindanao, has been established. The region includes not only parts of southwestern Mindanao but also some adjoining islands.

E. MBOBI

1163

Geology of Malaysia, Singapore, Brunei, and the Philippines

Despite being geographically close, the geology of Malaysia in the west and the Philippines in the east are very different. The Philippines is part of the "Ring of Fire" that borders the Pacific Ocean, so called because it is a belt of volcanoes in a region of high seismic activity. Malaysia is the most southeastern part of the Asian continental landmass and forms part of the Sunda Shelf.

Malaysia has no volcanoes and is tectonically inactive; unlike the Philippines, it is not located at a border between the moving tectonic plates that form the Earth's outer shell. By contrast, the geological history of the Philippines is complex, marked by the collision of the Eurasian Plate and the Philippines Sea Plate.

THE GEOLOGY OF MALAYSIA

Malaysia consists of Peninsular Malaysia and Eastern Malaysia (Sabah and Sarawak in the northern part of Borneo). It is composed from a variety of rock types dating from around 540 million years ago to recent geological times. Much of Malaysia is formed from sedimentary rocks (rocks that are laid down in layers) that were created by the accumulation and compaction of loose sediments, such as sand and silts produced by the erosion of the land during the Paleozoic era (about 545 million to 245 million years ago). One of the main Paleozoic sedimentary rocks in Malaysia is limestone, which is found in thick layers.

In a process called orogenesis (mountain building) at the beginning of the Mesozoic era (245 million years ago), the area was compressed, deforming preexisting rock layers and leading to the formation of a mountain range. This mountain belt extends from Myanmar (Burma) through Thailand and Peninsular Malaysia to the Bangka and Belitung islands of Indonesia. A common feature of orogenesis is the production of granite plutons (large elliptical masses of granite rock that are forced to the ocean's surface). During this process, high temperatures occur, superheating and altering the surrounding sedimentary rocks. The process of changing rocks through heating (or through chemical action) is called metamorphosis; heat forms ring-shaped metamorphosed areas called metamorphism aureoles.

In the Tertiary period, beginning around 65 million years ago, layers of limestone were laid down in what is now Sarawak. Heavy erosion of the easily eroded limestone has carved huge cave systems in the limestone deposits of Sarawak, including the famous Mulu Caves. Between around 34 million and 5 million years ago, material eroded from neighboring continental masses was laid down in lake basins and swampy environments to form sedimentary rocks. These recent sedimentary deposits, which are found in basins in Sabah and Sarawak as well as in the Malay Basin on the Malay Peninsula, contain significant quantities of oil and natural gas.

THE GEOLOGY OF THE PHILIPPINES

The Philippine Archipelago is a cluster of more than 7,000 islands, but two large mountainous islands, Luzon and Mindanao, make up about 65 percent of the total area. The westernmost group of the Philippine Islands comprises Palawan and its smaller neighbors. The Palawan region is different from the rest of the Philippines; its geological history is quite similar to that of Malaysia, although it did not experience orogenesis. Unlike the other regions of the Philippines, Palawan has no volcanoes and it does not experience strong earthquakes.

The rest of the Philippines has a complex geological and tectonic history. The archipelago is positioned in the zone of convergence between the Philippines Sea Plate and the Eurasian Plate. Several smaller plates, known as micro-plates, are also compressed in the convergence zone.

A subduction zone (a zone where one tectonic plate slides under another) lies off the western coast of the Philippines, where the Eurasian Plate plunges beneath the micro-plates of the Philippines Archipelago. A 560-mile (900 km) long trench associated with the subduction zone consists of the active Manila Trench, west of Luzon, and the inactive Sulu Trench, west of Mindanao. The subduction caused volcanic activity, and a volcanic arc (a line of volcanoes) formed about 10 million years ago during the Miocene era. The arc includes the active Taal volcano in the south, Mount Pinatubo in the center, and the Iraya volcano in the north. Both the Manila Trench in the west and the Philippines Trench in the east of the archipelago reach depths of over 16,400 feet (5,000 m).

To the east of the Philippines Archipelago, the Philippines Sea Plate is being subducted in a northwestward motion in a westward dipping subduction zone under the Philippines micro-plates. The volcanic arc associated with the subduction zone extends from the Balut volcano in the south to the Mayon volcano in the north. The Philippines has at least 21 active volcanoes.

Between the two subduction zones lies the Philippines Fault, an 800-mile (1,300 km) fault line that extends from northwestern Luzon to southeastern Mindanao. The convergence zone around the fault line, which is caused by horizontal slipping of compressed landmasses, is an area of considerable seismic activity. Crustal shortening—the thrusting of one block of crust over another and the folding of rock strata underneath—occurs in the convergence zone. The fault zone has been active since the Pliocene era (less than 5 million years ago) and the landmasses along the fault have moved as much as 62 miles (100 km).

Tectonic activity in the zone of the Philippines Fault and around the region's volcanoes causes hydrothermal fluids—hot fluids, mostly water, from the Earth's crust that are enriched with chemical elements—to rise, altering the surrounding rocks. The chemical elements are deposited in the rocks, forming ore-rich deposits. The abundance of volcanic rocks, combined with the hydrothermal activity in the Philippines, makes it the world's second-richest region in gold deposits after South Africa.

J. NEUBERG

Mount Pinatubo

Mount Pinatubo stands 5,741 feet (1,750 m) high and is situated 56 miles (90 km) from Manila, the national capital of the Philippines. It forms part of a volcanic arc that extends west of the Philippine Archipelago. Mount Pinatubo had been dormant since it last erupted in around 1380, but on April 2, 1991, local people reported explosions coming from the volcano. The area immediately around the volcano was heavily populated; about 515,000 people lived on its slopes, and 30,000 Americans lived in two U.S. military bases nearby. The first explosions were caused by seawater making contact with hot molten rocks, or magma. The explosions lasted for several hours and were followed for several days by increasing emissions of steam and ash. Scientists who studied material deposited after the initial explosions concluded that there could be further violent activity, with large-scale pyroclastic flows (avalanches of hot gas and volcanic particles) and extended lahars (volcanic material mixed with water, which moves like a mudflow, destroying anything its path). Increasing seismic activity caused by magma rising to the surface of the volcano forced the scientists to raise the alert level. By June 12, 120,000 people had been evacuated from the area. The biggest eruption occurred three days later on June 15, producing a 19-mile (30 km) high column of volcanic debris and ash, throwing rocks as far as 12 miles (20 km) from the cone. Heavy ash fell over the surrounding area, collapsing the roofs of buildings, and pyroclastic flows destroyed the U.S. military bases. Volcanic activity persisted throughout June, resulting in the expulsion of 16 million cubic feet (453,070 cubic m) of magma. The eruption caused only 300 deaths; rapid evacuation of the local population ensured that hundreds of thousands of people survived.

Mount Pinatubo erupts in June 1991 for the first time since 1380. Debris and ash reached 19 miles (30 km) into the atmosphere.

Climate of Malaysia, Singapore, Brunei, and the Philippines

The broadly equatorial tropical climate of Malaysia, Singapore, Brunei, and the Philippines is characterized by dramatic weather systems including monsoons, cyclones, and typhoons. The climate in the region is consistently hot, with abundant rainfall for much of the year, usually accompanied by thunderstorms.

Eastern Malaysia (the states of Sarawak and Sabah), Brunei, and the Philippines are less exposed to air masses moving directly from continents than are Peninsular Malaysia and Singapore, so they have a more maritime (ocean-influenced) climate. The islands of the Philippines extend farther north from the equator, as far as 21°N, and include some subtropical forest vegetation as well as tropical forests. The Philippine Islands also have more distinct monsoon seasons than any other part of the region.

In common with the rest of Southeast Asia, the dominant influences on the tropical equatorial climate are the northeast and southwest Asian monsoon winds, which can reduce the high humidity and bring a wetter and a drier season. Tropical cyclones (areas of low air pressure that form violent storms) and typhoons are frequent features of the region and can cause significant damage when crossing land. The El Niño phenomenon (unusual warming of the North Pacific along the equator) also affects the region's climate, causing a dramatic reduction in rainfall during the drier season, which can lead to drought and agricultural losses, especially of the rice crop.

ASIAN MONSOONS

Two monsoon wind systems dominate Southeast Asia. The northwest monsoon winds blow from China and the North Pacific during November through March, bringing moist air and rain. From April through September, the southern monsoon winds blow from Australia. The dry winds from the Australian deserts produce a mostly dry season from June through September, although Indian Ocean breezes continue to bring some rain. March and October form two short transition seasons between the monsoons with light and variable winds and high humidity.

TROPICAL CYCLONES AND TYPHOONS

The particularly warm sea temperatures (exceeding 82°F, or 27.5°C) of the northwest Pacific allow the development of strong tropical cyclones, which move westward toward the Philippines. All but the most southern parts of the Philippines are affected each year by these tropical cyclones, which form a large low-pressure rotating weather system with strong winds, heavy clouds, and thunderstorms. Like hurricanes, typhoons are particularly strong tropical cyclones with winds of at least 74 miles per hour (119 kmph) and occur mainly from June through November, when the northwest Pacific is warmest. Typhoons originate from the Pacific Ocean. On average, up to 20 tropical cyclones may cross the Philippines each year, including one to three typhoons that cause storm damage, landslides, and flooding.

Tropical cyclones are powered by the energy released when water vapor that has risen from the warm surface of the sea reaches high into the atmosphere, where vapor condenses as it cools and releases energy as heat (called latent heat). For a tropical cyclone to form, there must be an initial weather disturbance, such as a local storm, warm ocean surfaces, or relatively weak winds high in the atmosphere. The high winds and low pressure of the tropical cyclone increase the supply of water vapor by increasing the evaporation of sea water. Under

The high temperatures and heavy rainfall in Sarawak support a dense rain forest canopy that includes strangler figs (left) and other jungle vegetation.

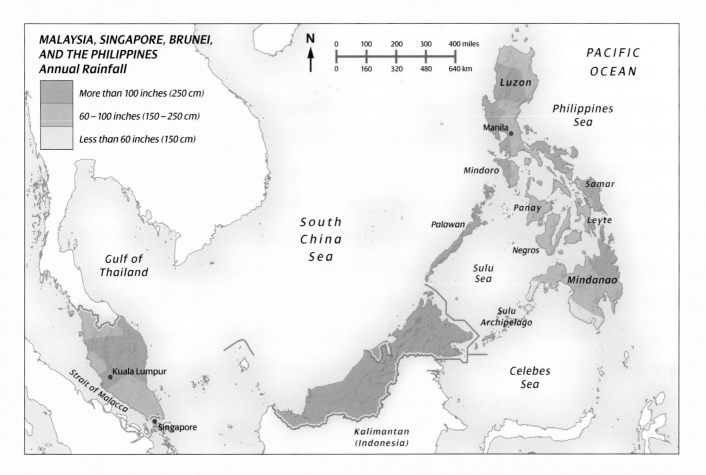

MALAYSIA, SINGAPORE, BRUNEI, AND THE PHILIPPINES
Annual Rainfall

More than 100 inches (250 cm)

60 – 100 inches (150 – 250 cm)

Less than 60 inches (150 cm)

these conditions, a tropical cyclone can develop strong winds, large waves, and torrential rains that can produce floods and devastation if it moves onto land. Once the cyclone moves onto land, it no longer has a supply of water vapor and therefore weakens, but it may still cause considerable damage.

THE MALAYSIAN CLIMATE

The broad climatic region formed by Malaysia, Singapore, and Brunei has a tropical climate that is consistently hot, with high and frequent rainfall. Locally, however, the climate is modified by the presence of mountains that may shield some areas from the monsoon winds that bring rain. In general, there are two peaks in the rainfall pattern over the year, with the heaviest rains falling from March through May and between September and November. Malaysia may be divided into three main types of climatic-geographic regions: highlands, lowlands, and coastal regions. Singapore and Brunei experience much the same climate as the coastal regions of Malaysia.

MALAYSIAN COASTAL REGIONS

The coastal regions of Malaysia tend to be consistently humid and hot. Penang, on the western coast of Malaysia, is typical of the western coastal lowland areas with year-round high

temperatures. Average maximum temperatures are 90°F (32°C) during the day, dropping to an average minimum of 73°F (23°C) at night. There are over 4 inches (about 10 cm) of rainfall every month, with the wettest season being from August through November, when over 12 inches (30 cm) of rain falls per month. The climate is sunny with an average of seven to eight hours of sunshine a day except during the cloudier, wetter season, when there are five to six hours of sunshine a day. The eastern coasts of Malaysia have a climate with similar average temperatures but with less variation in the seasonal rainfall throughout the year.

Singapore has around 6.5 inches (17 cm) of rain per month for most of the year, with a slightly wetter season from November through January and around 10 inches (25 cm) of rain per month. There are about five to six hours of sunshine a day on average throughout the year, with a humidity of between 70 percent and 80 percent.

MALAYSIAN LOWLANDS

Kuala Lumpur is typical of the inland lowlands of the Malay Peninsula, with average daily maximum temperatures of 90°F (32°C) and average minimum temperatures at night of 73°F (23°C). Humidity is high in the morning at around 97 percent, dropping to around 65 percent later in the day. The rainfall has a more distinct pattern with two peaks during the year: one in

April with nearly 12 inches (30 cm) in the month, and a second from October through November with around 10 inches (25 cm) per month.

MALAYSIAN HIGHLANDS

In the mountains in both Eastern and Peninsular Malaysia, the climate tends to be cooler and wetter, with greater temperature contrasts between day and night. The Cameron Highlands, part of the Main Range in the Malay Peninsula, are typical, with cooler, wetter conditions. Average maximum daytime temperatures throughout the year are 72°F to 73°F (22°C to 23°C), dropping to an average minimum temperature of 55°F to 57°F (13°C to 14°C) at night. The cooler temperatures in the highlands encouraged settlement by British colonists in the nineteenth century. Humidity is very high (over 95 percent) in the morning all year, but dropping to around 75 percent later in the day. There is heavy cloud cover throughout the year in the highlands, giving only four or five hours of clear sunshine each day.

Rainfall is over 4 inches (10 cm) every month, with two peaks in the year. The first peak of rainfall is just under 12 inches (30 cm) in April, and the second peak is over 12 inches (30 cm) per month in both October and November.

The tropical climate, with adequate rainfall for most of the year, supplemented where necessary by irrigation, allows the cultivation of two or three crops of rice a year in the Philippines.

THE CLIMATE OF THE PHILIPPINES

The Philippines Archipelago is a group of around 7,000 islands in the western Pacific, between 4° and 21°N latitude. The larger islands are mountainous, with peaks of up to 10,000 feet (around 3,000 m). The islands in the south have an equatorial climate similar to that of the Malay Peninsula, hot with significant rain through the year. Zamboanga, in the island of Mindanao, is typical of the southern islands, with rainfall peaking in October at around 5.5 inches (14 cm) for the month and at least 2.5 inches (6 cm) per month during the rest of the year.

The islands in the center and north of the archipelago are more dominated by tropical cyclones, with the heaviest rain falling from tropical cyclones that occur mostly during July through October. Winds during the cyclone season are the southwesterly to southeasterly monsoon winds. Manila is typical, with high rainfall peaking at over 16 inches (40 cm) per month in July and August. Coastal regions that face northeast tend to have a rainfall peak from November through March.

HEALTH RISKS AND CLIMATE CHANGE

Some parts of the region are free from malaria, but the warm, humid climate allows a malarial mosquito cycle in rural Malaysia and also in the Bohol, Catanduanes, Cebu, and Manila districts in the Philippines. Dengue fever (an acute viral fever that is transmitted by mosquitoes) is also present in the same areas due to the warmth and humidity.

Climate change in the form of a global increase in average temperature is predicted to have significant repercussions in the region. The main repercussions are likely to be caused by rises in the sea level and effects on freshwater resources. It is predicted that the equatorial regions will receive slightly increased rainfall during both the rainy and dry season. However, the increase in temperature will increase the rate of evaporation of water so that the increase in rainfall will not lead to an increase in the amount of water available for consumption. The amount of water projected to be available by the middle of the twenty-first century falls far short of the projected increases in demand for irrigation and consumption during the dry season. Some parts of Malaysia and the Philippines, such as the states of Kedah and Perlis, already face seasonal water shortages, so future shortages are likely to be far more severe. Rice production is also likely to be significantly affected, which will have economic consequences.

The predicted increase in rainfall—and particularly of intense rainfall—during the northeast monsoon rainy season would also increase flooding along the river plains throughout the region, including the densely populated western lowlands of Malaysia, which are home to the largest Malaysian cities. Floods would also increase in frequency and affect larger areas.

Sea-level rises of 1 to 6 inches (3–15 cm) are expected by 2010 and rises of around 35 inches (90 cm) by 2070. Unless protected by sea defenses, a rise in the sea level of 35 inches (90 cm) would cause widespread erosion and flooding of coastal Malaysia and the low-lying regions of the Philippines, as well as great social and economic damage. Tourism, agriculture, fishing, and mangroves in these coastal regions would be severely affected.

M. FELTON

CLIMATE

KUALA LUMPUR, MALAYSIA
3°12'N 101°55'E Height above sea level: 29 feet (9 m)

	J	F	M	A	M	J	J	A	S	O	N	D
Mean maximum												
(°F)	90	93	91	93	91	91	91	91	90	90	90	90
(°C)	32	34	33	34	33	33	33	33	32	32	32	32
Mean minimum												
(°F)	73	73	73	75	75	73	73	73	73	73	73	73
(°C)	23	23	23	24	24	23	23	23	23	23	23	23
Precipitation												
(in.)	6.7	6.4	9.7	11.9	9.4	6.2	5.3	7.5	9.4	11	13.1	9.8
(cm)	17.1	19.1	24.6	30.2	24	15.7	13.4	19	23.8	27.9	33.4	24.9

MANILA, THE PHILIPPINES
14°63'N 121°02'E Height above sea level: 52 feet (16 m)

	J	F	M	A	M	J	J	A	S	O	N	D
Mean maximum												
(°F)	86	88	90	93	91	90	88	88	88	88	87	86
(°C)	30	31	32	34	33	32	31	31	31	31	31	30
Mean minimum												
(°F)	75	75	77	79	81	79	84	79	79	79	77	75
(°C)	24	24	25	26	27	26	29	26	26	26	25	24
Precipitation												
(in.)	0.7	0.3	0.4	0.8	6.5	10.4	16.5	19.1	13	10.6	5.1	3
(cm)	1.9	0.8	1.1	2.1	16.5	26.5	42	48.6	33.0	27.0	12.9	7.5

SINGAPORE
1°22'N 103° 48'E Height above sea level: 59 feet (18 m)

	J	F	M	A	M	J	J	A	S	O	N	D
Mean maximum												
(°F)	86	88	88	88	88	88	88	88	88	88	88	86
(°C)	30	31	31	31	31	31	31	31	31	31	31	30
Mean minimum												
(°F)	73	73	75	75	77	77	75	75	75	75	75	73
(°C)	23	23	24	24	25	25	24	24	24	24	24	23
Precipitation												
(in.)	7.8	6.1	6.7	5.6	6.2	5.5	5.7	5.6	6.8	6.6	9.9	12.0
(cm)	19.8	15.4	17.1	14.1	15.8	14.0	14.5	14.3	17.7	16.7	25.2	30.4

Flora and Fauna of Malaysia, Singapore, Brunei, and the Philippines

Drenched with monsoon rains for much of the year, the region from Peninsular Malaysia east through the states of Eastern Malaysia in Borneo to the Philippines is cloaked with wet tropical forest.

The rain forests of the region include some of the most biodiverse habitats on Earth. However, vast tracts of the forests have been badly degraded by human activities and if logging continues into the twenty-first century at the same rate that tree cover was lost through the 1980s and 1990s, almost all the forests of Malaysia and the Philippines will have disappeared within a generation.

COASTAL FORESTS OF PENINSULAR MALAYSIA

Much of coastal and estuarine Peninsular Malaysia is fringed by deep mangrove beds. Sediment builds up behind the mangroves to form peat, on which a forest of hardy trees grows. The trees are able to tolerate the acidic, anoxic (low-oxygen), and nutrient-poor soil. Strangler figs are characteristic peat forest plants. A fig starts life as a seed in bird droppings in the canopy. Roots snake

Heath Forests of Northern Borneo

Peat forests occur along the coast of northern Borneo and around large bodies of fresh water, like Lake Mahakam. Inland from the peat forests in Sarawak, Brunei, and Sabah lie dry, well-drained heath forests. Heath forests consist of low, small-leaved trees of a relatively uniform height that are densely packed together and swaddled with epiphytes (plants that grow on other plants but are not parasitic). Like the soils of the peat forests, heath forest soils are acidic, and nutrients are hard to come by. Many plants of the heath forest have evolved sophisticated insect-capture devices to counter the shortage of nutrients. They include pitcher plants that have deep basins of insect-digesting liquid, bladderworts that wash insects into smaller bowls, and the sticky leaves of sundews. Rather than capturing insects through stealth, ant-house plants instead offer them a home. Ants make their nests inside chambers at the base of the plant and dump their trash and decomposing dead in separate chambers. The plant absorbs nutrients from the ant refuse through the chamber walls.

down the trunk of the host tree to the ground below. The fig then grows a canopy of its own that shades out the host, while encircling it with thick roots. Starved of light, the host dies and rots away, leaving a vertical tunnel of sturdy fig roots that can reach 150 feet (45 m) or more in height.

Peat forests along the coast are important for waterbirds and fish, the prey of brown fishing owls and gray-headed fish eagles. The forest is also important for mammals such as the Malayan water shrew, which occurs only in the state of Selangor in the west of the Malay Peninsula. The feet of this little shrew are fringed by stiff hairs that allow the animal to power itself through the water in pursuit of aquatic invertebrates.

INLAND FORESTS IN PENINSULAR MALAYSIA

Further inland, the peat forests give way to richer freshwater swamps and then to lowland rain forests. Dipterocarps (a family of giant tropical trees that have two-winged fruits and a distinctive "cauliflower" top that grows up to 130 feet, or 40 m high) draped with orchids and ferns are abundant, and there is a rich layer of shade-tolerant herbs below the canopy, although vegetation is sparse at ground level.

A small population of tigers still roams the forests; their prey includes mouse deer (or chevrotains), Malayan tapirs, and sambars (deer), as well as the exceptionally rare Sumatran rhinoceros. Other animals in the forests include Asian elephants, gaurs (wild oxen), clouded leopards, and sun bears.

In more mountainous regions, the dipterocarps peter out, to be replaced by oaks, chestnuts, and rhododendrons. Many lowland animals also live in these highland forests, where they are joined by a variety of mountain-living specialists, such as siamang gibbons, red-cheeked squirrels, and lesser moon rats. The beautiful crested argus is one of many birds that are endemic to the woodlands.

SABAH AND SARAWAK

The flora and fauna of northern Borneo—the Malaysian states of Sabah and Sarawak, as well as the small independent nation of Brunei—are similar to those of the Malay Peninsula and

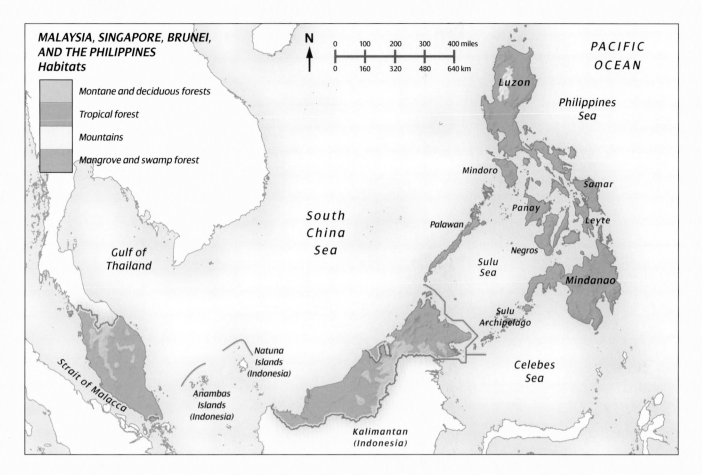

MALAYSIA, SINGAPORE, BRUNEI, AND THE PHILIPPINES
Habitats

- Montane and deciduous forests
- Tropical forest
- Mountains
- Mangrove and swamp forest

N

| 0 | 100 | 200 | 300 | 400 miles |
| 0 | 160 | 320 | 480 | 640 km |

PACIFIC OCEAN

Luzon

Philippines Sea

Mindoro

Samar

Panay

Palawan

Leyte

Negros

Sulu Sea

Mindanao

South China Sea

Sulu Archipelago

Gulf of Thailand

Celebes Sea

Strait of Malacca

Natuna Islands (Indonesia)

Anambas Islands (Indonesia)

Kalimantan (Indonesia)

Sumatra to the west, but they are more diverse than either. The lowland dipterocarp-dominated rain forests of northern Borneo are among the richest habitats in the world, with as many as 240 different species of trees in every 2.5 acres (1 hectare). The forests lack some of the larger predators of the Malay Peninsula, such as tigers; in the absence of large predators, smaller carnivores, such as sun bears, clouded leopards, and Sunda otter-civets, are the top mammalian predators.

Other predators include a variety of reptiles, such as snakes including Malayan pit vipers and king cobras, large lizards including Dumeril's monitors and Malay water monitors, and estuarine crocodiles. The lowland forest of Sabah also contains populations of elephants and Sumatran rhinoceroses, as well as a small population of elusive, endangered Bornean orangutans. The orangutan is not the only primate in the lowland forests; there are also white-bearded and Mueller's gibbons, macaques, proboscis monkeys, langurs, and slow lorises, a nocturnal primate that uses toxic chemicals to repel predators, such as sun bears.

Like the mammals, the avifauna (birdlife) of Borneo is similar to that of mainland Asia, with a number of endemic species. Hornbills, woodpeckers, and pittas are highly diverse in the region, while black-browed babblers and white-crowned shamas are found nowhere else.

The forests of Sabah and Sarawak are under severe pressure from human activities, and vast areas have been deforested. Logging and clearance for agriculture is increasing at a fast rate.

The plight of these habitats came to international attention in 1997, when fires that had been started to clear forest for oil-palm cultivation caused a pall of smog to smother much of Southeast Asia and northern Australasia. Conservationists estimate that if current rates of destruction persist, the entire lowland forest of northern Borneo will have been destroyed by 2020.

THE MOUNTAINS OF SABAH AND SARAWAK

Northern Borneo's montane forests are better protected from the ravages of human activity, thanks to their remoteness. Cooler and damper, the highlands are isolated in a "sea" of lowland forest. As a result of the area's protected remoteness, explosive speciation (the formation of new species) occurred in the region. For example, 23 species of birds are endemic to the montane forests, including golden-naped barbets, spot-necked bulbuls, and mountain serpent-eagles. Unlike the dipterocarp-dominated lowlands, a wide range of trees compete to dominate the canopy, including oaks, podocarps, chestnuts, and laurels, with rhododendrons reaching nearly to the highest levels. The lower slopes are rich with animals, including orangutans and Sumatran rhinoceroses, while a range of endemic smaller mammals live at higher elevations, such as Kinabalu ferret-badgers, Hose's palm civets, Kinabalu black shrews, and Brooke's tree squirrels.

FORESTS IN THE SOUTHERN PHILIPPINES

The forests of the Philippines are incredibly diverse and are the haunt of many groups of plants and animals that are found nowhere else. However, many of the unique habitats of the islands have been badly affected by human activities; in the entire Sulu Archipelago, for example, only the eastern portion of the island of Tawi-Tawi retains any primary woodland. The relict lowland dipterocarp forest on Tawi-Tawi contains small populations of a number of endangered or restricted-range animals, including Sulu bleeding-hearts (a species of dove), Sulu hornbills, Philippine cockatoos, and Tawitawi rats.

The large southern island of Mindanao and its smaller satellite islands have more forest cover, although in much of the highlands the dipterocarp forest has been almost completely destroyed. Around the coasts, some forest of stunted trees and bamboos remains. In the mountain foothills, the dipterocarps give way to a mixed montane forest of oaks and figs. A unique forest of giant tree ferns and dwarf trees covered with lichens, mosses, begonias, and other epiphytes grows near the summits.

Almost 80 percent of the mammals in the Mindanao forests are endemic, including Philippine colugos (also known as the flying lemur; a mammal that has a membrane of skin between its limbs, allowing it to glide) and Philippine tarsiers (small primates with large eyes and large feet). Several more widespread

The chevrotain or mouse deer is a solitary nocturnal animal that lives in forested regions of the Philippines. Only 10 inches (25 cm) high, the mouse deer may seek refuge on the lower branches of trees when it is threatened.

species that are critically endangered elsewhere, such as mottle-winged fruit bats, Philippine warty pigs, and Philippine deer, also survive in Mindanao. The forests contain a wealth of exotic birds, such as azure-breasted pittas, red-eared parrot-finches, and McGregor's cuckoo-shrikes, plus a range of hornbills, Mindanao scops and eagle owls, and spotted imperial pigeons.

PALAWAN AND THE VISAYAN ISLANDS

In contrast to the Sulus and Mindanao, Palawan retains much of its lowland rain forest. The west of Palawan has a wet lowland dipterocarp forest; mountains along the spine of the island cast a rain shadow, and as a result, the eastern half of the island is drier with a range of drought-tolerant semideciduous trees. Palawan and nearby islands share elements of both the Borneo and Philippine faunas, as well as many endemics of their own, such as Palawan soft-furred mountain rats, Palawan fruit bats, Palawan tree shrews, Palawan stink badgers, and Palawan binturongs (also known as civet cats). Some species that live in Borneo, such as pangolins and porcupines, also live in Palawan.

The Visayan Islands, the central group of the Philippine Archipelago, have suffered serious deforestation, particularly the islands of Negros, Panay, and Cebu, although Negros and Panay still retain a little of their original forests, mainly oak and chestnut, and thinner woodlands at high elevations. The Visayan Islands are home to some rare animals, including Visayan warty pigs and Philippine spotted deer, which are both critically endangered, as are Negros shrews and Panay cloud rats. Cloud rats are a unique group of large rodents that occur in the

Philippines and nowhere else. Negros is also home to a relict population of endangered Philippine crocodiles, a small, heavily armored species of which fewer than one hundred adults remain. On the Visayan island of Sibuyan, one-half of the original forest cover remains, and the tiny island contains six endemic mammals and three endemic birds.

By the early twentieth century, Cebu had been almost completely deforested, resulting in a cataclysmic effect on the island's wildlife. Some 39 species of birds are assumed lost on Cebu, including at least nine endemic subspecies. However, in the 1990s, conservationists realized that a few tiny fragments of forest had survived the destruction. Miraculously, these still held tiny populations of birds that were assumed long-extinct, like Cebu black shamas, Cebu hanging parakeets, and Cebu coppersmith barbets. However, of the 11 remaining native species of birds on Cebu, just one has a population of more than one hundred birds. Cebu flowerpeckers may be the world's rarest bird, with as few as four individuals left in 2005.

LUZON AND ITS NEIGHBORS

Deforestation has also occurred farther north in Luzon and its neighbors. Mindoro, for example, now has primary forest only along its mountainous central spine, with stands of endemic Mindoro pines at the peaks. These fragmented forests hold small populations of mammals, such as Philippine warty pigs, hairy-tailed cloud rats, and tamaraws, a species of dwarf water buffaloes.

The largest island in the group, Luzon, retains the largest tracts of primary forest remaining in the Philippines, despite being home to more people than any other Philippine island. Some coastal forests and mangrove beds occur along the shores, while the inland lowland rain forests are dipterocarp-dominated. Dipterocarps are replaced above about 3,300 feet (1,000 m) by oaks and laurels, with pandan vines hanging from their moss-encrusted boughs. The Luzon forests retain a rich small mammal fauna; rodents are particularly diverse, with a host of endemic rats and shrew-mice, and several types of cloud rats. The forests are also home to populations of Philippine brown deer and long-tailed macaques, as well as golden-crowned fruit bats, the largest bats in the world. Birds are similarly diverse, and there are many species unique to the island, such as Luzon racquet-tail parrots, Luzon bleeding-

The proboscis monkey lives only on the island of Borneo, in the Malaysian states of Sabah and Sarawak in the north and in Indonesian Kalimantan in the south. These monkeys live in mangrove swamps in groups of between about 10 and 30.

hearts, Luzon redstarts, and Luzon button-quails, while the forests support the world's largest population of great Philippine eagles.

One of the most unusual habitats in the region, the Luzon pine cloud forest, lies near the peaks of the island's highest mountains. Cool and wet, yet prone to regular fires in the dry season, this unique habitat consists of stands of saleng pines separated by grassland; a subspecies of common crossbills lives here, a species familiar in pine forests throughout the United States.

J. MARTIN

History and Movement of Peoples

Early Malay States and the First European Intervention

The Malay Peninsula has been inhabited for at least six to eight thousand years. Historians disagree as to whether there was large-scale migration from China and Tibet during the third millennium BCE, displacing earlier inhabitants, or whether there was a smaller-scale process of infiltration by groups who imposed their culture and language on the previous inhabitants.

During the first millennium CE, Malay traders and seafarers from Borneo and Sumatra settled in the Malay Peninsula and became the region's dominant population. The first states emerged in the region in the second and third centuries CE. The geography of the peninsula imposed limits on these states; there are no wide, fertile plains, so large densely populated states, such as those that developed in some other parts of Southeast Asia, were not viable. As a result, up to 30 small states rose and fell, mainly along the eastern coast of the Malay Peninsula, during the first millennium CE.

THE EMERGENCE OF EARLY STATES

The early states were heavily influenced by concepts of religion, government, and the arts that were brought by Indian traders, mainly from the port of Amaravathi on the Coromandel Coast, the southeastern coast of India. By the first century BCE, Indian and Chinese traders had established strong trading links with the Malay Peninsula. Both Hinduism and Mahayana Buddhism were influential, and these religions combined with traditional animism to form a belief system, traces of which still survive in Malaysian culture. The most important early state was called Langkasuka and, although its precise location is now unknown, Langkasuka controlled much of the northern Malay Peninsula. A significant complex of Indian-style temple ruins has been found in the northwestern state of Kedah, and it may be the site of the ancient kingdom.

The peninsula at this time was an important source of both gold and tin, and there was much trade among China, Indochina (modern Vietnam, Cambodia, and Laos), Java, Sumatra, Borneo, the Moluccas, Celebes (modern Sulawesi), and even eastern Africa. The early Malay states were small and at times fell under the influence and control of larger empires, such as Buddhist Sumatra-based Srivijaya and the Hindu Javanese state of Majapahit. Their impact added to

various cultural influences that were affecting Malayan society at the time, promoting both Buddhism and Hinduism. Traces of this influence can still be found in Malay political ideas, social structures, the arts, and ritual, despite the later influence of Islam. Both the Thai kingdom of Ayutthaya and the Khmer (Cambodian) Empire, centered in Angkor, also at times attempted to assert their control over the Malays, as did the Cholas from southern India, who attempted an invasion in the eleventh century CE.

Two major developments that changed Malay history occurred in the period beginning in the thirteenth and fourteenth centuries. The first was the arrival of Sunni Islam (the branch of Islam that is followed by the greatest number of adherents worldwide); the second was the rise of the great port-city of Malacca (modern Melaka) on the southwestern coast of the Malay Peninsula.

THE ARRIVAL OF ISLAM

The arrival of Islam in the region was gradual. Chinese records tell that an embassy from Sumatra to the Chinese emperor's court in 1283 was led by two Muslims. The earliest archaeological evidence of Islam from the Malay Peninsula is an inscribed stone dating from the fourteenth century found in Terengganu state. It is possible that Islam spread to the eastern part of the peninsula from China, rather than from Sumatra or India.

Islam was at first a religion of the elite. The Bengali and Gujarati traders who brought Islam to the western part of the peninsula were respected for their wealth and sophistication. Once the Malay elites converted to Islam, the ordinary people followed, although the influence of the earlier religions remained strong, and few Malays became strict or orthodox Muslims until the rise of reform movements during the nineteenth century.

MALACCA

The rise of Malacca began around 1400. Parameswara (c. 1344–1414 or 1424), a prince from Srivijaya, left Sumatra in 1396 and became the ruler of the island of Temasek, now known as Singapore. He fled northward, driven by constant attacks from the allies of Majapahit, and by 1402, he had founded the kingdom of Malacca. He was still ruler there when the port was visited by the Chinese admiral Cheng Ho (1371–1433) in 1409. Malacca's origins were humble: at first it was an insignificant fishing settlement that paid tribute to the Thai king of Ayutthaya, but Parameswara developed the port, which became a great regional center for trade. In Malacca, the government was stable and trade was free.

Malacca lies at a trading hub along a strategic strait. The prevailing winds change with the seasons, and during the two monsoon periods it was a vital stopover point for trade between India and China. At its height in the late fifteenth century, when

St. John's Fort in Malacca was built in the mid-eighteenth century to protect the Dutch from raids by Malay forces.

Malacca was the center for trade throughout the Southeast Asian region, it attracted merchants from China, Arabia, Persia, India, Java, Borneo and other East Indian islands, Burma, and Cambodia. Malacca is known to have been home to around 15,000 merchants from throughout the region.

Malacca was not just a trading port; it dominated most of the Malay Peninsula and the eastern coast of Sumatra. When necessary, it fought to preserve its independence, for example, against the Thais, but it did not seek to antagonize its more powerful neighbors and was always eager to preserve good relations with China. On occasion, Malacca won additional territory through warfare, and sometimes the state gained land through a judicious marriage of its ruler; also, neighboring states sometimes requested to be annexed by Malacca for protection.

Although Malacca was an important regional center for the dissemination of Islam, it was also a cosmopolitan and tolerant society. Peoples of many different ethnic groups lived peacefully there, including Malays, Muslim Indians, Hindu Indians, Chinese, Javanese, Turks, Arabs, Burmese, and Thais. The city became a major center for Malay culture and literature. However, the city-state fell in 1511, when the Portuguese invaded.

THE PORTUGUESE CONQUEST

From the fifteenth century, the Portuguese sought a sea route to the East. Gradually, Portuguese ships made their way down the west coast of Africa, and in 1488, Bartholomeu Dias (c. 1450–1500) rounded the Cape of Good Hope. In 1497, Vasco da Gama (c. 1469–1524) reached India and afterward established permanent bases there. The Malay Peninsula was soon within their reach. The Portuguese were eager to take control of Malacca, which they saw as the ideal center for trade throughout the entire Southeast Asian region.

On September 1, 1509, five Portuguese ships sailed into Malacca. At first they were welcomed, but Indian merchants, who saw the Portuguese as rivals, pressed the authorities in Malacca to attack them; the Indians had also heard of the intolerance of the Portuguese toward Muslims in India. The

The Italian artist Giulio Ferrario depicted the port and town of Malacca in this illustration, dated between 1820 and 1830, from one of his travel books.

forces of Malacca attacked the Portuguese fleet; two of the five ships were destroyed and around 20 Portuguese were captured. However, in 1511, a much larger Portuguese fleet, commanded by Alfonso de Albuquerque (1453–1515), attacked Malacca and captured it, overthrowing its ruler.

A son of the last independent ruler of Malacca fled to the southern tip of the Malay Peninsula, where he founded Johor, which grew into a strong state that challenged the Portuguese in Malacca over the next 130 years. However, unable to recapture Malacca, the rulers of Johor expanded in other directions, building one of the largest Malay states and taking possession of the Riau Islands between Temasek (modern Singapore) and Sumatra.

THE PORTUGUESE IN MALACCA

The Portuguese campaign against Malacca was not just a reprisal for the earlier attack on the Portuguese fleet; the Portuguese were aware of Malacca's importance as a trading

center and wished to control it themselves. However, the Portuguese mission had another purpose: their ships carried the Christian sign of the cross on their sails, and the Portuguese intended to convert the peoples of Asia to Roman Catholicism. The Portuguese had emerged from Muslim occupation during a long campaign through the eleventh and twelfth centuries and they were not tolerant of Islam. As a result, many Muslim merchants left Malacca, unwilling to accept high taxes and religious intolerance, and the port began to decline.

Johor and Atjeh (a strong sultanate in northern Sumatra) had both taken advantage of Malacca's loss of local power to expand their influence through the region. Portugal strengthened the defenses of Malacca, building a massive fort, demonstrating its determination to remain, and enabling the port city to withstand numerous assaults. However, the raids on Malacca by the Atjehnese, who wanted to expand into the Malay Peninsula, sometimes led the Portuguese, Johor, and other Malay states to ally against their common enemy, Atjeh.

It was not Portuguese policy to acquire large areas of territory but rather to establish firm bases from which they could trade and control the local seas. Portugal did not have the financial or other reserves to do more; there were never more than six hundred Portuguese troops in Malacca, and often the number was much lower. However, despite the relative weakness of their military presence in the region, the Portuguese could not help but become involved in local power struggles. Johor, Atjeh, and the major Muslim states in Java all were at times a challenge to the Portuguese. Johor was a particular threat, as its ruler repeatedly tried to recapture Malacca. The Portuguese responded, capturing forts and destroying the major Johor center at Bintang in 1526. Continued attacks on Portuguese shipping by the sultan of Johor led to the sacking of his capital, Johor Lama, in 1587.

THE DUTCH CHALLENGE

Eventually the tide turned against Portuguese power in the region. The small European country was finding it difficult to protect its vast trading empire. Then, in 1580, the extinction of the hereditary male line of the Portuguese royal family led to the annexation of Portugal by its neighbor, Spain. The Portuguese and Spanish colonial empires effectively merged. The Dutch had formerly been under Spanish rule, and Spain continued its efforts to recover the Dutch provinces in the northern Netherlands; as a result, the Dutch attacked the Spanish Empire and its trade, including the former Portuguese possessions in Asia. By the beginning of the seventeenth century, Portugal's Asian possessions were greatly reduced and were unable to resist the rise of the Dutch East India Company (Verenigde Oostindische Compagnie, known as the VOC). In the seventeenth century a number of European countries established trading companies similar to the VOC, aimed at colonizing and establishing monopolies over the supply of particular products. In 1641, the Dutch moved against the Portuguese, who had regained their independence and the remains of their colonial

empire in the previous year. The Dutch seized control of Malacca with the help of the sultanate of Johor, Portugal's long-time enemy in the Malay Peninsula.

Dutch rule in the region was different from Portuguese rule. Although they did not develop Malacca's trade, preferring to redirect it through Batavia (modern Jakarta in Indonesia), the main Dutch base in the East Indies, Dutch relations with the local population were much better than those of the Portuguese with their Malay subjects and neighbors. Whereas the Portuguese had aggressively tried to promote Roman Catholicism in the region, the Dutch did not interfere with local religions or customs. The Dutch gradually extended their rule through the East Indian islands (modern Indonesia); Dutch rule, although confined to the Malacca district on the Malay Peninsula, indirectly affected the whole peninsula.

THE BUGIS

The inland areas of the Malay Peninsula had never been heavily populated, and a series of small states existed in the coastal fringes; the exception was Johor, which was larger and more powerful than its neighbors. Dutch rule spread through the East Indies, and in the seventeenth century the Dutch established a foothold in Sulawesi, leading to the large-scale emigration from the island of a people known as the Bugis. Bugis established settlements in various parts of the Malay Peninsula, and they became powerful along the western coast in Selangor, Kedah, Perak, and Johor. The strength of Bugi influence in the region limited the success of Dutch trade and, in 1756, the Dutch waged an inconclusive war against the Bugis.

The Riau Islands became the Bugis' powerbase, dominating trade in the region and increasingly isolating the Dutch in Malacca from political and commercial influence in the Malay Peninsula. As a result, the Dutch again went to war against the Bugis, taking the Riau Islands in 1785. Bugi power in the Malay Peninsula was broken, but the Dutch triumph was short-lived.

THE ARRIVAL OF THE BRITISH

The British had become the dominant power in India and were turning their attention farther east. In 1786, the British established a presence on the Malay island of Penang. During the Revolutionary and Napoleonic Wars in Europe (1793–1815), the Dutch were forced into an alliance with the French, and their overseas possessions were gradually taken by the British. Some Dutch colonies, including Malacca, were returned to the Netherlands after the Napoleonic Wars. In 1819, the British gained a foothold in Singapore, which was part of Johor, and in 1824 the sultan of Johor ceded Singapore to Great Britain. In the same year, the British exchanged their settlement at Bencoolen in Sumatra for Dutch Malacca. From that time, the British were the only colonial power active in the Malay Peninsula.

A. J. WOOD

The Spanish in the Philippines

Every Philippine village has a Catholic church, many of which date back to the Spanish colonial period. Roman Catholicism is one of the most enduring legacies of Spanish colonial rule in the Philippines, a period of 333 years that shaped a culture that made the archipelago different from the other nations of the region.

Christianity was first introduced to the Philippines when the Portuguese explorer Ferdinand Magellan (c. 1480–1521) landed on the island of Cebu on March 17, 1521. Under the patronage of the Spanish crown, Magellan had set out to chart a western route to the Spice Islands of the East Indies (modern Indonesia), the source of spices that were commercially very desirable in Europe. Spain wanted a presence in the region and a share of the spice trade. Initially, the inhabitants of Cebu welcomed Magellan. Soon after his arrival on the island, Magellan presided over a lavish ceremony in which the local Muslim chieftain Raja Humabon (dates unknown), his wife, and many of his followers were baptized. However, when another of Cebu's Muslim leaders, Lapu-Lapu (dates unknown), attacked the Spanish forces, Magellan was killed.

Magellan's death caused a temporary suspension of Spanish activity in the islands, but in 1542, Ruy Lopez de Villalobos (c. 1500–1572) led an expedition to the islands of Leyte and Samar, which he collectively called Felipina for the Spanish crown prince, the future King Philip II (reigned 1556–1598). A longer version of the name, Las Islas Felipinas (the Philippine Islands), later became the name of the whole archipelago. The next major Spanish expedition, led by Miguel López de Legazpi (c. 1510–1572) arrived in the islands in 1565. After encountering some hostility from local people, Legazpi established permanent settlements in Cebu and later in Luzon.

MANILA

By 1570, the Spanish had taken control of the thriving Muslim settlement on the present site of Manila, where Legazpi established the first capital of the Philippines. He and his successors exploited the site and its fine natural harbor to extend Spanish rule and trade through the archipelago. To protect the new city of Manila from attacks by Muslims, they built strong city walls, which still exist. In modern times, the district within the walls is called Intramuros (literally, "within the walls"). The walled city came to symbolize the permanent presence that the Spanish believed they had established in the region. Within the walls, they constructed grand buildings to symbolize their power: the stone cathedral, the palaces of the archbishop and the governor-general, and large private homes.

Before the Colonial Era

There is evidence of hunter-gatherers in the Philippines over 30,000 years ago. From around 3000 BCE, Malays from the south entered the islands, and the earlier peoples, Negritos and Igorots, were pushed into remoter areas. In time, different local Malay groups emerged, such as Tagalog, Cebuano, and Bikol peoples, based on language and culture. The islands lacked any cohesive political system. Society was based on the *barangay*, a kinship group usually numbering 200 to 500 people. The *barangay*, headed by a *dato*, or chief, was the principal political unit. Except in parts of Luzon where there were settled communities, most people were shifting farmers whose villages were abandoned as new settlements were built, when people moved to new land. Other communities were hunters or fishers.

The lack of larger political units was, in part, attributable to the nature of the archipelago; the small islands were isolated from one another, while mountains divided communities on the larger islands. The linguistic diversity of the archipelago also discouraged the formation of larger units. The different peoples followed traditional religions, worshipping nature spirits and honoring ancestors. Their society was divided into three classes: a ruling class that comprised the chief and his family; a landowning class; and a lower rank that included servants, sharecroppers (small farmers who paid rent in the form of a proportion of their crop to landowners), and slaves. These small communities were not, however, totally cut off from other peoples in Asia; from the eighth century, Chinese merchants visited the islands.

Beginning in the fifteenth century, this social pattern started to change in parts of Mindanao and in the Sulu Archipelago, as Islam entered the region from northern Borneo. Muslims organized the first states in the Philippines: sultanates (hereditary monarchies ruled by a monarch called a sultan). The sultans developed cities around their mosques and palaces and markets, and ports grew. In 1457, an Arab who had been born in Johor in the Malay Peninsula arrived in the Sulu Archipelago, where he founded the sultanate of Sulu. The sultanate became one of the most powerful Muslim states in the region, soon controlling many of the islands that surround the Sulu Sea. The influence of the sultan of Sulu, and of other Muslim monarchs in the southern Philippines, spread through the central Visayan Islands, and by the time the Spanish arrived in central Luzon, they found a Muslim *dato* ruling the *barangay* on the site of modern Manila.

Over the course of the following centuries, Manila became the center of Spanish economic and political activity in the Philippines. The city was inhabited by a diverse population that included the Spanish, the Creoles (Filipinos of Spanish ancestry), Chinese, mestizos (people of mixed Spanish and local parentage), and the original local inhabitants, known to the Spanish as the *indios*. The Chinese and Chinese mestizos played an important role in the economic and cultural life of Manila and eventually in the movement for independence from Spanish rule.

Manila Cathedral, which was rebuilt in the twentieth century, is in the walled Intramuros district, the original Spanish colonial city.

The Spanish used Manila as a base for the conquest of the archipelago. While they never fully conquered the large southern island of Mindanao (at that time largely Muslim) and the northernmost parts of the Philippines, they met little opposition in central and southern Luzon and the Visayan Islands. The absence of a cohesive, integrated political system in the islands, the linguistic diversity of the peoples, and the willingness of many chiefs to cooperate with the Spanish led to the rapid colonization of the Philippines. During the sixteenth century, political authority in the Philippines was exercised by the viceroy of Nueva España (modern Mexico) and only indirectly by the representative of the Spanish crown in the archipelago.

José Rizal (1861–1896), the leader of the nationalist movement against Spanish rule in the Philippines, spoke 22 languages and, in addition to being a journalist, poet, novelist, and historian, was interested in architecture, economics, music, sculpture, sociology, and education.

THE NATURE OF SPANISH RULE

The Spanish made great efforts to convert the people of the archipelago to Christianity. One of the striking features of Spanish colonialism was the inseparable union of church and state. Papal concessions to Spanish monarchs had given them sweeping powers over the administration of church revenues and a deciding voice in ecclesiastical appointments. In return, the Spanish crown undertook the task of converting the local people, most of whom came into direct contact with the Spanish state through a Spanish friar. After the formal establishment of the Spanish colonial regime in 1565, the first missionaries, the Augustinians, arrived. Fransciscan friars followed in 1577, the Jesuits in 1581, Dominican friars in 1587, and Recollect friars in 1606. Friars controlled education and public works, supervised tax collection, conscripted local people into the army, and acted as censors of reading material. They were the most powerful officials in the villages.

Building on their previous experiences of colonization, the Spanish adopted many of the same institutions they had used in Latin America to govern the Philippines. To entice Spanish settlers, Legazpi and his successors distributed *encomienda*s (land trusts) to colonists. An *encomienda* was land entrusted rather than granted as private property as a reward for services to the Spanish crown. The land holder, an *encomendero*, was expected to resettle the original inhabitants of the district in permanent communities and to establish a system of law and order. In return, the *encomendero* was entitled to collect tributes from the people, to exploit their labor for public works, and to impose quotas on their produce for his use.

By the middle of the seventeenth century, Roman Catholicism had a strong foothold. The use of elaborate ceremonies helped convert the Filipinos to the new religion. Before the colonial era, the *dato* or chief was the center of village life, but new kinship relationships were fostered through Christian baptism—godparents still play an important role in Philippine society. However, Filipinos did not completely abandon all the old ways; many folk customs were Christianized as Filipinos fused their old animist beliefs with their new faith.

TRADE AND SOCIETY

From the sixteenth through the eighteenth centuries, the principal economic enterprise of the colony was the galleon trade from Manila to Acapulco in Mexico. Chinese ships brought silk and other luxury goods to Manila for export by Spanish galleons to Europe via Mexico. However, by the late eighteenth century, the Philippines was a supplier of raw materials directly to Spain. The islands produced tobacco in the Cagayan Valley of Luzon, rice and sugar in central Luzon, and sugar in the Visayan Islands. The frontier of agriculture expanded, and local people, who practiced traditional farming, were forced off the land and into the cities.

A new landed commercial elite emerged alongside an increasingly impoverished urban and rural population. By the nineteenth century, local revolts and uprisings were common as conflicts between landless peasants and the landlords intensified. Discontent created the conditions for the emergence of a nationalist movement.

THE REFORM MOVEMENT AND RIZAL

After three centuries of Spanish rule, the Philippines was transformed into a complex society with a flourishing economy, a powerful Roman Catholic church, and tension between different classes and racial groups. By the late nineteenth century, anti-Spanish sentiments converged into a coherent ideology and a growing nationalist movement.

One of the main proponents of Philippine nationalism was José Rizal (1861–1896), who came from a Chinese mestizo family. He attended the foremost universities in the Philippines before going to Spain to study medicine, and his experiences outside the Philippines shaped his nationalist ideas. The contrast between the harsh reality of colonial life in the

Philippines and the more liberal atmosphere that he encountered in Spain made Rizal highly critical of Spanish rule in his native land.

Rizal and his fellow Philippine students and exiles, who like him came from elite mestizo backgrounds, thrived in the openness of Spanish urban society, but they were regarded in Spain as members of a lower class there. They founded the Propaganda Movement, which provided a forum for political discussion and for a campaign to reform Spanish rule in the Philippines. Initially, the members of the Propaganda Movement did not seek independence for the colony from Spain but instead advocated that the indigenous peoples of the Philippines should enjoy the same rights guaranteed to Spanish citizens in the islands. They supported a series of reforms including freedom of speech, Philippine representation in the Spanish legislature (the Cortes), and the appointment of Filipinos to the church and the colonial bureaucracy. They also started a newspaper, *La Sociedad* (Society), as a vehicle for their political aspirations.

Rizal and his companions wrote about the Philippines to instill in their readers a sense of pride in being Filipino. In 1887, Rizal published his first novel, *Noli me tangere* (Touch me not), a scathing indictment of the role of the Spanish church in Philippine society. He described the social conditions in the Philippines, pointing out that the grievances of the Filipinos were unheeded by the Spanish. The novel was banned in the Philippines, and Rizal was placed under close supervision by the Spanish authorities.

Ultimately, the Propaganda Movement failed to deliver reform in the Philippines. The authority of the colonial power remained intact, while the *indios* were denied rights. Rizal did not live to see the fulfillment of his dreams. In 1892, the Spanish arrested Rizal and banished him to Mindanao, fearing that his radical ideas would spark a revolution against Spain. However, banishment did not stop his political activities. When the Katipunan revolt broke out in 1896, the Spanish immediately blamed Rizal and his nationalist ideas. Consequently, he was arrested, tried, and executed. Rizal was killed by a firing squad on December 20, 1896; he was 35 years old. The death of Rizal effectively stalled the reform movement in the Philippines.

BONIFACIO AND THE KATIPUNAN

In 1892, on the day that Rizal's deportation to Mindanao was announced, a new revolutionary movement was formed, the Katipunan. The movement was formed by nationalists who were convinced that legal campaigns were futile to effect change. Founded by Andres Bonifacio (1863–1897), the Katipunan was composed primarily of ordinary Filipinos and a few supporters from the landowning elite. The movement was far more radical than the Propaganda Movement and advocated complete independence from Spain by means of armed revolution rather than through peaceful reform. By 1896, the Katipunan claimed thousands of members, and Bonifacio was recognized as the leader of the revolutionary movement.

The Katipunan founded a newspaper, *Kalayaan*, the Tagalog word for "freedom"; the paper published nationalist songs, poems, and treatises urging Filipinos to rise against the Spanish colonists. The rapid growth of the movement alarmed the Spanish authorities, and a crackdown by the Spanish Guardia Civil (paramilitary national police force) led Bonifacio and his associates to raise the flag of rebellion openly in August 1896. In a dramatic act of resistance, they tore up their residence permits (*cedula*), a symbol of the subject status of the Filipinos, to indicate their rejection of Spanish colonial rule. The revolt spread from Manila to nearby provinces in Luzon as members of the Katipunan fought a series of battles against Spanish forces. However, Spain's military superiority led to the defeat of the rebels; by the end of September, hundreds of rebels had been killed, arrested, or exiled, and Bonifacio himself was forced into hiding.

DISUNITY AND DEFEAT

From September 1898, internal divisions emerged within the Katipunan that led to its eventual demise. After a series of disagreements, fellow revolutionaries chose Emilio Aguinaldo (1869–1964), one of the Katipunan's military leaders, to head a revolutionary government, undermining Bonifacio's leadership. Refusing to recognize the results of what he perceived as a plot against him, Bonifacio challenged Aguinaldo's leadership and the actions of his political opponents. The challenge was condemned as treason by the war council of the Katipunan. After an illegal trial, in which Bonifacio and his brother were found guilty, the Bonifacio brothers were executed in a forest clearing. Bonifacio, the leader of the armed revolt against Spanish rule, met his end at the hands of fellow Filipino revolutionaries.

However, the struggle for Philippine independence continued. By 1898, Spanish colonial power had been severely weakened not only through frequent clashes with Filipino revolutionaries but also as a result of Spain fighting a war in the Caribbean region. In the Spanish-American War (1898), U.S. forces were fighting to evict the Spanish from Spain's last large American colony, Cuba. The effects of the distant war drained Spain's resources and its resolve in fighting the nationalists in the Philippines. Soon, the revolutionaries were in control of most of the Philippine Archipelago.

On June 12, 1898, Filipino revolutionaries under Aguinaldo issued a declaration of independence at Cavite, marking the end of 333 years of Spanish rule and the hoped-for birth of an independent nation. The new Philippine Republic then began the process of establishing its own government. Aguinaldo was declared the first president of the republic, and the first Philippine constitution was drafted. However, the republic was short-lived. U.S. forces defeated Spain in the Spanish-American War, and in December 1898, the Philippines came under a new colonial power, the United States.

V. A. LANZONA

The British in the Malay States

During the eighteenth and nineteenth centuries, Great Britain gradually extended its influence in the Malay Peninsula. Initially a regional trading force, the British increasingly intervened and eventually became a colonial power. The effects on Malay society were far-reaching and often damaging.

British interest in Southeast Asia changed over time. Until the mid-nineteenth century, Great Britain's interests were commercial and strategic. Other European powers, especially the Dutch in the East Indies (modern Indonesia), tried to monopolize trade in their colonies to allow them to buy local produce cheaply; as the leading industrial nation of the time, Great Britain was eager to undermine these monopolies and establish its own. The British set up free ports (ports that are open to commercial shipping from all nations on equal terms) at Penang (in 1786), Malacca (modern Melaka; 1795), and Singapore (1812). In 1826, the British organized these territories as the Straits Settlements, although the settlements did not become a formal British colony until 1867. The British trading stations were immediately successful in attracting merchants and smugglers, and Chinese, Indian, Arab, and Malay traders settled, particularly in Singapore. Possession of the Straits Settlements also allowed Great Britain to guard the strategic sea route through the Strait of Malacca that connected China in the east with India and Europe in the west.

RULING FROM A DISTANCE

At first the British were not interested in controlling large territories in Southeast Asia, because they wished to avoid the heavy costs in finance and personnel involved in administering formal colonies. Under the terms of the London Agreement (1824), Great Britain agreed to recognize Dutch control throughout the East Indies archipelago so long as British traders were guaranteed access in the region. The British found it much more profitable to concentrate on trade, selling textiles from British-ruled India and manufactured goods, including guns, from Great Britain, in exchange for Southeast Asian opium and spices, such as pepper, cloves, and nutmeg, for resale in Europe or China.

The British and other traders in the Straits Settlements were also interested in business opportunities in the Malay sultanates of the interior. They were particularly attracted by Malaya's rich tin deposits as the demand for tin rose after the invention of commercial food canning. Competition to control this new source of wealth led to armed conflict between factions in the local Malay aristocracy and royal families. Various Malay factions allied to Chinese businesspeople, who provided the labor to work the mines. As a result, some of the Malay states became destablized by conflict.

To protect their economic interests in tin mining, the British intervened to establish effective control of the Malay sultanate of Perak in 1874. The sultan of Perak became obliged to act on the instructions of a British "adviser," also called a resident, in all matters except those dealing with Malay custom and religion. As a result, Perak became a protected state and was effectively a colony in all but name. The same arrangement was then imposed on other Malay sultanates as British investment in the region expanded; by 1889, Selangor, Negeri Sembilan, and Pahang all had British residents. The ruler of Johor state, situated north of Singapore, initially avoided this fate by giving British and Chinese investors full legal protection and by modernizing the administration of his state.

SARAWAK

At the same time as the British authorities gained control of the Malay Peninsula, British entrepreneurs were acting independently to gain footholds elsewhere in the region. The earliest such intervention was by James Brooke (1803–1868), a wealthy entrepreneur who purchased an armed schooner to pursue his activities in the region. Learning that the chief minister of the (Malay) sultan of Brunei, in northern Borneo, was in revolt, Brooke sailed to Brunei and helped suppress the rebellion. As a reward, in 1841, the sultan granted Brooke the right to govern the Sarawak River district in northwestern Borneo, confirming upon him the title of raja.

In 1846, the sultan of Brunei recognized Brooke's title as hereditary. Brooke established a dynasty of so-called "white rajas," who ruled Sarawak as an independent state; in 1850, the United States was the first country to recognize Sarawak's independence. Brooke extended his control northward at the expense of Brunei until Sarawak attained its present borders, making Sarawak many times larger than Brunei. He developed the economy of the territory, which became one of the world's leading producers of pepper.

Brooke, who reigned from 1841 to 1868, insisted that his European officials become fluent in Malay, and he divided functions according to ethnicity: Malays worked in the administration, Ibans (indigenous peoples of Sarawak) in the militia, and Chinese as workers in plantations. The program worked well and became a model for later British-led administrations in the Malay Peninsula. The Brooke dynasty of three rajas ruled their state in a paternalistic manner until 1946.

James Brooke (1803–1868) helped end a revolt in Brunei, receiving western Sarawak from the sultan of Brunei in return for his support. Brooke ruled Sarawak as raja (monarch) from 1841. The United States recognized Sarawak's independence in 1850; 14 years later, Great Britain acknowledged Sarawak's sovereignty.

THE BRITISH IN NORTH BORNEO

In 1881, the British North Borneo Chartered Company, a commercial trading company, gained a large territory in the north of Borneo. The company appointed a governor, and later a legislative council, to administer the territory, but the final authority in what became known as British North Borneo (now called Sabah) was the company's directors in London. In 1888, the territory gained a status similar to that of a British protectorate, although the company continued to administer the territory's internal affairs and had sovereignty over it. From 1884 through 1898, the company acquired additional land from the sultan of Brunei, reducing Brunei to its present borders.

Through the development of plantations, the British North Borneo Chartered Company's rule had a great impact on North Borneo. The company's control of the area eventually ended in 1946, after World War II (1939–1945), during which North Borneo was occupied by Japanese forces. Under Japanese occupation, the territory suffered considerable damage. The British North Borneo

Chartered Company was bankrupted by the war and so, unable to repair the damage, ceded sovereignty to Great Britain, and the British government took over full responsibility for the territory. In the same year, Great Britain acquired the independent Sarawak from the last Brooke raja, whose government also lacked the resources to rebuild Sarawak after the war.

CONSOLIDATING BRITISH RULE

The patchwork growth of British influence in the Malay Peninsula was gradually consolidated toward the end of the nineteenth century. In 1895, the Malay states under British control in the peninsula—Negeri Sembilan, Pahang, Perak, and Selangor—were brought under a single British-controlled administration known as the Federated Malay States. However, each state remained autonomous in internal affairs.

In 1900, the Duff Development Company purchased a trading concession in the northern Malay state of Kelantan from the Thai government. British interest in the northern Malay Peninsula increased and in 1909, the northern Malay sultanates of Kelantan, Terengganu, Kedah, and Perlis, which were governed by Thailand but had British advisers, were peacefully ceded to British rule by treaty. These four states, along with Johor in the south, became known as the Unfederated Malay States. Effectively ruled by the British, these states continued to have their own autonomous internal administrations.

The unevenness of this political development mirrored imbalances in the pattern of economic and social development. The economies of the states that were most directly under British control developed rapidly. In the early nineteenth century, the small states along the western coast of the Malay Peninsula were thinly populated districts whose Malay inhabitants were mainly rice farmers and fishers. However, in a matter of decades, the tin mines in Perak and Selangor made Malaya the world's largest producer of tin, a position it held until 1905. Then, when the U.S. automobile industry developed its insatiable demand for rubber tires, large tracts of land were devoted to rubber plantations, and Malaya became the world's largest producer of rubber. The prolonged economic boom produced large profits for the owners of the tin mines and plantations, but the new development was concentrated in one region; the eastern and southern Malay states were not developed. The transformation of the local economy caused severe social problems associated with an influx of Chinese and Indian migrants and imbalances in the distribution of wealth.

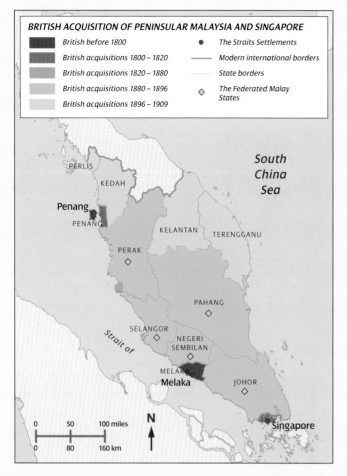

BRITISH ACQUISITION OF PENINSULAR MALAYSIA AND SINGAPORE

- British before 1800
- British acquisitions 1800 – 1820
- British acquisitions 1820 – 1880
- British acquisitions 1880 – 1896
- British acquisitions 1896 – 1909
- ● The Straits Settlements
- — Modern international borders
- State borders
- ◇ The Federated Malay States

IMMIGRATION

At the beginning of the nineteenth century, the population of the Malay Peninsula was thin and scattered in small settlements along the coasts and the main waterways. The peninsula was home to about one million people, concentrated in the northern sultanates. By the end of the century, the population was about 2 million, and by the 1930s, it had risen to 4.3 million. This huge increase was due to immigration from China, Sumatra, Java, and India into the southern and eastern districts of the peninsula. The immigrants came to escape poverty in their home countries and were attracted by the prospect of work in the tin mines, on plantations, or the possibility of opening up new farmland. The British encouraged immigration into Malaya until the economic downturn of the Great Depression hit Malaya in the 1930s. In the areas where the new industries developed, the population became ethnically mixed. In Perak, for instance, where there were large tin mines and extensive rubber plantations, more than one-half of the population of the state were Chinese immigrants by the 1930s. The more immigrants settled in a district, the more it was seen by the British as successfully developed.

Immigration had serious results for the development of Malay society, bringing to the same territory groups of people who had different cultures, who spoke different languages, and who followed different religions. The Malay Peninsula became an outstanding example of a "plural society"—one in which members of distinct and separate groups live alongside but separately from each other. Locally born Malay-speaking Muslim rice farmers had little in common with immigrant Buddhist Chinese-speaking tin miners or Hindu Tamil-speaking Indian contract workers living on a rubber plantation. The differences of employment, religion, culture, and language ensured that there was virtually no opportunity for social mixing or intermarriage between the groups.

The British authorities classified the population of the Malay Peninsula into three main racial groups: Malays, Chinese, and Indians. In fact, the divisions were more complicated. The loyalty of Malays to their state was strong, and they tended to see themselves as subjects of one of the Malay rulers rather than as Malays. The Chinese grouped according to their different languages, depending on where they had come from in China; some spoke Mandarin, others Cantonese, and yet others spoke Hokkien Chinese. In the Straits Settlements there were also Chinese whose families had lived in Malaya for generations and who spoke Malay as their mother tongue. The category of "Indians" included poor Tamil plantation workers, Bengali clerks, and Sikh police officers, although Tamil migrants from southern India formed a large majority.

A DIVIDED SOCIETY

The Malays were recognized by the British as the indigenous people. The British also recognized the Malay sultans as the ceremonial heads of their states. Although the sultans had surrendered practical power to the British "advisers," and later to a more centralized British-run administration, they became wealthy because of the generous pensions the British authorities paid them. The British encouraged the sons of the Malay royal families and nobility to get an English education, and in 1905, the colonial authorities set up a school modeled on the elite boarding schools in England to educate young Malay aristocrats, who could then move into government posts. Malay commoners were also offered education, but only in the Malay language and at an elementary level. The aim was to make ordinary Malays better farmers and fishers but to avoid giving them too much education for fear that this might make them dissatisfied with their position.

The British, working through the Malay rulers, also tried to protect Malays from the effects of rapid development by reserving tracts of agricultural land that could be owned only by Malays. Keeping Malays on the land also suited the British, who needed cheap food for the immigrant Chinese workers in the mines and Indian workers on the plantations. Over time, these policies kept rural Malays poor and combined to increase the class division in Malay society, trapping Malay commoners in the poorer rural sectors of the economy.

At the same time, the British felt no great responsibility toward the Chinese, whom they regarded as temporary migrants. Chinese immigrants were largely left to look after their own affairs as long as they did not break the law. The conditions under which Chinese immigrants worked were poor; most were young men who fled dire poverty in southern China to try to fare better in Malaya. Many arrived deeply in debt to bosses who had paid their fares. They were encouraged to seek escape from their hardships by smoking opium, gambling, and other activities that also helped keep them in debt. Those who escaped the vicious cycle typically set up shops or became traders in the rapidly growing towns. A few became very rich. The government did not provide schools for the Chinese, but the children of some wealthier Chinese who lived in the towns learned English at Christian missionary schools. Some of the poorer Chinese attended poorly staffed private Chinese schools, but overall levels of education and literacy among the ethnic Chinese population were very low.

The Indian plantation workers were recruited on contract from southern India, which was then also under British rule. They were sent to work on isolated plantations where they would be treated more or less as slaves. The roads and railroads of Malaya were also built by gangs of Indian laborers. When the contracts of plantation workers and other laborers expired, most were shipped back to India.

In the racially divided plural society, there was no sense of common interest or broad community. British Malaya was a territory thrown open for economic development almost regardless of the social costs. In the nineteenth century, one-quarter to over one-half of all government revenue came from opium licenses or sales, and although the British authorities received substantial revenue from the Malay territories, they spent less than one-tenth of that revenue on education. Each of the ethnic communities was preoccupied with its own affairs. In the early twentieth century, Malay-language newspapers encouraged their Malay readers to break down state differences and to develop a sense of shared Malay identity; this was spurred by fear of competition from the Chinese settlers. The growth of Malay national feeling was not initially anticolonial, because the Malays viewed the British as protectors of their rights as the indigenous people. In the first two decades of the twentieth century, Malay intellectuals were also caught up in the excitement of reforming their Islamic religion, as new ideas flooded in from the Islamic centers of Cairo, in Egypt, and Mecca, in Saudi Arabia.

Some Chinese settlers thought of Malaya as their homeland, but the majority were more interested in political developments in China. Feelings of nationalism were directed toward China. The establishment of the Chinese Republic in 1911 had strong support among "overseas Chinese" in Malaya and elsewhere, and overseas Chinese had seats in the new Chinese republican legislature. The National School Movement, which taught in Mandarin, the newly designated national language of China, also developed and helped break down barriers between different Chinese language groups in Malaya. Chinese nationalism reached new heights in the 1930s when Japan invaded China. The Chinese in Malaya raised money to support the war effort and boycotted Japanese products.

The sultanates

Until 1946, the administration of the Malay Peninsula under British rule was split among a British colony (the Straits Settlements, which included Penang, Malacca, and Singapore), the four Federated Malay States (Negeri Sembilan, Pahang, Perak, and Selangor) with a central administration in Kuala Lumpur, and the five Unfederated Malay States (Johor, Kedah, Kelantan, Perlis, and Terengganu), each a separate British-protected state. Although the federated and unfederated states had a different legal status, both were British protectorates in which the British controlled defense and, effectively, the economy. The governments of the sultans retained power over some domestic issues, subject to the "advice" of British residents, in effect colonial governors.

The sultanates varied in size between Pahang, which with an area of 13,886 square miles (35,964 sq. km) is about the same size as Maryland and Delaware combined, to Perlis, which with an area of only 310 square miles (803 sq. km) is four times the size of Washington, D.C. The states also greatly varied in population and economic importance. Among them, the Federated Malay States contributed a high percentage of the world's tin and were a major producer of rubber in the 1930s.

The personal and political allegiances of ethnic Malays were primarily toward the local state, and the sultans did nothing to change this situation. British rule maintained the authority of the sultans and made them wealthy through generous pensions. Although the monarchs accepted British protection, some discontent was evident. Terengganu was transferred from nominal Thai rule to British rule in 1909; a British resident was not installed in the state until 1919, but the loss of independence was resented, and Terengganu rose in revolt in 1928.

The powers retained by the sultans were largely symbolic, for example as head of the Islamic community within their state. In time, the British removed the administration of some states from the seat of the sultan and established a new state capital; as a result, some states have state and royal capitals. For example, Kuantan is the capital of Pahang, whose royal capital is Pekan.

THE EFFECT OF COLONIAL RULE

The impact of British rule, economic development, and immigration was uneven. The Malay-dominated agricultural states in the north and east of the Malay Peninsula were hardly affected. Sarawak and British North Borneo experienced some development, and Sarawak gained a large Chinese community. The impact of colonialism was greatest in the areas along the western coast of the Malay Peninsula, where large-scale immigration produced a pattern of Chinese-dominated cities surrounded by a poor Malay-dominated countryside. The colonial period left Malaya with serious racial imbalances and without a coherent society. These problems were made worse under Japanese rule from 1942 through 1945 during World War II and later presented a huge challenge to nation-building in independent Malaya after 1957.

I. PROUDFOOT

U.S. Involvement in the Philippines

From the 1830s, an elite group of traders and landowners, often of mixed Spanish and Chinese or indigenous heritage, emerged in the Philippines. This landed class became a national political force that challenged various aspects of colonial rule. However, their nationalist agenda was not realized, because in 1898 Spanish rule was replaced by a U.S. administration.

In 1898, the United States declared war on Spain, primarily as a result of developments in the Spanish colony of Cuba. The U.S. media represented the Spanish-American War as a struggle by the United States to liberate the Cubans from Spanish colonial rule. During the war, Filipino rebels, led by the landed elite, launched their own popular anticolonial rebellion against the Spanish, seizing control of virtually the entire Philippine Archipelago outside Manila, the national capital. The victorious Filipinos declared an independent republic.

However, the United States sent a naval expedition to the Philippines, and by May 1898, U.S. forces had captured the antiquated Spanish fleet and occupied Manila. A swift campaign in which U.S. forces gained control of much of the Philippines precipitated a debate in the United States about what to do with the archipelago. Opinion was divided between supporting Philippine independence or turning the Philippines into a U.S. colony. A forceful minority of Americans argued that the Filipinos were not yet capable of self-government. There was also an influential anti-imperial lobby that was nevertheless worried about granting political rights to people of largely non-European descent. In December 1898, Spain ceded the Spanish colonies of the Philippines, Puerto Rico, and Guam to the United States; by that time, the U.S. administration of President William Howard Taft (1857–1930) had decided to colonize formally all of the Philippines. The United States launched a war of conquest against those Filipinos who remained committed to the formation of an independent republic.

Manuel Quezon, seen here after his inauguration as first president of the Commonwealth of the Philippines in 1935, was an uncompromising advocate of Philippine nationalism. He once said "I prefer a country run like hell by Filipinos to a country run like heaven by Americans. Because, however bad a Filipino government might be, we can always change it."

ESTABLISHING AMERICAN RULE

Filipino nationalists resisted the imposition of U.S. rule, and the Philippine-American War began in 1899. After around 5,000 U.S. and more than 200,000 Philippine losses, the U.S. government increasingly changed its position from 1901; instead of seeking an all-out military victory it looked to set up a structure of collaboration with those members of the landed elite who were thought to be sympathetic. The landowners, in turn, consolidated their support among the peasantry in the countryside and helped to suppress the fighting. The Americans required the landowners to mediate with the mass population, while the elite needed the Americans to restore political and social order and bolster their leadership of Philippine society and their control of the colony's economy. The worst of the fighting

was over by the end of 1902, but sporadic resistance continued until 1913. In 1907, an elected Philippine assembly opened, and in 1916, the U.S. government promised the Philippines independence at some (unspecified) time in the future.

Meanwhile, the U.S. administration in the Philippines expropriated more than 400,000 acres (162,000 hectares) of agricultural land from the Spanish religious orders who had been major landowners in the colonial era. The land was auctioned publicly, and at the same time, the United States placed restrictions on American property ownership in the Philippines. In practice, this meant that virtually the only people able to buy the land that had formerly belonged to the Church were members of the existing landed elite, who were able to expand their holdings dramatically. As a result, the small class of wealthy landowners grew more powerful under U.S. rule.

AUTONOMY

The U.S. administration in the Philippines developed an autonomous political system in stages, mirroring the American system with a Congress and a Senate. The Congress was elected from districts, each returning one member on a winner-takes-all basis. In 1935, the Philippines became a commonwealth with almost complete internal autonomy; full independence was projected, although no date was given. An elected president headed the Commonwealth; the first occupant of the post was Manuel Quezon (1878–1944), who had become a leading member of the nationalist movement after he was first elected to the Philippine assembly in 1907. The right to vote, which was restricted to men, was initially based on a property franchise; the system suited the property-owning elite and more or less limited elections to competing rival landowners.

THE EFFECTS OF U.S. ADMINISTRATION

Elsewhere in Asia, colonial rule operated through large bureaucracies that were dominated by officials born and educated in the imperial homeland; however, the United States did not establish a centralized bureaucracy of colonial officials in the Philippines. Once the government of the United States and the relatively small group of U.S. administrators on the ground were confident of the landed elite's self-interested loyalty to American rule, they established a civil service with a bare minimum of U.S. citizens and gave most of the administrative posts in the territory to Filipinos.

Many Filipino politicians, most of whom were landowners, used their political power to obtain low-rate or interest-free loans. The landowner-politicians discovered that political control of the treasury and senior judicial appointments was a strong guarantee of their own continued dominance. The elite prospered, and, in 1909, the Philippines was given privileged access to the U.S. market, and Philippine agricultural exports, particularly sugar, were purchased in the United States at prices above those being paid elsewhere. However, the majority of small farmers, who were in share-tenancy agreements (paying a share of the crop as rent), suffered hardship, struggling to meet rising payments. As a result, disaffected tenant farmers rebelled in Luzon in the 1920s and 1930s.

The development of the Philippines in the 1920s and 1930s was shaped not only by the particular character of the U.S. colonial government but also by the political and economic collaboration of the Filipino landowners with the administration. Some historians observe that the political dominance of a small landed class blocked or limited the development of democracy despite the early establishment of a legislative system in the Philippines. Although a middle class developed, most Filipinos remained poor. However, under U.S. rule education and health care dramatically improved, such that by the 1930s literacy rates had doubled, and many communicable diseases had been almost eradicated.

The progress toward full independence was broken in December 1941, when Japanese forces invaded the Philippines during World War II (1939–1945). Quezon and his government left Manila, and within a few weeks, the vast majority of U.S. colonial and military officials had been ejected from the Philippines. Quezon fled to the United States and died in 1944.

M. T. BERGER

U.S. Attitudes toward Philippine Independence

From 1898, when Spain ceded the Philippines to the United States, U.S. attitudes toward the acquisition of a large Asian colony were ambivalent. Many Americans felt that it was wrong in principle for the United States to become a colonial power. The archipelago was acquired with some reluctance, and in 1899 the British poet Rudyard Kipling (1865–1936) wrote the poem *Take Up the White Man's Burden* to encourage the U.S. government to colonize the Philippines formally. There was an opinion shared by many members of the U.S. administration that the Philippines was not ready for independence. This perception eventually persuaded the United States to become a colonial power.

U.S. governor-general Francis Harrison (1873–1957; in office 1913–1921) was an opponent of colonialism. Appointed to the Philippines by President Woodrow Wilson (1856–1924; in office 1913–1921), Harrison actively promoted the cause of Philippine independence. Democrats in the U.S. Senate sponsored the Jones Act (passed in 1916), which would have set a date for Philippine independence, but the measure was rejected by the House of Representatives. In its final form, the Jones Act recognized that Philippine independence was a long-term aim "as soon as stable government can be established." More important, the Jones Act created an elected senate, which replaced the Philippine Commission, a unelected body chosen by the U.S. president.

The U.S. authorities in the Philippines promoted education and the participation of Filipinos in the administration. By the mid-1920s, only around 6 percent of the civil service in the archipelago was American. Initially, many U.S. teachers were sent to the Philippines, but by the 1920s, Filipinos formed the overwhelming majority of the teaching profession in the islands. The nature of the U.S. administration had changed by the mid-1920s; the administration was in the hands of Filipinos, and after 1935, the governor-general was replaced by an elected Philippine president, although the Philippines was still denied full independence.

War in the Malay States, Singapore, and the Philippines

On December 7, 1941, during World War II (1939–1945), the Japanese attacked the U.S. Pacific Fleet at Pearl Harbor in Hawaii. The attack signaled the beginning of a rapid Japanese campaign to conquer the Malay Peninsula, Singapore, and the Philippines.

The Japanese military campaign of 1941 through 1942 had two main objectives. The primary objective was to occupy territories that would provide Japan with the raw materials desperately needed by Japanese war industries. The secondary aim was to crush European and U.S. influence in Asia, making Japan dominant in the region.

Malaya, an important British colonial possession, was a major source of rubber and tin; the Malay states (British protectorates and colonies) occupied a strategic position along the sea route between India and China. The British colony of Singapore was one of the world's greatest ports and had an important role in controlling shipping traffic from India through to the Pacific and around the oil-rich Dutch East Indies (modern Indonesia). The Philippines had been under U.S. administration since the end of the nineteenth century, but by 1941, the archipelago was on its way toward independence. Although the Philippines gained internal self-government as a commonwealth in 1935, it still formed a vital base for the U.S. Navy in the Pacific. Japan therefore had to take the Philippines to weaken U.S. influence in the region and to control the north-south shipping lanes to the Dutch East Indies, which it also intended to conquer.

INVASION

On December 8, 1941 (the same day as the Japanese attack on Pearl Harbor, but on the other side of the international date line), Japanese forces invaded northern Malaya and began driving the British and Malayan defenders southward. The highly trained and motivated Japanese troops overran their enemies; on January 11, 1942, Kuala Lumpur, the Malayan capital, fell, and by the second half of January, the British were squeezed into the southern tip of the Malay Peninsula. The British could not hold the mainland and, on January 31, the last British troops in the peninsula evacuated across the straits between Johor and the island of Singapore. On February 9, Japanese troops crossed the straits, and after a brief, bloody engagement, British forces in Singapore surrendered on February 15. To secure the region, Japanese forces had also occupied the British-controlled territories of northern Borneo: British North Borneo (now Sabah), the protectorate of Brunei, and Sarawak, legally an independent state ruled by the Brooke family from Great Britain.

While Malaya collapsed, other Japanese units overran the Philippines. Amphibious landings in Luzon, the most northerly large island in the Philippines, began on December 10. Nine days later, Japanese forces also landed on Mindanao, the second-largest Philippine island after Luzon, in the far south of the archipelago. Filipino and U.S. forces led by General Douglas MacArthur (1880–1964) were unable to stop the Japanese onslaught, and Manila, the capital of the Philippines, fell on January 2, 1942. The bulk of the U.S. and Filipino troops retreated into the Bataan Peninsula west of Manila and held out there until April 9; however, by early May, Japanese forces occupied all of the Philippines. The president of the Philippines, Manuel Quezon (1878–1944), was forced to flee to the United States during the occupation.

OCCUPATION

The Japanese forces and administrators in Malaya and the Philippines tried to present themselves as liberators from colonial oppression rather than aggressors. They had initially encouraged the nationalist movements that were already thriving within the two countries, but they soon demonstrated that independence was the last thing they wanted for their newly conquered territories. In Malaya, all the main nationalist groups, such as the Union of Young Malaya (UYM) and the Malayan Communist Party (MCP), were banned by June 1942; only the collaborationist Indian Independence League was allowed to continue its activities.

The brutal actions of the Japanese in Malaya, much of them directed against Malaya's large Chinese population, soon disillusioned any remaining sympathizers; Japan had been at war with China since 1937, and the ethnic Chinese in the Malay states were a particular target for the Japanese. Tens of thousands of people were deported from Malaya and Singapore for forced labor in New Guinea and in Thailand, where more than 40,000 Malays died during the war. Food supplies were diverted to Japanese troops rather than hungry civilians. Any dissent resulted in arrest, torture, and execution. In response, the prohibited political groups formed the Malayan People's Anti-Japanese Army (MPAJA), which conducted a guerrilla war against Japan from 1942 through 1945, with British government backing. The Chinese population of northern Borneo also launched a major rebellion against Japanese occupation in 1943, but the revolt was crushed with the loss of thousands of Chinese lives.

Filipinos had a similar occupation experience to the peoples of Malaya and Singapore. Nationalist hopes that the Japanese would bring complete independence were quickly quashed. In 1942, a group of influential Filipino politicians and officials tried to negotiate the creation of a new national government, but this resulted in nothing more than a Japanese puppet administration. Resistance flourished through guerrilla groups, such as the Hukbalahap (Communist-led guerrillas who, after the war, declared their Communist sympathies and conducted a campaign against the Philippine government). Other groups, including the movement known as President Quezon's Own Guerrillas, also confronted the Japanese. Unlike other Pacific guerrilla movements, the Filipino guerrillas had a considerable impact on the Japanese, not only through military action but also through the invaluable intelligence they provided to the United States.

LIBERATION

By 1943 the war was beginning to turn against Japan. With increasing desperation, the Japanese attempted to promote local nationalism in the hope of winning civilian loyalty in the occupied countries. The Philippine puppet government under José Laurel (1891–1959) was offered a more genuine independence in July 1943, and a new constitution was ratified in September that year. However, all the members of the new government were pro-Japanese, and Japan had made the offer of independence conditional on a declaration of war against the United States. Such conditions would soon become immaterial, however. On October 20, 1944, U.S. forces under General MacArthur landed on the island of Leyte and began the reconquest of the Philippines. By March 1945, after fighting that cost around 100,000 civilian lives, Manila was back in U.S. hands, and by July 1945, the Philippines was effectively under U.S. control again. Following the war, the Philippines was granted full independence in 1946.

Malaya and Singapore remained in Japanese hands until September 9, 1945, when the British took back their former possessions after the official Japanese surrender in the Pacific. The Japanese occupiers had attempted a last-ditch program to promote Malayan independence in July 1945, encouraging

Japanese forces march through the downtown area of Singapore in February 1942, following the surrender of the city by the British.

Malays to join the pro-Japanese Indian National Army based in Singapore. However, the brutalities of Japanese occupation and their impending defeat bought the occupiers little support. Although the Japanese in Malaya surrendered in September 1945, the MCP fought an independence war with the British between 1948 and the late 1950s.

O. C. McNAB

1189

The Malay Emergency

When World War II (1939–1945) ended, the Malay Peninsula, Singapore, British North Borneo (now Sabah), Sarawak, and Brunei faced an uncertain economic and political future. The period of Japanese occupation during the war had also made it clear that British rule was neither inevitable nor permanent.

Japanese rule during World War II exacerbated ethnic tensions in the region. Ethnic Chinese guerrillas fought against the Japanese in Malaya, while a Chinese revolt in British North Borneo had briefly threatened Japanese control. The Chinese perceived themselves to have been greater opponents of the invaders than the Malays.

A POLITICAL JIGSAW

By 1945, much of the region had been devastated by war, and a coordinated recovery was made more difficult by the fact that the region formed several separate political entities. The Malay Peninsula was divided into three different political units: the Straits Settlements, the Federated Malay States, and the Unfederated Malay States. The Straits Settlements was a British colony that comprised the Malay states of Penang and Malacca (now Melaka), as well as the island of Singapore. The colony also included the island of Labuan off the northern coast of Borneo and Christmas Island and the Cocos (Keeling) Islands, which lie south of the Indonesian island of Java.

The Federated Malay States was a federation of four states ruled by sultans: Pahang, Perak, Selangor, and Negeri Sembilan. The federation was established in 1895 by Great Britain, which was responsible for its defense and foreign affairs, while the state governments were responsible for home affairs. However, a British official advised on internal matters in the states, which were bound by treaty to follow his decisions. The Unfederated Malay States (Johor, Kedah, Kelantan, Perlis, and Terengganu) were separate states under British protection. Each was ruled by a sultan, but the effective ruler was a British adviser. There was no overall administration for the Unfederated Malay States.

The sultanate of Brunei in northern Borneo was a British protectorate that had considerable internal autonomy. British North Borneo was a British protectorate, and Sarawak, a huge territory in northern Borneo, was the personal possession of the British Brooke family, one of whose members, James Brooke (1803–1868), became raja (monarch) of Sarawak in the 1840s.

FIRST ATTEMPTS AT FEDERATION

While the disparate nature of the administration of these territories was an obstacle to reconstruction after World War II, there was also a growing sense of Malay identity and nationalism. The British colonial authorities in the region encouraged the creation of a Malayan Union that would have included all the territories under British rule or protection. However, most Malay nationalists resisted the British project, which would have brought large minorities of Chinese, Indians, and different indigenous peoples in Borneo into the federation. The majority population of the Malay Peninsula sought a more distinctly Malay entity, and Singapore was soon excluded from the project. A British proposal that the minorities of the region should have equal citizenship with the Malays also failed to win favor.

In 1946, as a result of Malay opposition to the project for a "greater" Malay Union, the United Malays National Organization (UMNO) was formed by Malay nationalist leader Dato Onn bin Ja'afar (1895–1962). UMNO became the political voice of the Malays whose opposition to regional unification became clear through strikes and demonstrations.

The Straits Settlements colony was divided in 1946. Singapore became a separate British colony; Labuan became part of British North Borneo; and Christmas Island and the Cocos (Keeling) Islands were transferred to Australian rule. The Brooke family lacked the resources to rebuild Sarawak after Japanese occupation and the damage caused by the war, and the last raja of Sarawak ceded the sovereignty of his territory to Great Britain. This action was opposed both by his heir and by the Malay population of Sarawak, and the first British colonial administrator appointed to Sarawak was assassinated. In 1946, the Federated and Unfederated Malay States joined with Penang and Malacca to form a federation under British rule.

FEDERATION AND INSURGENCY

Negotiations between the British and UMNO secured the creation of the Federation of Malaya in 1948. The federation had limited internal self-rule and entrenched the role of the Malays, whose rights were protected. The powers of the sultans were also guaranteed. The federation was opposed by many of the ethnic Chinese in Malaya, who were denied full citizenship and the right to vote. As a result, some members of the (largely Chinese) Communist Party of Malaya, which had formed the greater part of the armed opposition to Japanese occupation, again went underground and launched a guerrilla movement—the Malay Races Liberation Army (MRLA) led by Chin Peng (born 1924)—against the new federation.

In the 12-year period of guerrilla activity that is usually called the Malay Emergency, the MRLA conducted a violent campaign that was resisted by the infant forces of the new federation, and by much larger British forces with the support of some British Commonwealth countries. The guerrillas attacked tin mines and rubber plantations, the rural infrastructure, and roads and railroads. Although only a minority of Malaya's ethnic Chinese supported the insurgency, the tactics adopted by the British were initially unpopular. The British uprooted many rural Chinese, forcing them into so-called New Villages on the edges of cities where they were more easily defended and where the activities of the inhabitants could be more easily monitored.

Eventually, reforms rather than military activity helped end the emergency. The Chinese who had been relocated to the New Villages were given land rights. The colonial authorities distributed free food and made medical care available, gradually winning over the Chinese. At the same time, the brutality of the MRLA greatly damaged their cause. In 1951, the MRLA killed the British high commissioner in Malaya. His successor, Gerald Templer (1898–1979), reinforced the campaign against the guerrillas from 1952 through 1954 while promoting reforms, such as enfranchising Malaya's ethnic Chinese. With declining support and the arrival of troops from Australia and New Zealand to fight the insurgency in 1955, Chin Peng, realizing the fight could not be won, sought negotiations.

In August 1957 Malaya gained independence, with Tunku Abdul Rahman Putra (1903–1990) as the first prime minister. The dispirited insurgents gradually surrendered or abandoned their campaign. The struggle that had initially been an anticolonial movement lacked rationale now that Malaya was independent and the ethnic Chinese who had been the principal supporters of the MRLA had won land rights, the vote, and other reforms. The last serious action in the insurgency was in 1958, and in 1960, when the Malayan government declared the emergency over, Chin Peng fled to China.

For subsequent history, see pages 1199, 1215–1217, 1245-1247, and 1277–1278.

P. FERGUSSON

During the Malay Emergency (1948–1960), some 40,000 troops from Commonwealth countries (including these British soldiers) and more than 200,000 Malay full-time and part-time forces confronted an unknown number of Communist guerrillas.

Peoples of Malaysia, Singapore, Brunei, and the Philippines

The countries of the region are ethnically diverse, although Malays and peoples whose languages are related to Malay are dominant. The Malays and the main cultural-linguistic groups in the Philippines all speak languages that belong to the Austronesian (Malayo-Polynesian) family.

Throughout the region, peoples whose ancestors have migrated from the Indian subcontinent or from China—and in the case of Malaysia and Singapore, from both regions—form sizable minorities. The peoples of the region follow a number of different religions: Malaysia and Brunei both have a Muslim majority, and the Philippines has a Roman Catholic majority.

THE MALAYS

The Malays are thought to have originated in Borneo, from where they spread along the coast of Sumatra and into Peninsular Malaysia in the first millennium CE. The Malay language is closely related to Bahasa Indonesia, the national language of Indonesia, but there are several Malay dialects. Malays account for 51 percent of the population of Malaysia, although about 58 percent of Malaysians speak Malay (Bahasa Melayu). Although they are a majority in Peninsular Malaysia, Malays form only about one-eighth of the population of Eastern Malaysia (Sabah and Sarawak).

In Malaysia, Malays and the non-Malay indigenous peoples of Sabah and Sarawak, such as the Iban, are known as Bumiputras (or Bumiputeras), which means "sons of the soil." More than one definition of Bumiputra exists, but the term is generally understood to exclude ethnic Chinese and non-Muslim Indians. The Malaysian constitution defines the Bumiputras as those who profess Islam, speak the Malay language, and practice Malay culture. Since independence (of Malaya) in 1957, the government has enacted legislation that is collectively known as the Bumiputra Laws, which define measures in favor of the Bumiputra community. The laws stipulate quotas for admission to higher education and employment, as well as positive measures to assist Bumiputras in home and business ownership.

Malays account for 67 percent of the population of Brunei and 14 percent of the population of the city-state of Singapore. All Malay peoples are Muslim, following Sunni Islam, and most live in villages and small towns. Many of the major cities of Malaysia have an ethnic Chinese majority. Malay culture was influenced by Hindu Indian, Thai, Javanese, and Sumatran culture. Malay society typically has clear class distinctions. The majority of Malay states have a sultan or raja as chief of state and Malaysia is a monarchy. Although officials are now appointed or elected, members of the nobility and junior members of the Malay royal families occupy many important roles.

ETHNIC CHINESE AND INDIANS

Chinese traders settled throughout the region from around the tenth century CE, although settlement greatly increased during the second half of the nineteenth century when trade in rubber, tin, and other commodities grew, industries were founded, and mining developed. In modern times, ethnic Chinese account for 77 percent of the population of Singapore, about 24 percent in Malaysia, 15 percent in Brunei, and a small minority in the Philippines. The Chinese have played a major role in business and finance in these countries. In Malaysia, ethnic violence occurred in the late 1940s and 1950s and occasionally since, in part because of tensions raised by the lack of civil rights of the Chinese minority until the late 1950s and because of Malay disquiet concerning the dominance of the Chinese in commerce. Singapore has a Chinese majority, and about 35 percent of Singaporeans speak Mandarin Chinese as a first language; there are also substantial minorities speaking Hokkien Chinese and Cantonese. The majority of Chinese in the region are Buddhists, but many follow Chinese traditional religions, including Taoism.

Peoples of Indian descent form sizable communities in both Malaysia (7 percent of the population) and Singapore (8 percent). Indians came to the Malay Peninsula from the end of the nineteenth century, mainly to work in plantations and other industries. Around 85 percent of the region's ethnic Indians are Tamils, whose ancestors came from southeastern India. Telegu, Punjabi, and other peoples are also represented. The region is also home to peoples of mixed ancestry, Eurasians who descend from British, Dutch, Portuguese, and (in the Philippines) Spanish colonists who intermarried with local peoples.

INDIGENOUS PEOPLES OF EASTERN MALAYSIA

Around 11 percent of the population of Malaysia and 6 percent of the population of Brunei are non-Malay indigenous peoples who are classed as Bumiputras. There is also a small non-Malay

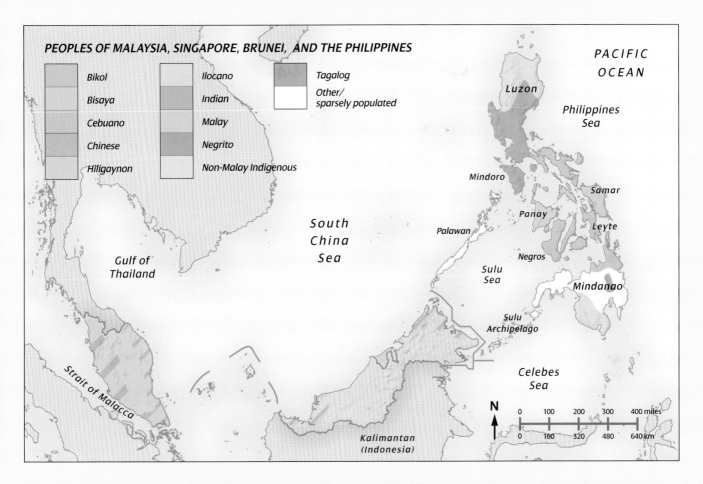

PEOPLES OF MALAYSIA, SINGAPORE, BRUNEI, AND THE PHILIPPINES

Bikol
Bisaya
Cebuano
Chinese
Hiligaynon

Ilocano
Indian
Malay
Negrito
Non-Malay Indigenous

Tagalog
Other/ sparsely populated

PACIFIC OCEAN

Luzon

Philippines Sea

Mindoro

Samar

Panay

Leyte

Palawan

Negros

South China Sea

Sulu Sea

Mindanao

Gulf of Thailand

Sulu Archipelago

Celebes Sea

Strait of Malacca

Kalimantan (Indonesia)

N

0   100   200   300   400 miles
0   160   320   480   640 km

indigenous group in Peninsular Malaysia known as the Orang Asli. The peoples of Eastern Malaysia are members of many different ethnic and linguistic groups, the largest of which is the Iban. However, they share some cultural similarities. Many of these peoples, who form a majority in the state of Sabah, follow traditional beliefs.

THE PEOPLES OF THE PHILIPPINES

The majority of Filipinos descend from Malays who migrated to the islands from around 1,500 years ago. The original inhabitants of the Philippines were peoples variously known as Negritos, pygmies, or Aetas, who now form a small minority in the eastern part of the southern island of Mindanao. The Malay Filipinos are diverse; some are predominantly Malay, while others have Chinese, Spanish, or American ancestors (Spanish and later American colonists were active in the islands and some intermarried). Although most Filipinos have a common Malay ancestry, several major ethnolinguistic and cultural groups are recognized.

The Tagalog people are the largest cultural-linguistic group in the Philippines, accounting for 28 percent of the population. They live in central Luzon, the largest Philippine island, and on neighboring islands, such as Mindoro. The Tagalog language is the basis for the Philippine national language, Filipino

(Tagalog). Centered around Manila, the Philippine national capital, the Tagalog people have a dominant role in commerce, administration, and the professions. The Tagalog are Westernized, with many elements of Spanish and American culture and, like most Filipinos, they are Roman Catholics.

The Cebuano people (who are also known as Cebuan or Sugbuhanon) live in the islands of Cebu, Bohol, Negros, Leyte, and the northern parts of Mindanao. The second-largest cultural-linguistic group in the Philippines, they account for 13 percent of the nation's population. Most Cebuano people are farmers.

Centered in the Ilocos Region and the Cagayan Valley in Luzon and in parts of Mindanao, the Ilocano people (also known as the Iloko or Iloco) are the third-largest cultural-linguistic Philippine group, accounting for 9 percent of the population. Originally from coastal Luzon, the Ilocano have migrated to the other islands. The Hiligaynon people of the Western Visayas are closely related to the Cebuano. Also called the Ilongo or Panayan, the Hiligaynon form 8 percent of the Philippine population. Their language, a member of the Visayan or Bisayan group of Malay-Polynesian languages, is closely related to the Bisayan languages spoken by the Bisaya/Binisaya peoples of the eastern Visayan Islands. There is also a small Bisayan population in Sarawak. The Bikol (or Bicolano) people live in the Bicol Peninsula of Luzon and on neighboring islands. They account for around 6 percent of the population of the Philippines.

C. CARPENTER

Brunei

Brunei was once a powerful sultanate that ruled the greater part of northern Borneo. However, from the sixteenth century, the country declined, losing the region that became British North Borneo (now called Sabah) and the large southern territory of Sarawak, which was ceded to the Brooke family of Great Britain, who ruled it as sovereigns until 1946. By the 1880s, Brunei was reduced to its present area, about the size of Delaware. In 1888, Brunei became a British protectorate, although the sultan retained autonomy. The state was occupied by Japanese forces from 1941 through 1945 and returned to British rule after World War II (1939–1945). The discovery of oil in the 1920s transformed Brunei's economy. By the 1960s and 1970s, the nation had laid the foundations for a welfare state in which education and health care are free and many facilities are heavily subsidized by the state. In 1959, Brunei was granted complete internal self-government, and the state regained independence in 1984. The nation, which is divided into two separate blocks by Malaysian territory, is oil-rich and has a high standard of living, and it remains an absolute monarchy.

GEOGRAPHY

Location	Southeastern Asia in northern Borneo
Climate	Tropical wet climate
Area	2,226 sq. miles (5,765 sq. km)
Coastline	100 miles (161 km)
Highest point	Bukit Pagon 6,070 ft (1,850 m)
Lowest point	South China Sea 0 ft (0 m)
Terrain	Coastal plains rise to hills in the west and mountains in the east
Natural resources	Petroleum, natural gas, timber
Land use	
Arable land	0.6 percent
Permanent crops	0.8 percent
Other	98.6 percent
Major rivers	Belait, Tutong, Brunei
Major lake	Tasek Merimbun
Natural hazards	Flooding

NEIGHBORS AND LENGTH OF BORDERS

Malaysia	238 miles (383 km)

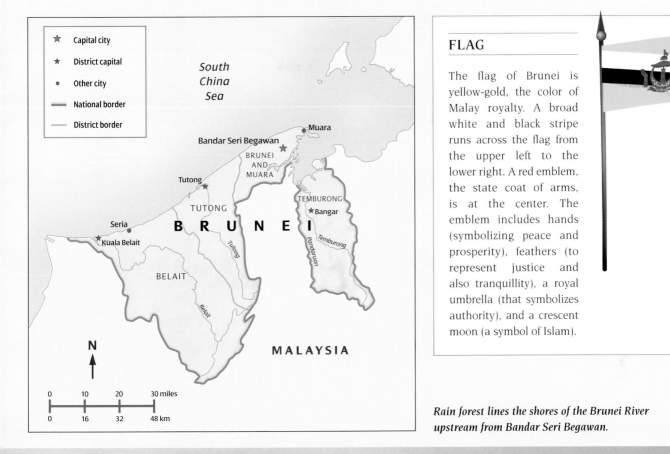

FLAG

The flag of Brunei is yellow-gold, the color of Malay royalty. A broad white and black stripe runs across the flag from the upper left to the lower right. A red emblem, the state coat of arms, is at the center. The emblem includes hands (symbolizing peace and prosperity), feathers (to represent justice and also tranquillity), a royal umbrella (that symbolizes authority), and a crescent moon (a symbol of Islam).

Rain forest lines the shores of the Brunei River upstream from Bandar Seri Begawan.

METROPOLITAN AREAS, 2001 POPULATIONS

Urban population	87 percent
Bandar Seri Begawan	230,000
Bandar Seri Begawan city	27,000
Kuala Belait	21,000
Seria	21,000
Tutong	13,000

Source: Bruneian census, 2001

POPULATION

Population	333,000 (2001 census)
Population density	149.6 per sq. mile (57.8 per sq. km)
Population growth	1.9 percent a year
Birthrate	18.9 births per 1,000 of the population
Death rate	3.4 deaths per 1,000 of the population
Population under age 15	28.1 percent
Population over age 65	3.1 percent
Sex ratio	106 males for 100 females
Fertility rate	2.3 children per woman
Infant mortality rate	12.3 deaths per 1,000 live births
Life expectancy at birth	
Total population	75.0 years
Female	77.6 years
Male	72.3 years

ECONOMY

Currency	Bruneian Dollar (BND)
Exchange rate (2006)	$1 = BND 1.54
Gross domestic product (2003)	$6.8 billion
GDP per capita (2003)	$23,600
Unemployment rate (2005)	4.8 percent
Population under poverty line	N/A
Exports	$4.5 billion (2004 CIA estimate)
Imports	$1.6 billion (2004 CIA estimate)

GOVERNMENT

Official country name	Sultanate of Brunei Land of Peace
Conventional short forms	Brunei or Brunei Darussalam
Nationality	
noun and adjective	Bruneian
Official language	Malay
Capital city	Bandar Seri Begawan
Type of government	Absolute monarchy
Voting rights	None
National anthem	"Allah Pelihakaran Sultan" (God bless the sultan)

National day	National Day, February 23, 1984 (anniversary of the end of British protection; independence was achieved on January 1 in the same year)

TRANSPORTATION

Railroads	None
Highways (all paved)	1,569 miles (2,525 km)
Navigable waterways	130 miles (209 km)
Airports	
International airports	1
Paved runways	1

POPULATION PROFILE, 2005 ESTIMATES

Ethnic groups	
Malayan	67 percent
Chinese	15 percent
Borneo ethnic groups	6 percent
Indians, Eurasians, Europeans, and others	12 percent
Religions	
Sunni Muslim	67 percent
Buddhist	13 percent
Protestant Christians and Roman Catholics	10 percent
Chinese folk religions (including Taoism), Hindu, traditional religions, and nonreligious	10 percent
Languages	
Malay	67 percent
Chinese	15 percent
Languages of the Indian subcontinent and other minorities	11 percent
Languages of Borneo	6 percent
English	1 percent as a first language, but understood by the majority
Adult literacy	94 percent

CHRONOLOGY

1363	Brunei is founded by Awang Alak Betatar, who converts to Islam and changes his name to Muhammad Shah; he rules Brunei as sultan from 1363 through 1402.
15th and 16th centuries	Brunei becomes a powerful state, controlling most of northern Borneo (present-day Sabah and Sarawak) and nominally ruling much of the rest of the island, as well as the Sulu Archipelago in the Philippines.
16th century	As one of the principal Islamic centers in Borneo, Brunei becomes the focus of Catholic Spain's efforts to contain the spread of Islam in the region. Spain, the colonial power in the Philippines to the north, attacks Brunei in 1578 and briefly occupies its capital.
17th century	Brunei's power declines after a civil war that leads to the loss of territory in southern Borneo and in the Philippines.
1841	Omar Ali Saifuddin II (reigned 1829–1852) grants British entrepreneur James Brooke (1803–1868) territory in southern Sarawak in return for his support in crushing a rebellion. Brooke founds a dynasty that rules until 1946.
after 1841	Brunei falls into decline as Sarawak annexes much of the sultanate's remaining southern territory.
1846	Brunei cedes the island of Labuan to Great Britain.
1888	Great Britain makes Brunei a protectorate. The British Chartered North Borneo Company establishes control over northern Borneo (modern Sabah), removing the area from Bruneian influence.
from 1906	A British resident (colonial administrator) becomes the effective ruler of Brunei, while the sultan exercises reduced authority in internal affairs.
1929	Oil production begins off the coast of Brunei.
1941–1945	Japan occupies Brunei during World War II (1939–1945).
1959	Brunei's first constitution is adopted with provision for a partly elected legislature. The state becomes fully self-governing, although Great Britain remains in charge of defense and foreign affairs.
1962	After a revolt is put down by British forces, the sultan declares a state of emergency and rules by decree.
1963	Brunei resists pressure from Great Britain to join the Federation of Malaysia.
1967	Hassanal Bolkiah (born 1946) becomes sultan. Under his rule, Brunei becomes a welfare state, but its citizens are denied any participation in government.
1984	Brunei gains complete independence from Great Britain.
1998	Sultan Hassanal Bolkiah removes his younger brother, Prince Jefri Bolkiah (born 1954), as head of the Brunei Investment Agency. In 2000, a suit against Prince Jefri for misuse of state funds is settled out of court.
2004	Sultan Hassanal Bolkiah appoints a 21-member council and agrees to eventually restore a partially elected legislative council.

GOVERNMENT

Some international observers believe that political dissent in Brunei is largely absent due to the high standard of living, generous state subsidies, and welfare provision. Bruneians have a comfortable life but lack the right to vote.

The chief of state of Brunei is the sultan. The throne has been in the same family since the fifteenth century, but although succession normally passes from the sultan to his eldest son, the monarchy is not strictly hereditary. The sultan appoints his heir; if there is no appointed successor when the monarch dies, the Council of Succession (whose members are chosen by the sultan) decides which member of the royal family should succeed.

AN ABSOLUTE MONARCH

The sultan of Brunei since 1967, Hassanal Bolkiah (born 1946), is chief of state and also prime minister. He appoints all public officials, including the members of the cabinet with a maximum of 13 ministers. The sultan chairs the cabinet and all ministers are responsible to him. Sultan Hassanal Bolkiah, who ruled by decree from 1984 through 2004, is not only prime minister but also defense minister and finance minister. Other members of the royal family serve in the cabinet, including the heir to the throne, Prince Al-Muhtadee (born 1974), who is senior minister without portfolio, and the sultan's brother, Prince Mohamed (born 1948), who is foreign minister. The sultan is advised by several appointed councils, including the Privy Council, which advises on constitutional matters, and the Religious Council.

In 2004, Brunei's Sultan Hassanal Bolkiah signs a constitutional amendment that would allow the eventual establishment of a partly elected legislature.

THE CONSTITUTION

In 1959, when Brunei was still a British protected state, the sultan introduced a constitution. The constitution, amended in 1971 and 1984, established a legislative council and a government headed by a chief minister. The title of chief minister was changed when independence from Great Britain was achieved in 1984, and the sultan became prime minister. In the same year, a cabinet-style government was introduced. Under the constitution, the legislative council was empowered to scrutinize, but not initiate, legislation.

The 1959 constitution is still legally in force, although most of its provisions have been effectively suspended since 1962, when a rebellion was put down with the help of British forces. The last elections were held in 1962, and the constitutional provisions regarding elections were suspended. In 1984, the legislative council was disbanded and the sultan has since ruled as an absolute monarch. Two political parties were allowed to form in 1985, but one was banned in 1998 and the other has been subject to such harassment that it is now inactive.

In 2004, the sultan gave way to international pressure to reform, appointing a 21-member legislative council that is charged with reviewing but not proposing legislation. The council voted for an amendment of the constitution, calling for a 45-member council. As a result, the sultan amended the 1959 constitution, permitting a new legislative council with a maximum of 45 members, including 15 elected members. The entire cabinet will automatically be members of the council. In summer 2005, construction of a new legislative council building began in Bandar Seri Begawan, the national capital of Brunei, but the sultan has set no date for elections, instead urging caution. At present, Brunei remains a state in which citizens have no right to vote, and there are no elections.

LOCAL GOVERNMENT

Brunei is divided into four districts, one of which, Brunei and Muara (the district that surrounds the national capital), is home to nearly 70 percent of the population. By contrast, Temburong, the small detached eastern enclave, contains only 3 percent of the population. Appointed officials administer the four districts. Appointed municipal boards are responsible for the three main urban areas.

C. CARPENTER

MODERN HISTORY

Brunei was the largest state in Borneo in the fifteenth and sixteenth centuries, but gradually lost territory in the following centuries as the Brooke family established a personal fiefdom to the south and a British chartered company created its own territory to the north.

In 1839–1840, the British entrepreneur James Brooke (1803–1868) helped the Bruneians suppress a rebellion. In 1841, Brooke was rewarded by the sultan of Brunei, Omar Ali Saifuddin II (reigned 1828–1852), who named Brooke the raja of Sarawak, then a southern province of Brunei. Brooke used his new power base to extend his territory northward and eventually took most of southern Brunei. The sultan of Brunei ceded the island of Labuan to Great Britain in 1846. In 1850, the United States recognized Sarawak's independence; Great Britain followed 14 years later. While Brooke advanced through southern Brunei, the British Chartered North Borneo Company (established in 1882) annexed northern Brunei (now the Malaysian state of Sabah). As a result, Brunei was greatly reduced in size and divided into two unequal small territories.

THE BRITISH PROTECTORATE

In 1888, Sultan Hashim Jalilul Alam Aqamaddin (reigned 1885–1906) handed over control of the foreign affairs of his weakened state to Great Britain. Colonial influence was increased by a treaty of 1905–1906, under which a British resident was installed to advise on matters of state.

Oil was discovered in Brunei during the reign of Sultan Muhammad Jamalul Alam II (reigned 1906–1924). In 1927, there were major oil strikes near Seria on the northwestern coast of Brunei. The wealth generated from oil improved the quality of life for Bruneians, but also made the British protectorate a target for the expansionist Japanese, who invaded in 1941 during World War II (1939–1945). Brunei was severely damaged during the war and much of the state's infrastructure had to be rebuilt.

After the defeat of Japan in 1945, Brunei was returned to British rule, but the sultan exercised autonomy in many internal matters. In 1959, the country introduced a written constitution with provision for a partially elected legislature, and the resident became a high commissioner; the British were henceforth more genuinely advisers than rulers, although they did retain control of foreign policy. Under Sultan Omar Ali Saifuddin III (reigned 1950–1967), the Brunei Shell Petroleum Company began offshore drilling, and the sultan invested revenue to create the infrastructure of a welfare state. His reforms culminated in the final year of his reign in the creation of a national currency, the Bruneian dollar.

The vast palace of the sultan of Brunei in Bandar Seri Begawan symbolizes the wealth and the power of the nation's absolute ruler, who was the world's richest man in the 1990s.

In 1962, the Partai Rakyat Brunei (PRB) party won all the elected seats in the legislature and sought full democracy and an end to the monarch's powers. When the sultan refused their demands, the PRB launched an uprising that was put down with the help of British Gurkha forces. The constitution was suspended and further elections banned. The sultan subsequently came under pressure from the British to join Malaya, Singapore, Sarawak, and British North Borneo (now Sabah) in the new Federation of Malaysia. However, he decided that his state was economically strong enough to remain outside the federation.

INDEPENDENCE

On January 1, 1984, the state became fully independent. Brunei is ruled by its sultan, since 1967 Hassanal Bolkiah (born 1946), who is head of state and head of government. British Gurkha forces remain in Brunei to defend the country's oil installations. Oil wealth has given the citizens of Brunei one of the highest standards of living in the developing world.

H. RUSSELL

CULTURAL EXPRESSION

The sultanate of Brunei in northern Borneo has been an Islamic state since its foundation in 1363. Despite losing the greater part of its territory in the last two hundred years, Brunei has retained many of its traditions and customs but has also developed a new modern culture that has been shaped by the country's wealth from the exploitation of its large reserves of oil and natural gas.

The culture of Brunei is influenced by several different factors, including the Sunni Islamic faith that is followed by the majority of its citizens, by the small nation's rich history as a formerly powerful sultanate, and by a period as a British protectorate from 1888 through 1984. Modern Brunei is a cosmopolitan society in which different peoples—Bruneian Malays, Chinese, indigenous peoples of the interior, Indians, Europeans, and others—contribute to the cultural mix. These different traditions are also seen in the cooking of Brunei, which does not have its own cuisine. Food and drink in Brunei are mainly prepared and served according to Malay and Chinese traditions, but modern international dishes are readily available in the cities.

TRADITION

The preservation of culture and traditional protocol in Brunei is regarded as important by the authorities and is governed by *adat*, customary laws issued by the government in order to preserve, among other things, ceremony, dress, and heraldry. The Ministry of Religious Affairs, which fosters Islam, the main religion in Brunei, also oversees Brunei's culture. Although Brunei's official language is Malay, English is popularly used. For writing, Jawi, Malay written in Arabic, is widely used.

FESTIVALS AND CEREMONIES

Some public holidays in Brunei are celebrated according to the Islamic lunar calendar, while others are marked on the Western calendar or the Chinese lunar calendar. Brunei's rich culture is reflected in its festivals, beginning on February 23 with National Day, which is marked by parades before the sultan in the Hassanal Bolkiah National Stadium. Hari Raya Aidilfitri (Eid al-Fitr) is the time for celebration following Ramadan, the Islamic month of fasting during daylight hours. Celebratory meals are served, and the sultan opens the doors of his palace to the public for three days. Royal Brunei Armed Forces Day on May 31 is usually marked by military parades and air shows. This holiday is followed by Hari Raya Koran, when Muslims traditionally make pilgrimages to the Islamic holy city of Mecca in Saudi Arabia. Many Bruneian Muslims make a sacrifice of a goat or a cow to mark the holiday. The sultan's birthday on July 15 is a festival of parties, parades, and fireworks. The birthday of the Prophet Muhammad on the twelfth day of the Islamic month of Rabi-al-Awwal is also a public holiday. Chinese New Year, a two-week festival beginning on the eve of the lunar New Year, is celebrated by the sultanate's ethnic Chinese community, while Christians, mainly in Bandar Seri Begawan (the national capital) and in Seria, celebrate Christmas Day on December 25.

ART AND ARCHITECTURE

The skyline of Bandar Seri Begawan is dominated by the gleaming gold dome of the Omar Ali Saifuddin Mosque, built in 1958 and named for Sultan Omar Ali Saifuddin (reigned 1740–1780), who is often described as the creator of modern Brunei. The design of the mosque draws on world styles and materials, including Italian marble, English stained glass, Arabian and Belgian carpets, and granite from Shanghai, China. One famous feature of the mosque is a barge in the lagoon outside, a replica of the sixteenth-century *mahligai*, or royal barge; the replica has been used from the 1960s to stage religious festivals. Other well-known buildings in the city include the former official home of the British resident, the Bumbungan Duabelas (the House of Twelve Roofs), built in 1906; the ancient tomb of the fifth sultan, Suhan Bolkiah (reigned 1473–1521); and Lapau, also known as the Royal Ceremonial Hall, where the present sultan, Hassanal Bolkiah (born 1946), was crowned in 1968.

Bandar Seri Begawan's most prominent building is the Istana Nurul Iman, the sultan's palace. With more than 1,700 rooms, it is usually said to be the largest residential palace in the world. Its golden domes and parkland setting along the river are open to the public during the religious holiday of Hari Raya Aidilfitri.

The suburb of Gadong, Bandar Seri Begawan's commercial and shopping district, is home to the largest mosque in Brunei, Jame 'Asr Hassanil Mosque, built in 1992. Televisions inside the mosque show live pictures of Mecca, and the mosque can accommodate thousands of worshippers in prayer halls with separate spaces for men and women. The mosque has chandeliers, hundreds of carpets, and features the largest edition of the Koran in the world.

Brunei's traditional domestic architecture can be seen in the so-called water villages, including Kampong Ayer, which is part of the capital, Bandar Seri Begawan. In water villages, houses constructed of palm and wood stand on stilts in the river or the shallow coastal waters of the sea and are connected by boardwalks and wooden catwalks.

In the rain forests of the interior, some people still live in longhouses, huge structures that shelter whole communities. In a longhouse, each family lives in an *amin*, or apartment, along a central walkway that serves as an indoor main street. The longhouse is decorated with art, characterized by images of monsters and a reflection of the belief in an upper world and a lower world. Doorways are symbolic passageways between these worlds and are guarded by protective images and figures called *uyat*, consecrated with sacrificial blood and

The mahligai, *a replica of a sixteenth-century royal barge, outside Bandar Seri Begawan's Omar Ali Saifuddin Mosque, is used for various official ceremonies and religious festivals.*

crafted with human, animal, or dragonlike faces and features (similar to the way gargoyles were used in cathedrals of medieval Europe to ward away bad spirits). The most famous image is that of Aso, the dog-dragon, which combines elements of dog and dragon with images of forest vines. Aso appears frequently on traditional weapons, including the daggers and swords of the elite members of society, as well as in entryways. Traditionally, longhouses would have been made of wood, but in recent times, concrete is more commonly used.

Bandar Seri Begawan and the smaller city of Seria contain examples of modern international architecture. Jerudong Playground, a large state-of-the-art amusement park, is entered through the Crystal Arch, which looks like a giant diamond and opens onto numerous roller coasters, laser shows, and other attractions. In the national capital, wide boulevards lead to spacious modern government buildings and museums, such as the Malay Technology Museum. The Brunei Museum uses more traditional decoration; its exterior is ornamented in traditional Malay designs copied from tombstones found in the area.

DECORATIVE ARTS

Decorative artists in Brunei create decorated gongs as well as pots and urns made from silver and brass that may be inscribed with words from the Koran. Brunei's sultans have commissioned musical instruments, richly decorated items, and weapons, such as cannons, over the centuries, and many of the finest examples are displayed in the city's museums. Calligraphy is a popular art form, but the major collection of elaborately decorated Korans displayed in Bandar Seri Begawan comprises volumes imported into the country. The Arts and Handicraft Center preserves local decorative art traditions, particularly the weaving of *jong sarat*, sarongs woven from gold or silver thread, and the carving of the *keris*, a traditional dagger with a wavy blade shaped like a snake.

The indigenous peoples of interior Brunei are known for their distinctive and accomplished artwork, which makes use of animal and natural materials, such as antlers, horn, and wood, as well as more modern materials, such as metal and beads, some of which are imported from Europe. *Hudoq* are masks worn during ceremonies to protect and promote the rice crop.

MUSIC AND PERFORMING ARTS

The national dances of Brunei include *alus jua dindang* (literally, "beautiful melody"), a traditional song and dance about the unique customs of the Brunei wedding ceremony. *Benari*,

Bruneian musicians play traditional instruments, including a hand drum and gulintangan, sets of gongs.

another folk dance also known as *joget baju putih*, is performed at various celebrations, including weddings, the fulfillment of a promise or pledge, or a new start, such as moving to a new home. Usually *benari* is danced by three couples to the music of violins and the rhythms of the *dombak*, a traditional frame drum, or *rebana*, a goblet drum.

The Kedayan, a people from western Brunei, are known for the *aduk-aduk*, a harvest dance. *Adai-adai* is an Islamic work song and dance traditionally sung by fishers to the rhythm of paddling oars. The song is meant to calm and revive those who sing and hear it. Other dances involve *silat*, the Malay martial art form. As they perform, dancers tap coconut shells together to keep rhythm. *Alai sekap*, a regional dance from the Belait district, the westernmost part of Borneo, is similar to the bamboo dance of the Philippines, although it makes use of wood and is danced to the rhythm of *gedang* drums. Highly regarded by the Bruneians, the *alai sekap* dance is performed at the funeral ceremonies of the heads of Belait's clans or tribes. Another famous group dance is the *jipin*, in which six men and six women dance to the music of traditional instruments, such as the *rebana*, the *dombak*, and the *gambus dan biola*, a kind of lute. The dance is part of many ceremonies and celebrations. Its precise origin is unknown; it may have its roots in Arabia or perhaps even Brunei itself.

In the sixteenth century, Sultan Suhan Bolkiah always took a *gulintangan* orchestra with him on his ship when he went to sea. Now one of the best-loved forms of traditional music, the orchestra includes the *gulintangan* itself (a large set of gongs), the *tawak-tawak* and *canang* (gongs), a single gong, and *gendan labik* (traditional drums).

K. ROMANO-YOUNG

DAILY LIFE

The quality of everyday life in Brunei is defined by the wealth of the state, which exploits large reserves of oil and natural gas. As a result, the nation is one of the richest in the developing world, and its citizens enjoy a high standard of living and a comprehensive welfare state.

The Bruneian welfare state is well funded and extends its benefits to all citizens. There is a social security safety net for the poor, and the government subsidizes rice (the staple diet of the poor) and housing. More than one-quarter of all public spending is on social development.

HEALTH CARE

Health care is largely financed by the state, although there is a nominal charge for all treatment at the point of delivery; private medical facilities are also available. Funding for hospitals, equipment, doctors, nurses, and medicine is provided by the government and is also raised through individual insurance contributions. Employees pay a minimum of 5 percent of their monthly salary, and this is matched by an equivalent contribution from the employer (the amount contributed may be increased by individuals in consultation with their employer). Because Brunei now has universal health care, the incidence of communicable diseases has decreased, the infant mortality rate

has fallen, and life expectancy has increased. The Bruneian infant mortality rate fell from 38 per 1,000 live births in 1971 to 12.3 per 1,000 in 2006. Life expectancy increased over the same period, from 70.1 years for men and 72.7 years for women in 1971 to 72.3 and 77.6 years, respectively, in 2006.

PENSIONS AND WELFARE

The state administers an employees' trust fund that finances old-age and disability pensions. Bruneians qualify for an old-age pension from age 55. Temporary disability benefits are capped at two-thirds of the employee's average monthly earnings in the six months before incapacity. Bruneians become eligible for permanent disability benefits after having been unable to work

Traditional water villages built on stilts above rivers and coastal estuaries are still home to large numbers of Bruneians. Wooden bridges and catwalks connect the homes with each other and give access to the shore.

for 10 years. The permanently disabled receive a lump sum of 48 times the average earnings of the disabled person in the six months before the onset of the condition, up to a maximum level that is periodically raised in line with inflation.

In some circumstances, the money paid in contributions into the health care insurance program may be recovered by an employee and used for other specified purposes. Bruneians who want to invest in property for their own residence or wish to emigrate may access some of these funds.

HOUSING

Affordable public housing is a high government priority, and the administration of the policy is under the direct supervision of the chief of state, the sultan. Housing is generally subsidized for all citizens, but some groups are targeted for particular benefits. The national housing program, which provided 900 million Brunei dollars from 1996 through 2000, caters to homeless and indigenous people. One program targets indigenous peoples, living in Kampung Rimba, Kampung Tungku, and Kampung Madang in the interior. There is also a program to build housing for new converts to Islam, for people who have lost their homes in fire (a frequent hazard in Brunei because many houses are wooden), and for the poorer people. The private sector is also an important provider of housing; Brunei Shell Petroleum, the major oil corporation, operates a housing loan plan for its staff. Belait, where the company is based, has the second-largest population in the sultanate.

A Hierarchical Society

Brunei is a hierarchical state in which the different elements of society live largely separate lives. The royal family and its relatives and the Bruneian nobility are at the top of the social hierarchy, while the Chinese, Indian, and other ethnic groups live outside Bruneian Malay society, following their own customs and traditions. Thai, Bangladeshi, and various European foreign workers also form their own communities.

Bruneian Malay personal names are complex, reflecting the hierarchical nature of society, and titles are considered important. Names may contain up to 20 different elements, and for royalty and the nobility, names comprise four main parts: a title, a given name, the family name, and a description of the individual's male parentage. Royal titles are particularly complex; noble titles include Pehin (lord) and up to a dozen different additional forms that modify the title of Dato (the highest nonroyal title).

Etiquette demands that the exact name and title be used in correspondence to avoid causing offense, but in personal contact the form of address "Haji" (for a man) or "Hajah" (for a woman), indicating that the person has been on pilgrimage (hajj) to Mecca in Saudi Arabia, is a diplomatic alternative, as it suggests that the person is a good Muslim.

EDUCATION

The government of Brunei provides free education from ages 5 through 18. The state has 176 primary schools, 39 secondary (high) schools, 5 vocational colleges, 5 private schools, and 3 international schools. There is also an institute of technology. The University of Brunei—Universiti Brunei Darussalam (UBD)—was founded in 1985 and has approximately three thousand students. The university offers degrees in education, mathematics and computer science, electronics and electrical engineering, and management studies, among others. It does not offer degrees in engineering or medicine, but the government funds scholarships to enable those who wish to enter these fields to study abroad (most go to Malaysia, Great Britain, or the United States). At all levels the principal language of instruction is English although the national language is Malay. In the private Islamic religious schools, the language of instruction is Arabic.

THE ROLE OF WOMEN

Although Brunei is in many ways a highly traditional Muslim society, women are free and equal under the law: there is no segregation by gender in public, except in a few very traditional outlying villages, and wearing headscarves is not compulsory. Nevertheless, Sharia (Islamic law), which is unfavorable toward women, applies in family matters, including divorce, inheritance, and child custody. In other areas, the Bruneian legal system is based on English common law, and Islamic law does not apply to non-Muslims.

Women currently make up nearly two-thirds of the student body at the national university. The *tudong* head covering must be worn by all female students in public schools, but this does not attract particular attention in the street because most Malay Bruneian women normally wear the *tudong*. However, members of ethnic minorities, such as Chinese and Europeans, and the female members of the Bruneian royal family usually wear their hair loose.

Most women in employment work for the government, the nation's largest employer. Women with university degrees enjoy the same employment rights as their male counterparts, but less educated women work on less favorable terms: they usually have only monthly contracts and shorter annual leave. In theory, women have the same political rights as men, but because Brunei has been under a state of emergency since 1962, when the constitution was suspended, no Bruneians now have the right to vote. Thus, although women have no effective political voice, they are not disenfranchised on gender grounds: Bruneian men are equally powerless.

In 2004, the sultan announced plans to reintroduce a partially elected legislative council, but no timetable for the reform has been announced. However, women will have the right to vote when the suspended (and amended) 1959 constitution is eventually restored.

A Muslim Bruneian boy learns how to pray by watching a relative worshipping in the Omar Ali Saifuddin Mosque in Bandar Seri Begawan.

WORKERS' RIGHTS

Brunei has only three labor unions, all in the oil sector. However, the unions are powerless, partly because less than 5 percent of the workforce belongs to them, but mainly because strikes are illegal, at least for Bruneian citizens. Foreign workers can and have stopped work, notably garment makers protesting poor conditions and excessive payroll deductions. Foreign workers account for about 40 percent of the labor force and include Thais and Bangladeshis as well as Europeans.

RELIGION

The government of Brunei is officially described as a Malay Muslim monarchy. Islam, the state religion, is practiced by 67 percent of the population. There is freedom of worship for adherents of the other main religions, including Buddhism (followed by 13 percent of Brunei's citizens, mainly ethnic Chinese) and Christianity (10 percent). Ethnically, most citizens of Brunei are Malay (67 percent); the next largest groups are Chinese (15 percent), Ibans and other indigenous peoples of the interior (6 percent), and Indians, Eurasians, and Europeans (12 percent).

At the start of the twenty-first century, there was no great tension between the Islamic values codified in the constitution of Brunei and the more secular, Westernized outlook of its most affluent citizens, including some members of the ruling family. However, in 2000, civil proceedings were taken against Prince Jefri Bolkiah (born 1954), the sultan's brother, who was accused of the inappropriate use of the funds of a state body, the Brunei Investment Agency, to pay for an ostentatious lifestyle.

Although there is no religious persecution, the government has frequently been accused of refusing permission to build new non-Muslim places of worship and to perform essential maintenance of existing churches and temples. Brunei was criticized on these grounds by the U.S. State Department's human rights report in 2002. Evangelism and other forms of religious proselytizing are strictly forbidden in Brunei; residents who try to convert Bruneian Muslims may be expelled, and visitors who are suspected of intending to convert Muslims to other faiths are refused entry to the country.

Alcohol has been outlawed in Brunei since 1991, but it is nevertheless widely available. Beer appears on many restaurant and bar menus under the name "special tea," and it is brought to the table in teapots and poured into cups. The subterfuge is intended to avoid offending Islamic religious sensibilities, although no one is fooled. There is, however, a recognition that non-Muslim tourists and foreign workers drink alcohol, and the Bruneian authorities do not enforce the alcohol ban for foreigners, in part because the economy relies upon non-Bruneian workers, but also because the authorities are encouraging the tourist industry as part of the program to diversify the economy.

While the official approach to the future challenges facing Brunei is to take the nation closer to the West, fundamentalist Islam provides another, conflicting influence. As yet, radical Islam is politically insignificant in Brunei, but the movement exists. Although Muslim radicals are few in number, they are active in attempts to convert Ibans and other indigenous peoples in the interior to Islam. In response to the perceived fundamentalist threat, particularly since the terrorist attacks on the United States on September 11, 2001, the Bruneian authorities have closely watched the activities of the country's few radicals, and they have increasingly refused entry to radical Muslim clerics.

SOCIAL PROBLEMS

The oil and natural gas industries dominate the nation's economy and, after the state, are the main employers. In the 1990s, a revolution in technology has made many laborers redundant in the hydrocarbon sector, making unemployment a social problem to the sultanate for the first time. Although unemployment stood at only 4.8 percent of the labor force in 2005, the problem is a new challenge to Bruneian society. At the same time, there has been a possibly related increase in crime, which was historically restricted almost entirely to smuggling. Drug abuse has also risen and, although it is not yet a big problem by Western standards, a rehabilitation center has been opened in the Bandar Seri Begawan suburb of Gadong.

H. RUSSELL

Bandar Seri Begawan

Bandar Seri Begawan, the national capital of Brunei, was known as Brunei Town until 1970, when the city's name was changed. The first part of the new name, Bandar, is the Persian word for "harbor," while Seri Begawan, deriving from Sanskrit (the classical language of India), means "blessed one."

The metropolitan area of Bandar Seri Begawan was home to 230,000 people at the 2001 Bruneian census, while 27,000 lived within the city limits. The urban area contains about 70 percent of the nation's population. Kampong Ayer, a so-called water village, consists of traditional houses on stilts in shallow water along the shore. The village is home to around 24,000 people and stretches along the coast for one-quarter mile (400 m). To the east, hills restrict the spread of urbanization, and a ribbon of development spreads north and east along the coast.

A HISTORIC CITY

By the seventh century CE, a Malay fishing port and trading center stood close to the site of modern Bandar Seri Begawan. The first settlement was along the eastern bank of the Brunei River, while the modern city is centered on the opposite shore. By the fourteenth and fifteenth centuries, a town called Brunei was the center of a Malay sultanate of the same name, which controlled all of Borneo and part of the southern Philippines.

The water village of Kampong Ayer, built on stilts in the sea, adjoins the city of Bandar Seri Begawan.

The sultanate declined through the eighteenth and nineteenth centuries, and the population of Brunei Town shrank from its peak of 20,000 inhabitants. By the mid-nineteenth century, the sultanate was more or less confined to its present small area on the north coast of Borneo, and large numbers of people had moved away, some to the interior. The development of the present city began in 1906 when the British resident (colonial administrator) encouraged people to settle on reclaimed land on the western bank of the inlet. In 1909, the reigning sultan established a new palace on the west bank, and Brunei Town's Chinese traders arrived. Government buildings and the principal mosque were established along the western shore in the 1920s.

Brunei Town was overrun by Japanese forces in 1941 during World War II, and before the area was recaptured by Allied troops in 1945, most of the town was bombed. As a result, almost nothing remains from before the 1940s. In the 1950s and 1960s, oil wealth began to transform Brunei's national capital, and in the 1970s and 1980s, a number of large public buildings were constructed and a central business district was developed.

A MODERN CITY

The golden dome of the large Omar Ali Saifuddin Mosque dominates the downtown area of Bandar Seri Begawan. The interior of the mosque, one of the largest in the region, is lined with Italian marble. Other prominent public buildings include the royal palace (reputedly the largest residence used by a reigning royal family) and the Royal Regalia Museum, which displays the sultan's crown and throne as well as gifts received by him from other heads of state.

The modern city is a center of administration and commerce. Bandar Seri Begawan has some multistory office buildings but only one major shopping mall. The city has a university that was founded in 1985. Industries in the city include textiles, furniture, timber, and a wide range of decorative arts. Tourist attractions include the Brunei Museum, the Malay Technology Museum, and the water village of Kampong Ayer. Visitors and residents take water taxis across the inlet, while modern highways run along the coast and to the international airport, which is less than 1.5 miles (2 km) from the downtown district. Nearby Ulu Temburong National Park has raised walkways above the forest canopy from which visitors can watch birds and animals.

C. CARPENTER

ECONOMY

Brunei is a small nation that relies on the export of hydrocarbons (crude oil and natural gas). Revenue from oil and natural gas provides the people of Brunei with one of the highest standards of living in Asia and a comprehensive welfare state.

With an area of 2,226 square miles (5,765 sq. km), Brunei is comparable in size to the state of Delaware. At the 2001 census, the nation had a population of 333,000. Although Brunei is small in area and in population, it has a regional influence out of proportion to its size.

ECONOMIC CHALLENGES

Despite its oil wealth, Brunei faces a number of economic challenges, the most pressing of which is overreliance on the export of hydrocarbons, which supplies nearly one-half of the Bruneian GDP (gross domestic product, the total value of all the goods and services produced in a nation in a fixed period, usually one year). Revenue varies according to the price of oil and natural gas on the world market. Brunei was badly hit by the Asian financial crisis

Offshore rigs such as this one provide the greater part of Brunei's oil exports. Brunei and Malaysia dispute potentially oil-rich waters in the South China Sea.

of 1997 and 1998, and the collapse of the country's largest construction corporation in 1998 added to its economic problems. The government has made substantial investments of oil and natural gas revenue abroad to provide income when oil and natural gas reserves run out. However, the nation's economic base remains narrow, and government policy aims to increase industry and to promote banking and the tourist sector. To help diversify, the government encourages foreign investors to fund new projects, awarding tax-free status for the first five years.

Standard of Living

Brunei has one of the highest standards of living in the developing world. The per capita gross domestic product (GDP) was $23,600 in 2003; this figure is adjusted for purchasing power parity (PPP), a formula that allows comparison between living standards in different countries. No Bruneians are poor, but there are great inequalities in the distribution of wealth.

Brunei's generous welfare state is costly, and it is not certain that Brunei will be able to sustain the free health and education services and subsidized housing and rice for all its citizens in the future. Through membership in ASEAN (Association of South East Asian Nations, the regional trading organization) and other international bodies, Brunei is integrating its economy into the world economy, which may have effects upon the extent of state subsidies and government intervention in the economy.

The Bruneian economy is mixed: state intervention exists alongside investment by international corporations, while traditional agricultural activities still occupy many people who live in the villages in the interior. Social cohesion is a problem; Malays form a majority, but the ethnic Chinese minority, who account for 15 percent of the population, are prominent in commerce. The indigenous peoples of Borneo, who form about 6 percent of the population, live in rural areas and are less integrated in the modern economy of the nation than other communities. Brunei also has a substantial number of foreign workers from other Asian nations (particularly Thailand and Bangladesh), Europe, and North America, who work in the oil industry, in finance, and in other services. These temporary residents account for around 40 percent of the labor force. The

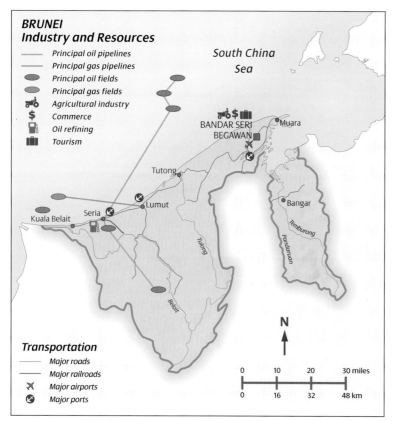

BRUNEI
Industry and Resources

— Principal oil pipelines
— Principal gas pipelines
⬭ Principal oil fields
⬭ Principal gas fields
🏍 Agricultural industry
$ Commerce
🛢 Oil refining
🏛 Tourism

South China Sea

BANDAR SERI BEGAWAN

Muara

Tutong

Lumut

Bangar

Seria

Kuala Belait

Tutong

Belait

Temburong

Pandaruan

N

Transportation
— Major roads
— Major railroads
✈ Major airports
✪ Major ports

| 0 | 10 | 20 | 30 miles |
| 0 | 16 | 32 | 48 km |

production peaked in the 1970s; since then, output has been reduced to prolong the life of the oil fields. Brunei produces 203,000 barrels of crude oil a day, and the nation has reserves of 1.26 billion barrels of crude oil. (One barrel is the equivalent of 42 gallons and is usually given in metric measurement as 0.16 cubic m.) Brunei Shell Petroleum (BSP), a joint venture between the Bruneian government and the Royal Dutch/Shell group, controls most of the oil industry in Brunei and operates the country's only oil refinery. Japan takes around one-half of Brunei's oil exports, followed by the United States, South Korea, and Thailand.

Since large reserves of natural gas were discovered in the 1970s, exports of natural gas have contributed almost as much revenue as oil exports. A gas liquefaction plant, one of the largest in the world, has made Brunei the fourth-largest exporter of liquefied natural gas (LNG) in the Asia-Pacific region. The nation produces 365.5 billion cubic feet (10.35 billion cubic m) of natural gas a year, about 90 percent of which is exported, almost all to Japan. A small amount of natural gas is used for domestic power generation. Brunei has reserves of around 11,125 billion cubic feet (315 billion cubic m) of natural gas.

Brunei's rivers are harnessed to produce electricity at two hydroelectric power plants. There are reserves of timber in the interior, but the export of timber is prohibited. Fish stocks support a fishing industry, but Brunei still imports a large part of its annual fish consumption.

Bruneian government regulates the migration of foreign workers, granting short-term work permits, and there is a program to train local people, particularly Bruneian Malays, to fill managerial roles currently held by foreign workers.

RESOURCES

The principal resource of Brunei is crude and natural gas. Oil was discovered in 1929 and natural gas in the 1960s. Most of the production comes from the Rasau and Seria-Tali offshore fields along the western coast, where Seria is the center of the nation's oil industry. Oil production fueled Brunei's economic development in the second half of the twentieth century, and

EMPLOYMENT IN BRUNEI

Sector	Percentage of labor force
Agriculture, forestry, and fishing	3
Oil and natural gas, and industry	61
Services	36

Source: Government of Brunei, 2003

In 2005, 4.8 percent of the labor force was unemployed.

AGRICULTURE

Only 0.6 percent of the land is arable and 0.8 percent is permanently cropped. Agriculture, forestry, and fishing employ 3 percent of the labor force and account for 5 percent of Brunei's GDP. The number of people involved in farming has decreased as rural workers leave the land for better-paying jobs in the cities. Rubber, once an important crop, is no longer cultivated. The government encourages the development of agriculture, and the nation is self-sufficient in eggs and poultry. Small farms grow rice, vegetables, and fruits and raise water buffalo. Most of the rest of Brunei's food needs are imported. The Bruneian government owns an Australian cattle ranch larger than Brunei itself, supplying most of Brunei's beef.

INDUSTRY

Most of Brunei's industry is related to the oil and natural gas industries. Industry (including oil and natural gas production) accounts for 56 percent of Brunei's GDP. The largest industrial plant is the liquefied natural gas (LNG) plant at Seria. There is also an oil refinery. Gas reserves will power new industries,

BRUNEI'S GDP

Brunei's gross domestic product (GDP) was $6.84 billion in 2003. The figure is adjusted for purchasing power parity (PPP), an exchange rate at which goods in one country cost the same as goods in another. PPP allows a comparison between the living standards in different nations.

MAIN CONTRIBUTORS TO BRUNEI'S GDP

Agriculture	4 percent
Industry	56 percent
Services	40 percent

Source: CIA, 2004

including an aluminum smelting plant under construction at Sungai Liang. The construction industry is a large employer that plays an important role in the development of the nation.

SERVICES

The government is the largest single employer; 48 percent of the labor force worked for the state in 1999. The services sector is expanding, and the government encourages the development of Bandar Seri Begawan, the national capital, as an offshore banking center. There is also a program to develop Brunei as a center for Islamic banking—fee-based financial services in

Downtown Bandar Seri Begawan is a modern service center housing the offices of finance corporations, banks, and airlines.

which banks neither charge nor pay interest, which Islam forbids. The government also encourages the growth of the tourist industry.

TRADE

Crude and refined oil and natural gas dominate the nation's exports. Brunei exported materials and goods worth $4.5 billion in 2004. The principal imports are machinery and transport equipment (including motor vehicles), consumer and manufactured goods (including domestic appliances and electronic goods), food, and chemicals. Brunei imported goods and services valued at $1.6 billion in 2004 and had a healthy trade balance. Brunei's main trading partner is Japan, which took 37 percent of its exports and supplied 7 percent of its imports in 2005. Other recipients of Brunei's exports include Indonesia (which took 19 percent in 2005), South Korea (13 percent), the United States (10 percent), and Australia (9 percent). The major source of imports to Brunei is Singapore, supplying 33 percent in 2005. Other sources of imports include Malaysia (23 percent), Japan, and Great Britain.

TRANSPORTATION AND COMMUNICATIONS

Brunei has 1,569 miles (2,525 km) of paved highways, 130 miles (209 km) of navigable waterways, and no railroads. The main ports are Muara, which is being developed as a container port, and Seria, the main center for the export of oil and natural gas. There is one international airport near the national capital. The nation has a modern telephone system with 90,000 lines in 2002. In 2004, 206,000 Bruneians had mobile cellular telephones. Around 56,000 people have Internet access.

C. CARPENTER

Malaysia

The British gradually established rule over the Malay Peninsula between the early nineteenth century and 1909. Great Britain ruled the different Malay states as colonies or protectorates, while North Borneo became a protectorate and the huge state of Sarawak was a personal possession of the Brookes, a British family. Japanese forces occupied the region from 1941 through 1945. After British rule was restored, the Federation of Malaya was formed in 1948, gaining independence in 1957. From 1948 to 1960, a state of emergency existed to counter a revolt by Malay Communists. In 1961, Great Britain withdrew from the region, and British North Borneo (renamed Sabah), Sarawak, and Singapore joined Malaya to form the new Federation of Malaysia, although Singapore withdrew in 1965. Today, Malaysia, which comprises 13 states and three federal territories, has a rapidly developing economy that depends on manufacturing and services rather than on mining and agriculture as it did in the past.

GEOGRAPHY

Location	Southeastern Asia on a peninsula south of Thailand, plus the northern third of the island of Borneo
Climate	Tropical wet climate; the southwest monsoon blows from April through October and the cooler northeast monsoon from October through February
Area	127,320 sq. miles (329,758 sq. km)
Coastline	2,905 miles (4,675 km)
Highest point	Mount Kinabalu 13,455 ft. (4,101 m)
Lowest point	Indian Ocean 0 ft. (0 m)
Terrain	Coastal plains in the Malay Peninsula and northern Borneo rise to hills and mountains
Natural resources	Tin, petroleum, copper, natural gas, iron ore, bauxite, timber
Land use	
Arable land	5.5 percent
Permanent crops	17.6 percent
Other	76.9 percent
Major rivers	Rajang, Pahang, Kinabatangan
Major lakes	Kenyir, Temengor
Natural hazards	Flooding, landslides

FLAG

The flag of Malaysia has 14 stripes (red and white) representing the 13 states of Malaysia and the federal territories. In the dark blue canton (the upper quarter next to the flagpost) are two yellow-gold emblems, a 14-point star and a crescent moon, a symbol of Islam. Blue symbolizes the unity of the peoples of Malaysia, while yellow-gold is the traditional color of Malay royalty.

METROPOLITAN AREAS, 2000 POPULATIONS

Urban population	70 percent
Kuala Lumpur	2,220,000
Kuala Lumpur city	1,298,000
Selayang Baru	188,000
Batu	178,000
Shah Alam	745,000
Shah Alam city	320,000
Subang Jaya	423,000

Kelang	632,000
Kelang city	385,000
Johor Baharu (Johore)	631,000
Johor Baharu city	385,000
Ipoh	574,000
Ipoh city	566,000
George Town	488,000
George Town city	181,000
Petaling Jaya	438,000
Kuching	424,000
Kuching city	152,000
Kota Kinabalu	305,000
Kota Kinabalu city	145,000
Seremban	291,000
Seremban city	246,000
Kuantan	289,000
Kuantan city	283,000
Sandakan	275,000
Sandakan city	220,000
Kuala Terengganu (Kuala Trengganu)	255,000
Kuala Terengganu city	251,000
Kota Baharu	253,000
Kota Baharu city	234,000
Tawau	214,000
Tawau city	145,000
Kajang	207,000
Taiping	199,000
Taiping city	183,000

Alor Setar (Alor Star)	187,000
Alor Setar city	115,000

Putrajaya, the new administrative capital, had a population of 7,000 at the 2000 census.

Source: Malaysian census, 2000

NEIGHBORS AND LENGTH OF BORDERS

Brunei	237 miles (381 km)
Indonesia	1,107 miles (1,782 km)
Thailand	314 miles (506 km)

There is also a short land border with Singapore along an artificial causeway that links the two nations.

POPULATION

Population	23,275,000 (2000 census)
Population density	182.8 per sq. mile (70.6 per sq. km)
Population growth	1.8 percent a year
Birthrate	22.9 births per 1,000 of the population
Death rate	5.1 deaths per 1,000 of the population
Population under age 15	32.6 percent
Population over age 65	4.7 percent
Sex ratio	107 males for 100 females

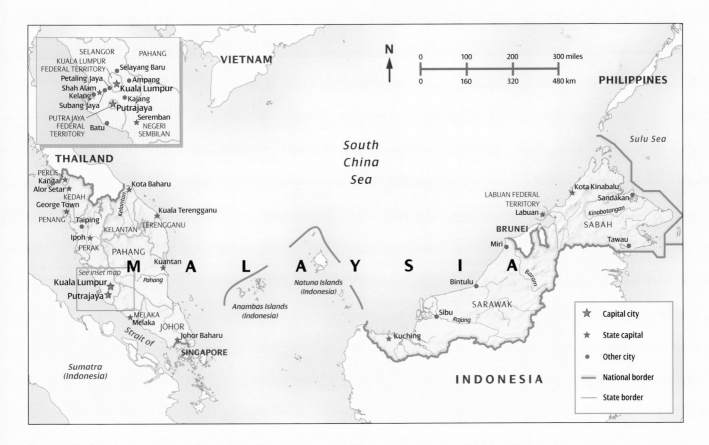

Fertility rate	3.0 children per woman
Infant mortality rate	17.2 deaths per 1,000 live births
Life expectancy at birth	
Total population	72.5 years
Female	75.4 years
Male	69.8 years

ECONOMY

Currency	Ringgit (MYR)
Exchange rate (2006)	$1 = MYR 3.54
Gross domestic product (2005)	$287 billion
GDP per capita (2005)	$12,000
Unemployment rate (2005)	3.6 percent
Population under poverty line (1998)	8 percent
Exports	$147.1 billion (2005 CIA estimate)
Imports	$118.7 billion (2005 CIA estimate)

GOVERNMENT

Official country name	Federation of Malaysia
Conventional short form	Malaysia
Former name	Malaya

Deer Cave in Sarawak is home to hundreds of thousands of bats.

Nationality	
noun	Malaysian
adjective	Malaysian
Official language	Malay (Bahasa Melayu)
Capital city	Kuala Lumpur
	(Putrajaya is the administrative capital)
Type of government	Federal constitutional monarchy
Voting rights	21 years and over, universal
National anthem	"Negera Ku" (My country)
National day	Independence Day, August 31, 1957

TRANSPORTATION

Railroads	1,175 miles (1,890 km)
Highways	44,633 miles (71,814 km)
Paved roads	34,769 miles (55,943 km)
Unpaved roads	9,864 miles (15,871 km)
Navigable waterways	4,475 miles (7,200 km)
Airports	
International airports	6
Paved runways	37

POPULATION PROFILE, 2005 ESTIMATES

Ethnic groups	
Malayan	50 percent
Chinese	24 percent
Sabah and Sarawak indigenous groups	11 percent
Indian	7 percent
Eurasians, Europeans, and others	8 percent
Religions	
Sunni Muslim	53 percent
Buddhist	17 percent
Chinese folk religions (including Taoism)	12 percent
Hindu	9 percent
Protestant Christians and Roman Catholics	6 percent
Others, traditional religions, and nonreligious	3 percent
Languages	
Malay (Bahasa Melayu)	around 58 percent
Chinese	24 percent
Tamil	4 percent
Iban	3 percent
English	1 percent as a first language, but understood by 31 percent
Telegu, Malayam, Panjabi, Thai, Dusun, Bajau, and other minorities	10 percent
Adult literacy	88.7 percent

CHRONOLOGY

1st millennium CE	Malay traders and seafarers from Borneo settle in the Malay Peninsula and become the region's dominant population.
10th century	Hindu and Buddhist coastal city-kingdoms develop in the Malay Peninsula.
14th century	Islam spreads through the region.
15th century	Malacca (now Melaka) becomes a powerful sultanate that controls most of the Malay Peninsula and neighboring areas by the early sixteenth century.
1511	The Portuguese arrive in Malacca and overthrow the sultanate, establishing a colony.
1641	The Dutch, allied with the sultan of Johor, take Malacca, expelling the Portuguese.
early 19th century	The British extend their influence through the Malay Peninsula, replacing the Dutch in Malacca in 1824. In 1826, the British establish the Straits Settlements territory that includes Malacca, Singapore, and Penang. In 1841, Sarawak becomes a possession of the Brooke family.
late 19th century	Great Britain establishes control over several Malay states and develops tin mining and rubber plantations. In 1888, the British North Borneo Chartered Company gains control of Sabah. In 1895, Pahang, Perak, Selangor, and Negeri Sembilan form the Federated Malay States under British rule.
1909	The northern Malay states of Kedah, Kelantan, Perlis, and Terengganu (all previously under Thai rule) become British protectorates, jointly known as the Unfederated Malay States.
1942–1945	Japan occupies Malaysia during World War II (1939–1945).
1946–1948	Great Britain unites its administration of Penang, Malacca, and the nine Malay states in 1946; two years later, these states become the Federation of Malaya.
1948–1960	The Malay Emergency: a (largely ethnic Chinese) Communist uprising against the federation is contained by Malay, British, Australian, and New Zealand troops. The Communists eventually lose support after full civil rights are granted to Malaya's ethnic Chinese minority.
1957	Malaya gains independence from Great Britain; Tunku Abdul Rahman Putra (1903–1990) becomes prime minister.
1963	The British colonies of British North Borneo (now Sabah), Sarawak, and Singapore join Malaya to form Malaysia, but Singapore secedes in 1965.
1969	Intercommunal rivalry and perceived favoritism by the Malaysian authorities toward ethnic Malays (Bumiputras) lead to riots.
1981–2003	Under the premiership of Mahathir bin Mohamad (born 1925), Malaysia rapidly develops a more diversified economy, but the rule of Mahathir becomes autocratic. In 1998, he removes his deputy, Anwar Ibrahim, who is tried and convicted on charges that many observers regard as politically motivated. Ibrahim is not released until 2004, when some of the charges are quashed.
since the 1980s	New industries bring increased prosperity, and Malaysia comes to depend on manufacturing.
2003	Abdullah Ahmad Badawi (born 1939) becomes prime minister.

GOVERNMENT

A federal constitutional monarchy, Malaysia has a parliamentary democracy. The position of chief of state, or king, rotates every five years among the leaders of the various states.

Malaysia comprises 13 states and three federal territories. Of the states, nine are monarchies whose chief of state is a sultan; the other four states each have an federally appointed governor. The nine state monarchs elect one of their number as Yang di-Pertuan Agong ("supreme ruler"), the ceremonial chief of state. for a single five-year term; the title is translated into English as "king." The election is a formality. When Malaya (the forerunner of Malaysia) gained independence in 1957, the sultans established an order of seniority, and they become king in a set order.

THE PARLIAMENT AND GOVERNMENT

The parliament of Malaysia has two houses. The upper house, the Dewan Negara or Senate, has 70 members, of whom 44 are appointed by the king on the advice of the government and 26 are elected by state legislatures (two from each state). Members of the upper house serve for three years. The lower house, the Dewan Rakyat or House of Representatives, has 219 members who are elected by universal adult suffrage for five year terms. Each constituency elects one representative. After a parliamentary election, the leader of the largest political party in the House of Representatives becomes prime minister.

POLITICAL PARTIES

All the major parties, most of which represent different ethnic groups, form a coalition called Barisan Nasional (BNP; the National Front). After elections in 2004, 198 of the 219 members of the House of Representatives were members of BNP. The largest single party within the coalition is Pertubuhan Kebangsaan Melayu Bersatu (United Malays National Organization, or UMNO); in 2004, UMNO had half the members of parliament. The other main parties in the National Front are the Malaysian Chinese Organization, the (Sarawak regional) Parti Pesaka Bumiputra Bersatu, the (centrist Penang-based) Malaysian People's Movement Party (Gerakan), the Malaysian Indian Congress, and regional parties from Sarawak and Sabah. Opposition is limited to the small Islamic Party of Malaysia (PAS) and the Democratic Action Party.

Mahathir bin Mohamad (born 1925; prime minister 1981–2003) dominated Malaysian political life, concentrating power in his hands. International observers viewed his rule as autocratic, and the opposition in Malaysia suffered restrictions

Peradana Putra, the premier's office, with its distinctive dome, is a landmark in Putrajaya, Malaysia's administrative capital.

on basic rights and political activity. The Barisan Nasional coalition continues to control most of the media. However, a 2006 report on Malaysia by the U.S. State Department Bureau of Democracy, Human Rights, and Labor stated that the country's human rights performance had improved although problems remained, including "abridgement of citizens' right to change their government."

LOCAL GOVERNMENT

The states have their own parliaments and governments, headed by a chief minister. State governments have limited powers, although Sabah and Sarawak enjoy greater autonomy. The states are divided into districts, some with elected city councils.

C. CARPENTER

MODERN HISTORY

Malaya achieved independence from Great Britain in 1957. This occurred toward the end of 12 years of guerrilla activity, usually known as the Malay Emergency, during which some members of the Communist Party of Malaya (with a largely ethnic Chinese membership) attempted to overthrow the Malay-dominated federation.

By 1957, the Malay Races Liberation Army (MRLA), the guerrilla force that had destabilized the Malay Peninsula since 1948, had been contained, and the security situation was stable enough for Malaya to become independent in 1957, although violence continued for another three years. The MRLA guerrilla action had been an anticolonial campaign, and once Malaya became independent, the principal reason for the MRLA's existence disappeared. The final serious incident in the emergency occurred in 1958, and in 1960 the government declared the emergency over.

INDEPENDENCE

The dominant political party in Malaya was the United Malays National Organization (UMNO), founded in 1946 to strive for independence from Great Britain and to protest a British proposal to grant equal rights to the different ethnic groups in Malaya. UMNO, which represented the interests of the Malay majority, came to dominate the nation's politics, and the party led every government of independent Malaya from 1957 through 1963; since 1963, it has been the largest element in the coalition governments of Malaysia.

At independence, 55 percent of Malaya's population was Malay, 35 percent ethnic Chinese, and 10 percent Indian. The federation consisted of 11 states; Penang and Melaka (formerly Malacca) were former British colonies, while the remaining nine states each had a hereditary monarch (usually called a sultan) as chief of state. Under the constitution of Malaya, the Malays maintained their privileges—Malay was the official language and Islam the official religion—and in return, non-Malays gained citizenship. The states retained some of their powers, and every five years the sultans elect one of their number to serve as Yang di-Pertuan Agong ("supreme ruler"), popularly known as the king of Malaya (now Malaysia). The Malays realized that independence was not viable without the cooperation of the other peoples of Malaya, and the UMNO party formed a coalition, the Alliance Party, with the Malayan Chinese Association (MCA) and the Malayan Indian Congress (MIC).

The prime minister who oversaw the successful transition to independence was Tunku Abdul Rahman Putra (1903–1990), who was premier until 1970. He was one of the founders of UMNO and a member of the royal family of the state of Kedah.

The new government consisted mostly of Malays with a smaller number of Chinese and Indians. There was an unwritten understanding that Malays would hold the main positions in government and politics, while the Chinese continued to dominate business and economic affairs. Government was consensual: difficult issues were resolved in private in order not to stir up racial tensions.

THE CREATION OF MALAYSIA

In the 1960s, the British were eager to decolonize the region. In northern Borneo, Great Britain governed British North Borneo (now called Sabah) and Sarawak as colonies and had a protectorate over the sultanate of Brunei. South of the Malay Peninsula, the city-state of Singapore was a British colony that had had internal self-government since 1959. The idea of an enlarged federation, Malaysia, gained support for security and economic reasons, and in September 1963, Malaysia was formed, although oil-rich Brunei declined to join. The inclusion of Sabah and Sarawak, with their population of Malays and various indigenous peoples, balanced the large Chinese population of Singapore.

Both Indonesia and the Philippines protested the creation of Malaysia. Early in 1963, Indonesia gave support to a rebel army in Brunei. Opposing Malaysia in Borneo, Indonesia's President Sukarno (1901–1970) adopted a policy of *konfrontasi* (confrontation), and from April 1963, Indonesians infiltrated Sabah and Sarawak. British forces supported the Malayan army against Indonesian guerrillas. The Philippines had a long-standing territorial claim to British North Borneo (Sabah), and although the Philippines did not engage in military activity in northern Borneo, the Philippine government did break diplomatic relations with Malaya.

After Malaysia came into being in September 1963, a border war continued in Borneo. In 1964, Indonesian agents made an incursion into Johor, in Peninsular Malaysia. By 1965, Australian and New Zealand forces fought alongside Malaysian and British troops in Borneo, and Indonesian forces openly engaged in the conflict. A coup in Indonesia in 1965 toppled Sukarno, bringing to power a new government, headed by President Suharto, that had no interest in continuing the confrontation. At peace talks in 1966, Indonesia accepted the creation of Malaysia; the

The Petronas Towers in Kuala Lumpur, the tallest building in the world from 1998 through 2003, came to symbolize Malaysia's economic progress in the late twentieth century.

Philippines also recognized Malaysia but never gave up its claim to Sabah. However, despite securing diplomatic recognition, the federation faced difficulties.

The Malays felt uneasy with the large number of Chinese added by the union with Singapore, and the Malay authorities also considered the Singaporean prime minister, Lee Kuan Yew (born 1923), too socialist. Singapore's ethnic Chinese majority became increasingly concerned that Malays received preferential treatment from the UMNO-dominated federal government. The relationship between the federal authorities in Kuala Lumpur and Singapore's state government broke down and the federation became unworkable. In August 1965, Tunku Abdul Rahman Putra, the federal prime minister, asked the national parliament to sever all ties with Singapore's state government. As a result, Singapore became an independent state.

ETHNIC UNREST

Even after the separation of largely Chinese Singapore, the political consensus did not last. The majority Malays were increasingly unhappy with the relative affluence of the minority Chinese community, whose members they considered to be immigrants. More extreme political parties sprang up, including the Pan-Malayan Islamic Party (PAS), which favored Malay interests, while many Chinese who had become disaffected with the Malay-dominated Alliance Party backed the Democratic Action Party (DAP). Matters came to a head after the 1969 parliamentary election, when non-Malays won a large number of seats. Malays rioted in Kuala Lumpur, and 143 Chinese and 25 Malays were killed (unofficial sources give higher figures).

A state of emergency was declared and parliament was suspended. A nine-member National Operations Council (NOC) was established to coordinate military and police action; the NOC consisted of leading Malay members of the government, army, police, and civil service, although the Chinese and Indians also had representatives.

Tunku Abdul Rahman Putra, whose powers were curtailed by the NOC, resigned in favor of his deputy, Tun Abdul Razak (1922–1976), who was an advocate of pro-Malay action. In 1971, the federal government under Tun Abdul Razak was restored. However, the new government was a controlled form of democracy: criticism of the government was restricted, and the authorities adopted more pro-Malay policies. The Alliance Party was replaced by a broader coalition of parties, the Barisan Nasional (National Front, or BNP), including members from the moderate Chinese and Indian parties.

THE NEW ECONOMIC PLAN

The new government's New Economic Plan (NEP) included targets to reduce poverty by 1990 and to remove the link between race and prosperity. The biggest problem was the economic weakness of the ethnic Malays, known as Bumiputras, who worked mainly in agriculture; only about 5 percent of the professional classes were ethnic Malays. The NEP envisioned an affirmative action plan in favor of the Bumiputras to help them into commerce and the professions. More Malays were appointed to posts in state-run financed corporations, and private companies were obliged to employ quotas of Malays and to allocate shares to Malays. The government also invested heavily in a schools program and in higher education for Malays.

The government was fortunate to introduce affirmative action at a time of economic expansion. The country experienced an average annual growth in gross domestic product (GDP; the value of all the goods and services produced in a country in a fixed period, usually one year) of 6.8 percent from 1971 to 1990. Malaysia's increased wealth lessened the resentment of non-Malays toward their perceived second-class status.

MAHATHIR BIN MOHAMED

After representative government was restored in 1971, the ruling UMNO party split into factions of Bumiputras competing for government favors. Supporters of the former premier Tunku Abdul Rahman Putra were unhappy at being sidelined, and the struggle for leadership intensified when Tun Abdul Razak's health began to fail and he died in office in 1976. The new prime minister, Datuk Hussein bin Onn (1922–1981), was also in poor health, and he was considered a stopgap.

Attention instead focused on the post of deputy prime minister, filled by Mahathir bin Mohamed (born 1925). A complex and charismatic personality, Mahathir was a strong advocate of pro-Bumiputra policies, yet he also addressed the needs and aspirations of the non-Malay communities. He introduced the New Development Policy (NDP) through which he intended to promote economic growth while being fair to all ethnic groups. Mahathir attacked a perceived attitude of dependency that came with reliance on government support and finance. He reversed the policy of creating state-financed corporations and began to privatize state-owned companies, some of which were handed over to individuals (without a public bidding process), leading to charges of favoritism.

Mahathir's biggest problems were not with the nation's non-Malay communities but with members of his own party. Between 1986 and 1987, members of UMNO rebelled against Mahathir's leadership, largely because of the cutback in patronage that his privatization policies had brought; there was also dissent because of his dominating personality. In domestic politics, Mahathir intensified the move toward centralization and became more authoritarian. He believed that a form of controlled democracy was necessary in an ethnically divided nation to ensure social stability and to minimize racial tension. In October 1987, Mahathir invoked the Internal Security Act (ISA) to arrest 106 people, including leading members of opposition parties. He also attacked the freedom of the press, shutting down three newspapers. The judiciary challenged Mahathir's use of the ISA. He responded by suspending the head of the judiciary, along with five members of the Supreme Court.

THE ASIAN FINANCIAL CRISIS

By the mid-1990s, Malaysia's economy was booming and the nation was one of the group of Asian countries that were known as "tiger economies" because of their powerful growth. Despite the nation's vigorous development, many Malaysian industries involve assembly rather than manufacture, creating a dependence upon other Asian countries, such as Japan and South Korea, to supply parts for assembly. As a result, when an economic crisis hit Asia in 1997, Malaysia was badly affected because the crash involved not only Malaysia but also its regional suppliers and the purchasers of its exports. As the crisis struck in 1997, currency speculators attacked the ringitt, the Malaysian currency. At first, Mahathir introduced policies

approved by the International Monetary Fund (IMF), and interest rates were sharply raised to persuade investors not to sell the Malaysian currency. However, the flexible exchange rate led to a fall in the value of the ringitt, and government cutbacks added to the recession. The deepening crisis led Mahathir to abandon IMF policies and introduce his own program, aiming to isolate Malaysia from foreign speculators. At the same time, Mahathir pushed ahead with plans to reinvigorate the economy by lowering interest rates to make borrowing easier and by spending $2.7 million on major projects to encourage growth.

Mahathir maintained financial stability and retained banking confidence. By maintaining subsidies and price controls, Mahathir also avoided ethnic tensions. Financial commentators condemned the program, arguing that investors would shun Malaysia in the future. Other critics thought that protectionism would allow the government to postpone reforming insolvent companies. Good foreign exchange reserves, a low foreign debt, and low inflation, together with an injection of government funds, lessened the worst of the recession, and the economy grew by 4.4 percent in 2002. However, Mahathir's handling of the financial crisis brought disagreement with his deputy prime minister and finance minister, and Mahathir's presumed successor, Anwar Ibrahim (born 1947).

Anwar Ibrahim backed IMF polices and also challenged Mahathir by initiating a campaign against alleged government corruption. As a result, Mahathir fired his deputy in 1998. Anwar Ibrahim subsequently faced allegations of sexual offenses and charges of corruption and abuse of power, and attempting to cover up misconduct. The charges were widely perceived to be politically motivated. Anwar Ibrahim protested his innocence but was sentenced to six years in prison and disqualified from political activities for a further five years. The trial was denounced by international and human rights observers. In 2004, an appeals court reversed the conviction and Anwar Ibrahim was released; however, he remained unable to participate in politics until 2007.

A CHANGE OF LEADERSHIP

In October 2003, Mahathir stepped down voluntarily after 22 years in power, to be succeeded by the deputy prime minister, Abdullah Ahmad Badawi (born 1939). Badawi won an overwhelming victory in the 2004 parliamentary election, with the BNP winning 199 of 219 seats in the lower house of parliament; within the coalition, UMNO won 110 seats. The opposition parties made little impression. Abdullah Ahmad Badawi's domestic policy has been characterized by measures against corruption; he sanctioned the arrest of several people who made fortunes through perceived cronyism during Mahathir's premiership, and in 2004 he allowed the release of Anwar Ibrahim. The new government also faces the rise of Islamic fundamentalism and has supported Islam Hadhari, a version of Islamic thought that sanctions technological development.

L. DOUGLAS

CULTURAL EXPRESSION

Literature

Malaysian literature is in its infancy. It draws upon Malay, Chinese, Tamil, and English traditions, which each contribute different elements to a new national literary expression.

Since the 1980s, the emergence of a vibrant economy and national prosperity in Malaysia has brought social changes that have been reflected in new forms of literature. The different ethnic and linguistic groups generally write in their own languages. Bahasa Melayu (Malay) is the official national language and is the first language of around 58 percent of the population. Chinese is spoken as a first language by 24 percent of Malaysians, while Tamil is the first language of 4 percent. English, the language of the former colonial power (Great Britain), is widely used as a literary language.

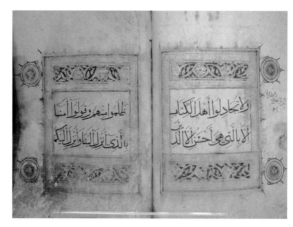

Islam has influenced Malay literature, and religious books, such as this Koran, are written in Arabic script.

MALAY

The Terengganu Stone, which is dated to 1303, is the earliest known narrative Malay writing; the stone is inscribed with an account of history, law, and romance. The *Hikayat Raja Pasai*, written in the fifteenth century, and the sixteenth-century *Sejarah Melayu* (The Malay annals) are major landmarks in early Malay literature. The first written Malay literature was in Arabic script, and early works were mainly histories composed for Malay royal families. The epic *Hikayat Hang Tuah* tells of the devotion of the warrior Hang Tuan to his sultan. At the same time, oral literature flourished; folktales were memorized and passed from one generation of storytellers to the next. Folktales such as *Hikayat Sang Kancil*, the story of a clever mouse deer, related stories of animals and people. Adventures adapted from Indian literature were also popular, including the epic *Ramayana*.

Munshi Abdullah (Abdullah bin Abdul Kadir; 1797–1854) is often called the father of Malay literature. His autobiography, *Hikayat Abdullah*, describes everyday life in the Malay states in the first half of the nineteenth century and the spread of British influence. By the 1920s, there was a division between the royal and noble Malays, who had been educated in English and read English-language literature, and the vast majority of Malays, who only heard or read Malay stories. Growing Malay nationalism was expressed in part through literature as Malay writers, many of whom were members of Malay-based literary associations, described ordinary lives, events, and popular discontent with colonial rule.

By the 1950s and 1960s, a number of women writers had gained popularity, including the poet Salmi Manja (born 1939) and the novelist Khadijah Hashim (born 1942). The race riots of 1969 were a strong influence on Malay literature, and subsequent writers explored social problems and economic inequality through the so-called Literature of Development.

CHINESE AND INDIAN LITERATURE

In the nineteenth century, Chinese migrants who settled in the Malay Peninsula brought their own fiction with them. The first local works published in Chinese appeared in 1911, but literary works from China remain popular. Since the 1950s, a vibrant Chinese-language press has flourished in Malaysia. Tamil, Telegu, and other Indian settlers in Malaya had their social and cultural roots in India; few Indians regarded the Malay Peninsula as their home until the late 1940s. As a result, ethnic Indians in Malaysia read works by Indian authors, and Malaysian Tamil writers take part in literary conventions and meetings in India. Authors from Malaysia, such as Lloyd Fernando (born 1926) and K.S. Maniam (born 1942), often write in English.

P. FERGUSSON

Art and Architecture

Malaysia has rich and varied traditions of building and decorative arts, reflecting its diverse population and the many cultural and political influences that have shaped the nation's history.

One of the best places to see the wealth of building types and styles that typify Malaysian architecture is the city of Melaka (formerly Malacca), which flourished as a center for the spice trade from the fifteenth century. In Melaka, the great wooden palace of Sultan Mansur Shah (reigned 1458–1477) has been reconstructed as the Muzium Budaya (Cultural Museum). Until recent times, wood was the principal material used for all Malaysian buildings, and it remains the main structural material for Malay *kampung* (village) houses, which are typically raised on stilts and thatched with palm.

The colonial heart of Melaka contains the Stadthuys (town hall) and Christ Church, built in brick by Dutch colonists, and Memorial Hall, constructed by British colonists in an unusual combination of baroque and Islamic styles. The influence of Chinese architecture is strong, from brightly colored and exuberantly decorated temples, such as the seventeenth-century Cheng Hoon Teng, to terraced shop houses (buildings that combine the function of a shop and a house), such as the ornately decorated Chan family shop house on Jalan Tun Tan Cheng Lock. Mosques also feature prominently; early examples, such as the Terengkera Mosque (rebuilt in 1856), were based on the traditional Javanese *pendopo*, pillared pavilions with tiered roofs.

MODERN ARCHITECTURE

In the capital, Kuala Lumpur, which dates from the nineteenth century, historic colonial architecture, such as the Sultan Abdul Samad Building, stands alongside innovative modern structures erected since independence in 1957. These new buildings range from the stunning National Mosque designed by Datuk Baharuddin bin Abu Kasim (born 1926) to the high-rise buildings of the Golden Triangle, the city's commercial district.

The Malaysian government plays a leading role in promoting modern building projects, including the landmark 1,483-foot- (452 m) tall Petronas Towers designed by U.S. architects Cesar Pelli & Associates and built in 1998, and Putrajaya (begun in 1995), a modern garden city that is being constructed as the main administrative center of the country. A number of Malaysian firms have been at the forefront of efforts to develop skyscraper designs that are responsive to the region's tropical climate.

Like architecture, painting and sculpture have been encouraged from the mid-1950s as a means of expressing national identity and success. Prior to this period, these arts were little developed, in part because of the predominance of Islam, which prohibits the portrayal of animal and human forms.

DECORATIVE ARTS

Malaysia has a long tradition of decorative arts, which range from intricate gold and silver jewelry associated with the Malay courts to mats, baskets, and hats woven by local peoples from rattan and palm leaves. Many fine examples of metalwork made for the courts of the local sultans survive from the eighteenth and nineteenth centuries, including the highly valued *keris*, ceremonial daggers that are traditional Malay weapons, and betel sets, comprising boxes, trays, and nut slicers for the ancient custom of chewing betel nuts. The sultans also commissioned weavers to make luxurious textiles, including *songket*, a patterned fabric woven from threads of colored silk and gold and silver. Kelantan and Terengganu are centers for producing *songket*, as well as traditional patterned fabrics such as batik.

Wood carving decorates buildings, from the posts, eaves, doors, and window panels of traditional Malay houses to the flamboyant ornamentation of Chinese houses and temples. Different forest-dwelling peoples in Sabah, Sarawak, and Selangor are known for their carved masks and images.

R. BEAN

Malaysian decorative arts include basketry, wood carving, metalwork, and batik.

Music and Performing Arts

Malaysia's diverse society and rich cultural history are reflected in a wide variety of musical genres. Although Islam, the religion of the nation's Malay majority, has strict views on what kinds of music are acceptable, Malaysia retains a great variety of theatrical, narrative, and dance genres.

Alongside a Malay majority, Malaysia is also home to ethnic Chinese and Indians, various upland and interior indigenous peoples, and the descendants of European settlers from the sixteenth century. Since each ethnic group maintains its own culture with considerable autonomy, the term "Malay music," strictly speaking, does not include the varied musical traditions of the non-Malay ethnic groups.

Malaysia's Chinese and Indian communities have their own music, including both traditional instruments and genres from China and the southern part of the Indian subcontinent and modern popular music from Hong Kong and Indian movies. Malay popular music is a fusion of the different cultural influences in the peninsula. The musician P. Ramlee (died 1973) helped create a Malaysian music that combined folk songs with Western dance rhythms and western Asian music. In the 1960s and 1970s, Malay popular artists copied Western styles, but recent Malaysian popular music owes more to local traditions.

TRADITIONAL MALAY MUSIC

From the tenth century CE, coastal city-kingdoms in the Malay Peninsula grew to become separate states, each ruled by a sultan. Music was cultivated at most courts for entertainment and ritual purposes. The *nobat* ensemble, imported from western Asia around the twelfth century, is virtually the only type of court ensemble that remains, consisting of an oboe (*serunai*), a trumpet (*nafiri*), two barrel-shaped drums (*gendang*), a kettle drum (*nehara*), and sometimes a knobbed gong and a pair of cymbals. One state, Terengganu, maintains a gamelan ensemble of bronze instruments derived from Indonesia, but the Malay gamelan style is much simpler than that of Java.

Of court origin, the *makyong* theater now survives as a folk practice, featuring female dancers and singers plus two male comedians, accompanied by a two-stringed fiddle (*rebab*), drums, and a pair of gongs. While the fiddle plays a highly ornamented melody in western Asian style, the drums and gongs mark a cycle of beats, which is of Southeast Asian origin.

Upland peoples in the mountains of the peninsula have a variety of small instruments, including jaw harps (small lyre-shaped instruments held in the mouth). The inland peoples of East Malaysia have several distinctive instruments, including a free-reed mouth organ with a gourd wind chest similar to instruments found in the mountains of Vietnam and northern Thailand.

A dancer performs the silat, *an elegant dance that derives from martial arts.* Silat *dancers spar in a stylized manner to the accompaniment of drums and other instruments.*

PUPPET THEATER

Shadow puppet theater, called *wayang kulit*, is popular both in the north and in Johor in the south. In the north, there are three forms: *wayang gedek*, which is the same as the southern Thai *nang talung*, and *wayang siam* and *wayang melayu*, both of which are indigenous forms. A puppeteer (*dalang*), seated in a small hut with a white cloth stretched across the front and lit from behind, manipulates cut-out leather puppets to perform a variety of stories, many from the Indian epic *Ramayana*, accompanied by a number of drums, gongs, cymbals, and one melody instrument, the *serunai*. In Johor, *wayang kulit jawa* is Javanese shadow theater performed by people of Javanese descent.

Several other forms of theater exist: *jikay* comedy, *manora* dance drama (from southern Thailand), and two forms of commercial theater that show influence from western Asia and popular culture, *boria* and *bangsawan*. Malaysia also has numerous dance genres, song and storytelling genres, music to accompany martial arts, general folk songs that accompany life-cycle events, and a healing ritual. Music played for its own sake is rare in Malaysia, and percussive instruments are far more numerous than melodic ones.

R. A. SUTTON

Festivals and Ceremonies

Malaysia is home to Malays, Chinese, Indians, and various indigenous peoples of the states of Sabah and Sarawak, and to Muslims, Buddhists, followers of Chinese folk religions, Christians, and Hindus. The principal festivals of the different peoples and religions are public holidays in Malaysia.

Some holidays in Malaysia are marked according to the Western calendar—these are mainly secular holidays—while others are calculated according to the Islamic or Chinese lunar calendar. Some holidays are celebrated throughout Malaysia, while others are unique to a particular state.

NATIONAL HOLIDAYS

New Year's Day (January 1), Chinese New Year, and Maal Hijrah, the start of the Islamic lunar year, are public holidays (although January 1 is not celebrated in all states). Chinese New Year is the principal annual festival for Malaysia's ethnic Chinese, who hold family parties and celebration meals and stage dragon dances and colorful firework displays on the holiday. Chinese New Year celebrations last for about two weeks, and on the holiday itself, people visit friends and family. Gifts of packets of money, called *ang pow*, are traditionally given on this holiday.

There are two secular federal public holidays in early summer: Labor Day (May 1) and the official birthday of the Yang di-Pertuan Agong ("supreme ruler," or the head of state) in the first week of June. The sovereign's official birthday is marked with ceremony and an annual honors list in which distinguished Malaysians receive awards or titles of nobility. The principal federal holiday is National Day, August 31, the anniversary of Malaya's independence from Great Britain in 1957. Formerly known as Independence Day, National Day is marked by military parades and other ceremonies in Kuala Lumpur, the federal legislative capital, and Putrajaya, the new national center of administration, and by parades in other major cities. Fairs, festivals, exhibitions, sports events, and parties are held on National Day, and children get free admission to movies. One secular federal holiday, Federal Territory Day, is celebrated only in Kuala Lumpur, Putrajaya, and Labuan.

RELIGIOUS HOLIDAYS

Islam is the state religion of Malaysia, and Muslim public holidays include the birthday of the Prophet Muhammad (c. 570–632 CE) and Eid al-Adha, the end of the Hajj, the annual pilgrimage by Muslims to Mecca. A healthy animal, usually a goat, is sacrificed and the meat is given to the poor. Hari Raya Puasa, or Aidilfitri (Eid al-Fitr), marks the end of Ramadan, the

month when Muslims fast during daylight hours. After prayers at the mosque, families gather for a celebration meal; children start the day by asking their parents for forgiveness for any bad behavior, and later in the day they receive a gift of money.

Christmas Day (December 25) and Vesak Day, the principal Buddhist holiday (in the spring), are public holidays. Vesak, known in Malaysia as Wesak Day, commemorates the birth and enlightenment of the Buddha and his entry into nirvana (final release from the cycle of reincarnation). Worshippers attend temples to pray, make offerings, and light incense, and the day ends with lantern parades.

Hindus celebrate Deepavali, known in India as Diwali, the festival of lights. Diwali celebrates the victory of good over evil and is believed to be the time when the souls of the dead revisit Earth. Hindus visit temples to pray in the morning before meeting with their family for a celebration. At the end of the day, lanterns are lit to guide the souls of the departed.

K. ROMANO-YOUNG

Young women carry the Malaysian flag in a street parade for the National Day celebrations.

Food and Drink

Malaysian cuisine is a blend of Malay, Chinese, Indian, Thai, Javanese, Sumatran, and Eurasian styles of cooking. Rice is an essential element in most Malay meals. Noodles are also served, and both are accompanied by a wide choice of spicy and tasty sauces and a selection of local vegetables.

Trade ships from across Asia and western Asia brought pepper, cardamom, star anise, and fenugreek to Malaysia. These were combined with fresh ingredients available locally, such as galangal, chilies, coconuts, kaffir lime leaves, pandan leaves, lemongrass, a variety of basil called *daun kemangi*, nutmeg, turmeric, and wild ginger buds, onions, and garlic to create the classic Malay flavors that characterize the cuisine not only of Malaysia but also Singapore and the Philippines.

A Malay breakfast may include *nasi lemak*, in which rice and coconut milk combine with curried chicken or beef. Nearly every Malay meal is served with rice. One popular dish, *nasi dagang*, is made from two varieties of rice—glutinous rice and cooking rice—cooked in coconut cream. It comes with side dishes or condiments, such as pickles and curries. While there are various dishes at any Malay meal, all are served at once, not in courses. Food is eaten delicately with the fingers of the right hand (never with the left which is used for personal ablutions) and Malays rarely use utensils.

MAIN INGREDIENTS

For many recipes, dried herbs and fresh savory ingredients are ground into a paste and fried in oil. Two versions of the popular street food *keropok* are made from fried ground fish, particularly in the state of Terengganu. *Keropok keping* is thin and crunchy, while *keropok lekor* is more substantial. Coconut milk may be added to rice, and the mixture that results is topped with chicken, beef, mutton, or fish (never with pork; Muslims, who form the majority of Malaysia's population, are forbidden to eat pork). Seafood dishes in Malaysia include shrimp, cuttlefish, and *pulut lepa* (a mash of onions, chilies, coconut, and boiled fish, cooked dry and used to fill glutinous rice rolls). *Ketupat sotong*, squid stuffed with glutinous rice, uses coconut milk as both a marinade and a sauce. The *nyonya* tradition of cooking features a mingling of Chinese dishes with Malay recipes and is the result of the interaction between the cultures of Chinese immigrants and local Malays that began four hundred years ago. *Nyonya* dishes are sweeter and richer than typical Chinese food, and they include more Malay spices.

A popular food that may be eaten instead of rice is the crepe-like pancake called *roti jala*. Made with a touch of turmeric, it is served with sauce and is eaten on special occasions. Other

Malaysians enjoy snacks of street food, such as this wok of spicy fried noodles.

popular foods are *rendang*, generally made with beef; satay, skewered meat served over rice and served with spicy peanut sauce; and fried noodles. One festival, the Lantern and Moon Cake Festival, celebrated in the eighth month of the Chinese lunar calendar, has its own food specialty, moon cakes. The cakes are eaten to commemorate the Chinese overthrow of their Mongol overlords in the fourteenth century; since the Mongols had banned meetings, the Chinese hid plans for a revolt in the cakes, which were then distributed to the conspirators.

DESSERTS

Desserts may be made at home or purchased on the street. Palm sugar, flour, and coconut milk combine to create a variety of pastries, cakes, and puddings. At a shaved ice stall, ice may be topped with beans, jellies, peanuts, coconut milk, and syrup. Favorite fruits include pineapples, papayas, bananas, mangoes, durians, and rambutans. Malay meals are accompanied by cool drinks, as well as tea and coffee. Coffee is served thick and aromatic, sometimes with condensed milk, and usually sweet.

K. ROMANO-YOUNG

DAILY LIFE

Religion

The state religion of Malaysia is Islam, which is practiced by 53 percent of the population. The central role of Islam in Malaysian daily life is a popular issue of debate, with some modern Islamic groups arguing that Islam should come before the interests of the state.

Malaysia's constitution guarantees freedom of religion. Although Islam is the official state religion, other religions are also practiced. Buddhists account for 17 percent of the population, followers of traditional Chinese folk religions (including Taoism) 12 percent, Hindus 9 percent, Protestant and Roman Catholic Christians 6 percent, and those who practice other religions or who are nonreligious 3 percent. In Malaysia, religion and ethnicity generally go together: ethnic Malays are normally Muslims; the ethnic Chinese are usually Buddhists or practice Taoism or folk religions; Indians are Hindus, Muslims, or Sikhs. Malaysia's Christians are drawn from different ethnic groups, although few Malays are Christian.

STATE RELIGION

Islam is not only the state religion but also benefits from discriminatory laws. Non-Muslim religious materials, including the Bible, cannot legally be printed in the Malay language. The Koran is often cited in political life, and Islam influences national law. Malaysia's dominant Malay culture largely follows Islamic dictates on diet, alcohol, family life, and personal behavior. Religious and cultural prohibitions dictate the availability of books and movies, and so on. Non-Muslim Malaysians claim discrimination, although the situation is complicated by affirmative action in education, employment, and business ownership in favor of Bumiputras (ethnic Malays who are Muslims). It is, therefore, difficult to differentiate religious from ethnic discrimination. Christians, in particular, meet obstructions to the construction and maintenance of their church buildings and schools.

Islam is part of the primary school curriculum for all students in public schools; at the high school level, non-Muslims study moral education instead. There is debate concerning teaching Muslim students about faiths other than Islam and about secular concerns. There is also controversy over the changes made to Islamic (Sharia) law in the last 50 years, since the emergence of a radical strict moral code introduced by the Egyptian-born Islamic cleric Yusuf Qaradawi (born 1926). Malaysia's few politically active Muslim groups include the traditional Kaum Tua and the reformist Kaum Muda Muslim groups. The youth organization Agnkatan Belia Islam Malaysia (ABIM), with its slogan "Islam first, Malay second," is shaping the outlook of some young people, encouraging followers to embrace customs that reflect an Arabic interpretation of Islam.

OTHER RELIGIONS IN MALAYSIA

The majority of Malaysian Christians are in Eastern Malaysia (Sabah and Sarawak), where there were conversions among the indigenous peoples of Borneo when the region was ruled by the British before 1963. Roman Catholics are concentrated in western Peninsular Malaysia, particularly around Melaka, where Portuguese traders were active from the sixteenth century. Although there is no law that forbids preaching to Muslims, the churches in Malaysia do not try to convert Muslim Malays. The large new city of Shah Alam is officially an Islamic city in which no Christian churches may be built.

Buddhism, the majority religion of Malaysia's ethnic Chinese, has been present in the region for centuries, but it has declined in practice. As a result, Buddhist organizations, such as the Buddhist Missionary Society, have simplified their message, attempting to interest young people. Several Buddhist sects operate, and efforts are being made to form a national Buddhist council to represent Buddhists and to coordinate activities.

Modern Hinduism was brought to the Malay Peninsula in the nineteenth century by plantation workers from southern India. There are two principal strands. So-called "folk Hinduism" became established in rural areas where the emphasis is on the worship of local gods or on the deity favored in the region from which the Indians originated; in the cities, there are larger temples, often devoted to the Hindu god Shiva.

K. ROMANO-YOUNG

Family and Society

Malaysia is a multiethnic nation of some 23.3 million people (at the 2000 census), and the largest group comprises ethnic Malays, who make up approximately 50 percent of the population. Ethnic Chinese account for 24 percent of Malaysians, and ethnic Indians approximately 7 percent. Indigenous peoples of Sabah and Sarawak make up 11 percent. Malaysian society is the sum of all these parts, but the ethnic Malays dominate.

Ethnic Malays are also known as Bumiputras (or Bumiputeras, meaning "sons of the soil") to indicate their indigenous status. The Malays can trace their history back to Borneo before the fifth century CE and through the influential Srivijaya kingdom in the Indonesian island of Sumatra, which unified various ethnic groups in the region between the seventh and thirteenth centuries. During this period, a Malay language and culture emerged, which borrowed Sanskrit words and concepts. The ethnic Chinese, on the other hand, were migrants from the southern coastal provinces of China and had traded in the region for centuries. They only began to settle in Malaya in large numbers during the nineteenth century, when they became laborers, traders, and merchants in the Malay Peninsula. Migrants from India came to the peninsula over hundreds of years, but they did not settle on a large scale until the nineteenth century. Most were Tamils and Telegu peoples who migrated from southern India to escape poverty and drought. Arriving in the British-ruled Malay states, many Indians found work as rubber tappers, while others built the infrastructure or worked as administrators and in business.

In addition to being multiethnic, Malaysian society is also multireligious. Ethnicity and religion are closely intertwined in Malaysia. An ethnic Malay person is constitutionally defined as a Malay-speaking Muslim and, although Malaysia has a secular constitution, Islamic values and interests are influential in shaping the politics and culture of the country.

ETHNIC CLASHES

There is an economic and political gulf between the Malays and other ethnic groups in Malaysia. For various political and cultural reasons, since the colonial era the Malays have lagged behind the Chinese in economic terms. This economic disparity persisted after independence in 1957 and, fueled by ethnic and religious elements, culminated in riots between Malays and Chinese in May 1969. These events prompted the Malaysian government to implement reforms in the New Economic Policy (NEP) from 1971 through 1991. The government discovered that the Malays controlled only 2.4 percent of the national economy, while other ethnic groups held 33 percent, with the remaining 63 percent of the economy owned by foreigners. The purpose of the NEP was affirmative action in favor of the Malays to redistribute national wealth in a 30:40:30 ratio among the Malays, other Malaysians, and foreign ownership.

Malaysia, along with neighboring Thailand and Indonesia, experienced rapid economic development from the mid-1980s to the mid-1990s, ending abruptly with the 1997 Asian financial crisis. This period saw the emergence of a middle class in Malaysian society. This group of well-educated, cosmopolitan Malays has been popularly termed Melayu Baru (New Malay) and has become the face of Malaysian economic progress. Nevertheless, even the expansion of the Malay middle class has not stemmed criticism that only a small number of urban-dwelling Malays have benefited from state patronage under the NEP. The rural-urban divide within the Malay community remains, while religion-based politics continue to hold great sway in Malaysian society, undercutting the political influence of the educated Malay middle class.

FAMILY

Family in Malaysia generally refers either to the traditional nuclear family unit of parents and children or to an extended network of familial relations that stretches across different households. In Malaysia, as in most of Asia, there is a strong emphasis on the family as a key unit of society and a fundamental feature of self-identity. It is both the political and cultural norm in Malaysian society to place the interests of the family over that of the individual.

Most Malaysian families are patriarchal; the belief that the man is in charge of the household crosses ethnic and religious lines. This expresses itself in various forms, from casual respect toward the male head of the family to domestic subjugation of women. Seniority is highly regarded in Malaysian households. Family members are addressed according to their position in the family, for example, "first brother," "third sister," and so on, and the eldest male in the family is usually greeted first. Children are expected to seek their parents' counsel, even after they are married, as a gesture of deference and respect. It is also common for both men and women to live with their parents until they

Rural communities, such as this water village near Kuantan in Pahang state, are now home to around 30 percent of Malaysians. There is a great difference in the standard of living as well as in family size between poorer rural Malaysians and city-dwellers, who live in smaller nuclear families or alone.

marry. The main religions in Malaysia—Islam, Buddhism, and Christianity—all stress the role of the family as part of a broader system of ethics and values.

Economic growth and modernization have slowly changed the traditional labor divisions between men and women. Greater opportunities for education and economic participation for women mean that they are increasingly prioritizing professional employment over traditional familial roles. In turn, this has affected the choices and expectations of both men and women in marriage and childrearing.

Malaysian society has also changed through urbanization. About 70 percent of all Malaysians now live in cities and this has resulted in an irreversible change in family structure. As Malaysians move from rural to urban settings, they lose intimate contact with their extended family and begin to form smaller family units. As a result, urbanization in Malaysia is creating more nuclear families.

THE CHANGING ROLE OF THE FAMILY

In Malaysia, as with most of Asia, it is a common assumption that care for the young and old is the family's responsibility. In Malaysia, it is generally assumed that the woman in a family will shoulder much of the burden of caring for the young and the elderly. As a result of changing attitudes toward the position of women in society, economic modernization, migration, and changing work and lifestyle patterns, the expectation that care is provided by the family is now under pressure. Although Malaysia is experiencing sweeping social and cultural changes that have gradually reduced larger family units to nuclear family units, the family unit continues to play an indispensable economic and social security role.

T. CHONG

Welfare and Education

Malaysia developed from being an exporter of raw materials, such as tin and rubber, to an assembler and exporter of electrical and electronic goods and a wide range of manufactures during the last quarter of the twentieth century. As a result, living standards rose, and the provision of health care and welfare, as well as education, similarly increased.

Malaysia has a growing elderly population as life expectancy increases. Many adult children live with their parents and help support them in their old age. Care of elderly parents is part of the culture of all Malaysians, in which age earns respect. There are also financial incentives for such care; adult children who live with their parents qualify for a tax rebate toward the expense of care, and they can also claim as tax deductions medical expenses incurred on their parents' behalf.

SOCIAL SECURITY

Apart from financial support from the family, there are two principal sources of funding for the elderly; some occupational pensions are available through the Employees' Social Security Act, but most people rely upon individual provision through the Employees' Provident Fund (EPF), to which people contribute for their retirement. Rising expectations of prosperity and the accessibility of payment from age 55 both put strains on the system, particularly as employees can withdraw 60 percent of contributions as a lump sum on retirement at age 55. A retired person may otherwise withdraw annual amounts. Each person's account in the EPF has three elements: 60 percent that can be withdrawn in whole or in part on retirement; 30 percent that is reserved for major expenses, such as buying a house; and 10

percent to cover medical expenses in old age. The EPF is funded by contributions from employees (12 percent of the weekly wage) and by employers (11 percent). However, the fund is often insufficient, particularly for people on low incomes, because the amount available depends on how much a worker has earned. Separate programs provide for those employed in the public sector and for members of the armed forces. The Old Age Pension Scheme (OAPS) provides a non-contributory pension for public sector employees.

HEALTH CARE

Malaysia effectively has a two-tier health care system. People with full health insurance—a minority because of the expense—and government employees have rapid access to private facilities. The majority must wait for non-emergency treatment, often for many months. The system emerged during the 1980s and 1990s, when private health care became more common. The establishment of private medical facilities created problems for state-run hospitals, which lost staff to better-paying jobs in the private sector. As a result, around 75 percent of the health care specialists in Malaysia are employed by private facilities, which cater to some 25 percent of the population.

In the state sector, patients get free treatment in exchange for a registration fee, a single payment of 1 ringgit (less than 30 cents). Hospitals, health centers, clinics, and other facilities are maintained by the federal Ministry of Health, and the standard of facilities and treatment is high. The government has implemented a program to establish clinics in remote areas that previously lacked adequate facilities, and state-funded health care is available in most rural areas. Thirteen major so-called nucleus hospitals provide specialist care in the cities.

The priorities facing the healthcare sector changed through the last quarter of the twentieth century, when the problem of communicable diseases lessened as preventive medicine and better standards of water treatment reduced the incidence of many diseases. At the same time, the incidence of noncommunicable diseases increased, giving Malaysia a health profile characteristic of developed nations, where heart disease, strokes, cancers, and road traffic injuries are among the most common conditions treated in hospitals. Traditional healers and alternative medicine also play a role in health care in Malaysia.

Housing

Traditional Malay houses, made from wood and bamboo, are ideally suited for the hot and humid climate. They encourage the circulation of air and are comfortable despite the heat. Many people still live in traditional houses, not only in the countryside but also in the city suburbs, where rapid urban development has overwhelmed former rural communities. Many Malaysians now live in modern housing, either individual houses or often apartments within a large development. There is a strong demand for low-cost housing in urban areas, and both the federal government and private corporations are involved in major programs to provide housing for low-income families. However, much of the smaller modern housing built in the cities is unsuitable for the climate and is poorly ventilated.

Muslim students attend the International Islamic University in Kuala Lumpur, which is one of a number of Malaysian universities that cater to particular ethnic or religious groups.

Both types of health care are popular with members of Malaysia's ethnic Chinese community as well as ethnic Indians and the indigenous peoples of Sarawak and Sabah.

EDUCATION

In 2005, 88.7 percent of Malaysians were literate. Expenditure on education increased 68 percent from 1998 through 2001 and has since continued to climb. Around 80 percent of Malaysian children receive some preschool education, although the preschool sector is not part of the formal education system; many preschool facilities are maintained by private or voluntary organizations. Preschool classes run by the Ministry of Education offer one or two years of education to children aged four or five whose parents cannot afford private facilities.

Only primary education, which begins at age six and lasts for six years, is mandatory. Children from different ethnic communities go to different schools and attend different classes. Ethnic Malays (Bumiputras) attend classes in the Malay language, English, math, Islamic studies and moral education, music, art, and health and physical education. In the final three years at primary school, Malay students also study science, life skills, and local studies. Chinese and Indian children study the same subjects, including Islamic and moral education, but they also study either Chinese or Tamil. Students take the primary school assessment examination (UPSR) at the end of six years.

After primary education, students enter lower secondary schools (junior high school) for a three-year course that includes Malay language, English, math, science, geography, history, physical education, health education, art and/or music, and integrated living skills. Muslim students study Islamic education, while non-Muslims study moral education. Chinese, Tamil, and Arabic are optional subjects. Increasing emphasis has been placed on computer literacy, and all schools are scheduled to have computer laboratories by 2010. Urban educational facilities are often more modern than those in rural areas, where some students still attend traditional Islamic schools.

Students take the lower secondary assessment examination (PMR) after the three-year course. Upper secondary education is a two-year course during which students may opt for chosen subjects. At the end of upper secondary education, students take the Malaysian Certificate of Education examination (SPM); successful candidates qualify to enter a postsecondary school for a one-year, or 18-month, course from age 18, which prepares students for the STPM, the matriculation certificate, examination that students must pass to qualify for entry into a Malaysian university. Both private and public sectors provide schools and colleges, although most primary schools are state-run. Private higher education institutions play a major role, although the state also provides universities. There is affirmative action in favor of the Bumiputras. For example, a university-level technical institution in the city of Shah Alam was established to cater to Bumiputras only. Some universities are solely for Muslim students. There are nearly 40 universities, including medical facilities, and technological universities. Two foreign universities that have established campuses in Malaysia.

V. MORRES

Kuala Lumpur

The largest city in Malaysia, Kuala Lumpur is a major commercial and industrial center. Since the national administration of Malaysia moved away to the new city of Putrajaya in 1999, Kuala Lumpur has been the legislative capital. The city remains the seat of the king of Malaysia and the national judiciary and home to foreign embassies and consulates.

Kuala Lumpur was founded in 1857, when the middle Klang Valley was opened to mining. A small group of Chinese prospectors established a successful mine, which soon attracted traders to supply them with provisions. A town grew around the mine near the confluence of the Klang and Gombak rivers. The British colonial authorities in Malaya appointed an official to control the mining town. The third holder of this office, Yap Ah Loy (1837–1885), was largely responsible for developing Kuala Lumpur as a commercial center in the 1860s and 1870s, and the

town soon became the largest center in the Malay state of Selangor. The city became capital of Selangor in 1880 and was rebuilt in brick after a disastrous fire in 1881. Sir Frank Swettenham (1850–1946), the British resident (governor) after 1882, played a major role in the redevelopment of the city, and in 1896, Kuala Lumpur became the capital of the (British) Federated Malay States.

Japanese forces occupied the city during World War II (1939–1945) from 1942 through 1945. Kuala Lumpur grew rapidly during the insurgency by Communist guerrillas (1948–1960), when many people from the countryside took refuge near the city. However, the main spur to the city's development was industry. When Malaya gained independence in 1957, as the Federation of Malaya, Kuala Lumpur became the national capital. In 1963, Malaya joined with Sabah (formerly British North Borneo), Sarawak, and Singapore (which withdrew from the federation in 1965) to form Malaysia, with Kuala Lumpur as federal capital. In 1974, Kuala Lumpur became a federal territory and ceased to be state capital of Selangor.

Shah Alam

Shah Alam dates from the 1970s, when the state of Selangor decided to build a new capital to replace Kuala Lumpur, which was the seat of the national government and a federal territory and, as a result, no longer part of Selangor state. A site among the Klang Valley's rubber and oil palm plantations was chosen for the new city, which was constructed around an artificial lake. The city is dominated by a huge mosque, Sultan Salahuddin Abdul Aziz Shah Mosque, which has a large central dome and four minarets. The mosque can accommodate 24,000 worshippers.

Because Shah Alam is so close to Kuala Lumpur, only 12 miles (20 km) to the east, the city is part of Kuala Lumpur's industrial and commercial region and benefits from the consumer market of its large neighbor. When the city was planned, it was decided that Shah Alam would not be just an administrative state capital but also a major industrial center. This is reflected in the choice of street names in the city, many of which are named for industrial tools or for professions. Automobile construction is the major industry in Shah Alam, which is home to Proton, Malaysia's car manufacturing corporation. A wide variety of other industries have developed.

Shah Alam has grown rapidly. Since the city became the state capital of Selangor in 1977, Shah Alam has spread across the surrounding countryside. At the 2000 Malaysian census, there were 320,000 people within the city limits, but the metropolitan area had a population of 745,000, making it the second-largest in the country. However, Shah Alam is effectively part of "Greater Kuala Lumpur," even though it is physically detached from the national capital. In time, as Kuala Lumpur and Shah Alam spread toward each other, Shah Alam is likely to become part of the Kuala Lumpur metropolitan area.

A MODERN CITY

Kuala Lumpur is a transportation hub, forming the center of the highway and railroad system in the western part of Peninsular Malaysia. The city suffers from traffic gridlock that has only partly been relieved by the construction of expressways and a three-line light railroad system. Kuala Lumpur International Airport is 20 miles (32 km) south of the city down the Klang Valley.

The city has an ethnic Malay majority, which is largely involved in administration and related activities. Ethnic Chinese dominate Kuala Lumpur's commerce, including banking and retailing. The city also has a large Indian population, many of whom are employed in industry, much of which is centered on the industrial suburb of Sungai Besi, which has metalworking, engineering, and other heavy industries. Other industries include food processing, soap manufacture, electrical and electronic engineering, timber processing, manufacturing railroad locomotives and rolling stock, cement and building materials, and a wide range of consumer goods industries. Much of the modern industrial development is based in the suburbs of Petaling Jaya and Batu Tiga, which have a range of high-tech industries.

The city has districts of traditional two-story Chinese houses with shops below, modern zones of small houses and apartment buildings, Malay *kampung*s (small villages) that have been overtaken by development, and districts, such as Kenney Hill, which contain villas that are owned by the wealthy. The commercial district of the city, which is Malaysia's national center for banking and finance, is known as the Golden Triangle. Kuala Lumpur is also home to several universities and other educational and research institutions.

TOURIST ATTRACTIONS

The 1,483-foot (452 m) Petronas Towers dominate the city. These twin high-rise buildings were the world's tallest until Taipei 101 was completed in Taipei, Taiwan, in 2003. Visitors enjoy a wide view across the city from the Skybridge that joins the towers. The view is sometimes obscured in late summer and early fall, when air pollution dramatically increases as a result of forest fires on the Indonesian island of Sumatra to the west.

High-rise office buildings tower over the downtown district of Kuala Lumpur, known as the Golden Triangle.

Much of central Kuala Lumpur is crowded and characterized by tall office buildings that dwarf the Jamek Mosque at the confluence of the Klang and Gombak rivers. The Moorish style mosque, built in 1909, is the oldest in the city. Lake Gardens, an extensive area of parkland and gardens on higher ground on the west bank of the Klang River, contains a number of important public buildings, including the national parliament, the Islamic Arts Museum Malaysia, and the National Museum. Dataran Merdaka (Independence Square) is the main central space used for ceremonies. Facing the square is the Moorish-style Federal Court, topped by copper domes and flanked by one of the tallest flagposts in the world. Other prominent buildings include the large modern National Mosque and the National Sports Complex, constructed to stage the 1998 Commonwealth Games.

The Istana Negara, the residence of the king of Malaysia, is a popular tourist attraction. The palace, which is fronted by colorful gardens, is the scene of a daily ceremony of changing the guards. Petaling Street in Chinatown is lined with shops selling textiles, Chinese traditional medicines, and a range of decorative items. It is also home to many Chinese restaurants. Central Market sells wood carvings, batik, jewelry, glass, and antiques.

C. CARPENTER

Putrajaya

Putrajaya was founded in 1995 and is the new administrative center of Malaysia. It is named for independent Malaya's (and later Malaysia's) first prime minister, Tunku Abdul Rahman Putra (1903–1990). Putra is a Malay title, equivalent to "prince."

Putrajaya was established to remove the main seat of government from the overcrowded, gridlocked city of Kuala Lumpur and to help spread development down the Klang Valley toward the coast. In the early 1990s, the Malaysian federal government entered negotiations with the state of Selangor to purchase enough land to build a new administrative center for the country. Construction began on October 14, 1995, and on June 4, 1999, Putrajaya became the national administrative center of Malaysia. It became a federal territory, the third after Kuala Lumpur and Labuan, on February 1, 2001.

The new city had 7,000 inhabitants at the 2000 national census, and development of the city is to be strictly controlled. When construction is complete after 2010, around 40 percent of the city will be open spaces, gardens (including botanical gardens), and water.

The Putra Mosque, Putrajaya, was completed in 1999. The mosque's minaret is 380 feet (116 m) tall.

A NEW CITY

The city is built around an artificial lake that covers just over 2 square miles (5 sq. km). The downtown district, called the Core Area, is divided into government, civic, commercial, mixed development, and recreational precincts that are linked by a central boulevard. There is no suggestion that the national parliament or foreign embassies will move from Kuala Lumpur to Putrajaya, effectively giving Malaysia two capitals. Surrounding the downtown area, there will eventually be 15 precincts, 12 of which will be residential. Each precinct will have schools, a hospital, a mosque, shops, and other amenities for the local community. The city will eventually have no more than 67,000 homes in total.

Putrajaya will serve only as a national center of administration. Nearby, a second new city, Cyberjaya, is under construction as the national center of information technology. Both cities are linked by a high-speed railroad to Kuala Lumpur farther up the Klang Valley to the north and to Kuala Lumpur International Airport. A monorail system is also being constructed in Putrajaya. Construction of the city slowed during the Asian financial crisis in the late 1990s but picked up speed early in the twenty-first century.

CITY SIGHTS

The dominating building in Putrajaya is Perdana Putra, the office of the prime minister of Malaysia. The complex, which houses most of the national administration, is a massive structure with a blue dome, combining both European and Malay architectural styles. The neighboring Seri Perdana, the official residence of the prime minister, incorporates traditional Malay and Indian Mogul design. A large square has been built to become the home of national events and celebrations.

The 381-foot (116 m) five-tiered pink-and-white minaret of Putra Mosque rises beside the lake. The mosque, which incorporates styles from Morocco and Uzbekistan, can accommodate 15,000 worshippers. Twelve massive columns support the central dome of the mosque, which houses a museum of Koranic manuscripts. The two-tiered bridge across the lake is modeled on an ancient bridge in Esfahan, in Iran. The upper tier carries a highway; the lower tier has a light railroad and is used by pedestrians.

C. CARPENTER

Ipoh

Ipoh in Perak state is a modern city that grew from the 1890s, when British mining companies began to exploit the reserves of tin in the Kinta Valley surrounding the settlement. At the 2000 Malaysian national census, the metropolitan area had a population of 574,000 inhabitants.

Ipoh is named for a tree that grows in the district, the *pohon epuh* or *pokok ipoh*, from whose sap a poison was obtained that was used in hunting. The Kinta River divides Ipoh into Old Town, the area built before World War II (1939–1945), and New Town, the district constructed since the war.

A MINING CENTER

A disputed succession to the throne of the Malay state of Perak in the 1870s led to British intervention, and a British resident was subsequently based in Perak state. Tin mining attracted Chinese workers to the area, and ethnic Chinese still form a majority in the city; it is estimated that nearly 70 percent of Ipoh's residents are Chinese. At the same time, Ipoh became a center for the rubber industry. Because Ipoh had developed with modern facilities, it became the base of the British administration in Perak and, as a result, the capital of the state. Ipoh grew rapidly in the 1920s and 1930s and gained the nickname "Millionaires' City" because many people made a fortune from tin mining in the district. The region around the city is marked with pits from which tin-bearing rock has been extracted.

A Taoist temple in Ipoh serves the city's largely ethnic Chinese population.

MODERN IPOH

The collapse of the price of tin on the world market in the 1950s led to the closure of many mines around Ipoh and a downturn in the fortunes of the city. However, Ipoh had grown large enough to have become a local route hub, a commercial center, and an administrative center, and it was in these roles that its prosperity continued when tin mining was no longer important. The city has a medical university and other educational establishments, including a polytechnic.

The main city landmark is the railroad station built by the British in the early twentieth century in a mixture of Moorish and Victorian Gothic styles; the result is impressive if architecturally confusing. There are several colonial style buildings in Old Town, as well as the Chinese shopping quarter, which attracts visitors. Old Town is also famous for its restaurants. The nineteenth-century Chinese settlers, most of whom came from southern China, brought their own cuisine, which fused with local Malay styles to produce a distinct Ipoh flavor of cooking that includes flat rice noodles and a variety of fish dishes.

Some tin mining continues, but on a much smaller scale than before. The government encouraged the growth of industry to take the place of mining, and an industrial park has a range of factories that produce electrical and electronics goods and consumer goods. The city has some wealthy suburbs that were home to the owners of tin mines in the past but have more recently attracted wealthy retired people from Kuala Lumpur and other cities. Ipoh now has the reputation of having a more elderly population than most Malaysian cities.

The region has a number of tourist attractions, including stretches of preserved forest and large limestone caves near the city. The caves have been converted into Chinese Buddhist temples at Sam Po Tong and Perak Tong, which contains a large statue of the Buddha and a long staircase built into the cave interior.

C. CARPENTER

Johor Baharu

Johor, officially Johor Baharu, is popularly known as J.B. The city is the capital of the state of Johor and is the major center of commerce and industry in southern Peninsular Malaysia. At the 2000 Malaysian national census, the metropolitan area had a population of 631,000, while 385,000 people lived within the city limits.

Johor Baharu was a small Malay fishing village when it was chosen by the sultan of Johor as the site of his new capital in 1866. Johor Baharu occupies a strategic position at the northern end of the two 0.75-mile (1.2 km) long causeways that link Peninsular Malaysia with Singapore. A six-lane highway and a railroad cross the main causeway, which carries most the direct traffic between Malaysia and Singapore. The city has two ports: Pasir Gudang (or Johor Port), which exports commodities and raw materials and imports oil, and Tanjung Pelepas, a major transshipment center where goods from across the Southeast Asian region are transferred from one ship to another for their onward journey to North America, Europe, or Australia. Johor Baharu also has an international airport (Senai International).

A REGIONAL CENTER

Sultan Abu Bakar of Johor (reigned 1862–1895) persuaded British and Chinese from Singapore to settle around Johor Baharu to establish plantations to produce pineapples, rubber, and oil palm. Ethnic Chinese founded many of the commercial undertakings in the city, and they still dominate its industrial, financial, and retail sectors and form the majority of Johor Baharu's population. Abu Bakar was actively involved in the city's planning, and some of the city's buildings are named for him, including the Sultan Abu Bakar Mosque. Among the principal buildings of Johor are the Istana Besar and the Bukit Serene palaces; the latter is the official residence of the sultan of Johor.

Routes from the southern part of the peninsula focus on Johor Baharu, bringing rubber and the agricultural produce of the region to the city, much of it for export to Singapore. Manufactured goods, raw materials for industry, and consumer goods are traded in the opposite direction across the causeway. Many industries have built up in Johor, including textiles, electrical goods, shipbuilding, and consumer goods. In modern times, the petrochemical and electronics industries have grown. Heavy industry is concentrated in the eastern suburbs of Pasir Gudang and Tanjung Lansat. Industrial parks line the highways toward the north.

SINGAPORE'S NEIGHBOR

In modern times, the proximity of Singapore is a major element in the economy of Johor Baharu, which is considered a satellite of the city-state to the south. High-rise office buildings line the waterfront looking across to Singapore. Singaporean corporations have established businesses in Johor Baharu, but one of the most profitable sectors is tourism. Two out of every three foreign tourists visiting Malaysia enter the country across the causeway from Singapore. Many Singaporeans visit, attracted by lower prices in the large central shopping district and the out-of-town shopping malls than in Singapore. Many of Johor Baharu's extensive shopping facilities cater to tourists from Singapore.

C. CARPENTER

A causeway connects Singapore (foreground) with Johor Baharu (background).

Kelang

Kelang (formerly Klang), is the third-largest metropolitan area in Malaysia. At the 2000 Malaysian census, Kelang's metropolitan area was home to 632,000 people, and there were 385,000 inhabitants within the city limits, which contain Port Kelang, Malaysia's largest port.

Kelang was once the capital of the Malay state of Selangor, but in 1889, the sultan moved his capital up the Klang Valley to Kuala Lumpur, which had prospered under British colonial rule. In time, Kuala Lumpur became the capital of Malaya and, after 1963, the capital of Malaysia. As a result, Kuala Lumpur became a federal territory, and Kelang became Selangor's capital again in 1974. During this time, the state of Selangor began building a new state capital, Shah Alam, and in 1977, Kelang lost its status for the second time in a century when Shah Alam became the state capital. The sultan of Selangor still has a palace in Kelang city, the Istana Alam Shah.

AN INDUSTRIAL CITY

Kelang is the center of an important agricultural region that produces rubber and fruit. The city's industries were originally based on the produce of the region and included pineapple canning and rubber processing. A footwear industry developed, based on local rubber, and Kelang also has a fertilizer industry that was originally established to supply local farmers.

The Klang River divides the city into Kelang North, a center of commerce and industry, and Kelang South, which is more residential. The city is a transportation hub where routes along the coastal plain and down the Klang Valley meet. The city benefits from its proximity to Kuala Lumpur, which is only 20 miles (32 km) away. Industrial parks and other facilities that supply Kuala Lumpur and its neighboring cities have developed.

A MAJOR PORT

In 1893, the British founded Port Swettenham, now known as Port Kelang, at the mouth of the Klang River, which is sheltered by two islands. The port was strategically placed along the Strait of Malacca, one of the world's busiest sea routes, at the point where natural routes down the Klang Valley, Peninsular Malaysia's main population center, reach the sea. Rubber, fruits, and other products of the Malay states were exported through the port, but Port Swettenham's growth in the nineteenth and early twentieth centuries was principally due to the export of tin.

After World War II (1939–1945), the port was improved; deepwater berths were constructed in the 1960s and 1970s and, more recently, Port Kelang built facilities to handle

A container ship enters Westport in Kelang, Malaysia's largest commercial port.

containers, which now account for much of its cargo. In modern times, the port has three sections, each of which has been separately privatized, although Northport and Southport are now under the same ownership. Southport is a free port, a zone into which imported goods intended for reexport may enter without having to pay duty. A large industrial park, Pandamaran, adjoins the port.

The major development at Port Kelang is at Westport, which would be Malaysia's biggest port even without Northport and Southport. Westport, which has 2.5 miles (4 km) of berths, handles only containers. When expansion is completed, the port will have 7 miles (11 km) of berths. In 2005, Port Kelang was the fourteenth-largest container port in the world and the second-largest in Southeast Asia after Singapore.

C. CARPENTER

ECONOMY

Malaysia has one of the strongest and fastest-growing economies in Southeast Asia. Since 1970, the government has shifted the focus away from the export of raw materials to providing communication services and developing its information sector. Malaysia is now a global leader in the electronic and electrical components industries.

Since the Federation of Malaya gained independence from Great Britain in 1957, there has been significant structural change in the economy. The move over the span of a few decades from a mainly agricultural and mineral-based economy to one dominated by manufacturing and services was mainly spurred by intense government efforts to seek a balanced and sustainable economy. These government measures ranged from the implementation of the New Economic Policy (NEP) in the 1970s—with the twin objectives of reducing poverty and regulating the economy through a policy of more government intervention—to the replacement of the NEP with the National Development Policy (NDP) in 1990. The current economic program, Vision 2020, aims to turn Malaysia into a fully developed nation by 2020.

ECONOMIC CHALLENGES

Despite steady progress, Malaysia's economy faces several challenges. The global recessions of 1981 and 1985, as well as the Asian financial crisis in 1997 and 1998, demonstrated how vulnerable Malaysia's economy is to a slowdown in demand for its exports. During the Asian financial crisis, output fell by 10.2 percent in 1998 due to weak external demand, particularly for semiconductors and similar hardware. The 1998 downturn was the first decline in output since the mid-1980s, and the crisis affected industries that cater to both the domestic and export markets. Malaysia imposed controls on capital flowing from the country in the aftermath of the Asian financial crisis. In order to manage national assets, the government established agencies known as Danamodal and Danaharta. Although the controls on capital have been loosened and the agencies were closed following the recovery of the economy, the management of the financial sector remains a key concern of the Malaysian government. However, in the twenty-first century, legislative amendments to allow mergers of commercial banks and financial companies—and permission given for a Singaporean company to hold a substantial stake in a Malaysian bank—point toward a gradual liberalization of the financial sector.

Despite the privatization of some state-owned corporations and undertakings since the mid-1980s, the state still owns many utilities and is involved in industry. The government advocates a partnership between the public and private sectors. The objective is the rationalization of the government sector to encourage more initiatives from the private sector, which is recognized as the driving force toward economic development. Government-linked companies (known as GLCs) still account for more than one-quarter of industry in Malaysia, and financing them remains a challenge. The government has introduced reforms to measure the performance of GLCs and to improve their productivity.

Corruption is a problem in several countries in the region. World Bank studies reveal that corruption increased in Malaysia from 1996 through 2004, but the problem is not as severe as it is in a number of neighboring states. The prime minister, Abdullah Ahmad Badawi (born 1939; in office from 2003), has stepped up efforts to eradicate corruption, but there is much to be done to boost public confidence.

Faced with increased competition from emerging economies, particularly from China, Malaysia also must ensure that, as well as being competitive, more of its industries complement those of other nations in the region. Since 2000, trade with China has more than doubled, suggesting that Malaysia may benefit from the growth of the giant Chinese economy. However, reliance on a few major trade partners, such as China (including Hong Kong), Japan, and the United States, reduces the Malaysian government's room to maneuver. Due to the volatility of demand for its exports, the Malaysian government has also recognized that there is value in promoting domestic consumption as an engine of growth. For example, real growth in 2004 was driven mainly by a 7.3 percent growth in domestic demand.

Standard of Living

Malaysia has a middle-income economy with a rapidly improving standard of living; in 1998, only 8 percent of the population lived below the official poverty line. The per capita gross national product (GDP) was $12,000 in 2005; this figure is adjusted for purchasing power parity (PPP), a formula that allows comparison between living standards in different countries.

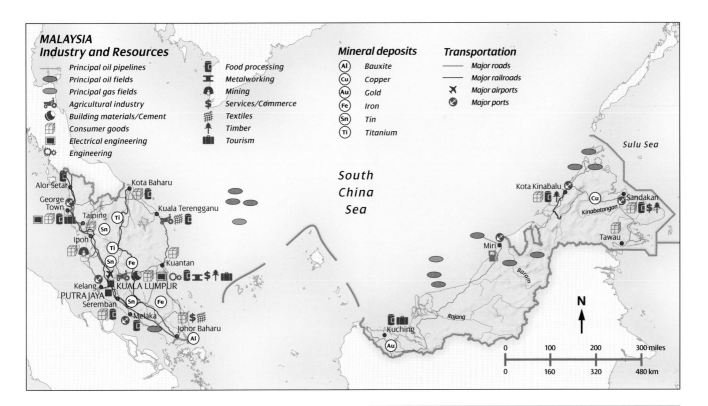

MALAYSIA
Industry and Resources

Principal oil pipelines
Principal oil fields
Principal gas fields
Agricultural industry
Building materials/Cement
Consumer goods
Electrical engineering
Engineering

Food processing
Metalworking
Mining
Services/Commerce
Textiles
Timber
Tourism

Mineral deposits
(Al) Bauxite
(Cu) Copper
(Au) Gold
(Fe) Iron
(Sn) Tin
(Ti) Titanium

Transportation
—— Major roads
—— Major railroads
✈ Major airports
◎ Major ports

A long-term challenge to the Malaysian economy continues to be the management of the government's Bumiputra (ethnic Malay) policies, under which contracts are granted to ethnic Malays to increase their participation in the domestic economy. The NEP program, in an attempt to reduce poverty, sought to restructure Malaysian society to remove the economic differences between the nation's ethnic groups. Many rural Malays were poor, while the urban minority Chinese community was wealthy. The program aimed to redistribute wealth through affirmative action in favor of the Bumiputra population to achieve equity of ownership of businesses in the ratio of 30 percent Bumiputra-owned, 30 percent foreign-owned, and 40 percent owned by non-Malay Malaysians. The goal was to be met through expansion of the economy so that no ethnic group should suffer through redistribution. The NEP program has been partially successful.

In the early twenty-first century, large numbers of Malaysian college graduates were unemployed. The figure has been estimated at 80,000, and economists are concerned that unless measures are taken to restructure the education and employment system, the problem of graduate unemployment will continue to create unrest and inefficiencies in the economy.

As Malaysians grew wealthier, many of the more poorly paid jobs were filled by illegal foreign workers. However, in the twenty-first century, a government campaign to reduce the number of illegal workers in Malaysia has brought about severe labor shortages in the construction industry, plantation work, and some basic service sectors. Hundreds of thousands of illegal workers from Indonesia were deported, leading to conflicts between the governments of Malaysia and neighboring Indonesia.

RESOURCES

Malaysia's natural resources include wood, rubber, natural gas, and crude oil. In 2004, oil and gas accounted for more than 10 percent of GDP (gross domestic product, the total value of all the goods and services produced in a country in a fixed time, usually one year); this was partly due to the rising price of oil in the world market. In 2004, there was an estimated 12 years of remaining oil reserves in existing offshore fields. However, new discoveries of oil fields enabled crude oil production to increase in the 1990s, and in 2005 Malaysia produced around 0.8 million barrels of oil a day. There are potentially additional reserves of oil in disputed sectors of the South China Sea that are claimed by Malaysia.

Great potential exists in natural gas development with joint ventures between Malaysia and Thailand in the South China Sea. There are also substantial gas fields off the coast of Sarawak.

EMPLOYMENT IN MALAYSIA

Sector	Percentage of labor force
Agriculture	14
Industry	36
Services	50

Source: Government of Malaysia, 2000

In 2005, government figures showed that only 3.6 percent of the labor force was unemployed.

Rice is harvested by machine on large Malaysian farms. However, some holdings are so small that mechanization is neither affordable nor practical.

In 2004, Malaysia's offshore gas fields had proven reserves of 78.8 trillion cubic feet (2.2 trillion cubic m) of natural gas. Between the first quarter of 2004 and the first quarter of 2005, Malaysia's production of natural gas expanded by more than 21 percent.

Tin and timber, two of the traditional exports of Malaysia, have declined. In the late nineteenth and early twentieth centuries, tin mining was the spur to economic development in the Malay states, but by the 1990s, tin exports, mainly from western Peninsular Malaysia, contributed only 1.7 percent of Malaysia's exports. Tin has been mined in the Malay Peninsula for two thousand years in a belt of tin-ore bearing deposits that stretches from George Town in the north to Melaka in the south. Around 90 percent of the current tin production comes from the states of Perak and Selangor. Most of Malaysia's tin production uses the gravel pump method, in which large quantities of water are sprayed on gravel, which is then pumped from pits and sorted into ore and waste. Since the 1980s, when tin prices fell, this method has been uneconomic in the small open-cast mines that characterize the Malaysian tin industry. Smaller mines have closed and production has decreased.

Timber was formerly exploited on a large scale; however, much of the forest of Sarawak and Sabah has been overlogged, and the industry has declined. In 2001, Sabah harvested 124 million cubic feet (3.5 million cubic m) of logs, but production fell to around 71 million cubic feet (2 million cubic m) in 2002. Around 1.2 percent of Malaysia's forest cover is felled annually.

AGRICULTURE

When Malaysia was formed in 1963, the nation had an economy mainly based on agriculture; until the late 1980s, a large proportion of the labor force was still employed in farming. Palm oil production in particular provided much dynamism from the mid-1970s owing to high export demand. A national agriculture policy was introduced in 1984 to boost the performance of the farming sector. The research and development efforts that followed have enabled Malaysia to retain a comparative advantage in this area, and the first quarter of 2005 saw a 27.5 percent rise in crude palm-oil production from the previous year, due largely to the increase in productivity as well as rising palm oil prices. This trend is expected to continue as some European countries begin to replace mineral oil with bio fuels such as palm oil.

Research and development efforts also led to an increase in rubber output under a rubber replanting program. In addition, the value of cocoa increased fivefold between 1981 and 1988 and continues to account for a significant share in the country's agricultural output. Continued strong growth is expected in the agriculture sector due to the government's plan to dedicate $4.2 billion in funding under the Ninth Malaysia Plan (2006–2010), which aims to modernize the farming sector.

Most Malaysian farmers are ethnic Malays who work small farms that grow rice (the main cereal), vegetables, fruits, and other crops. Rice yields have risen with the introduction of improved varieties of rice and the greater use of pesticides and chemical fertilizers. However, rice production has fallen overall because many farmers have left the land in favor of employment in the cities. In 2000, 14 percent of the labor force remained in agriculture, which supplied 8 percent of the GDP.

Fish is an important part of the Malaysian diet, and fishing in coastal waters, fish farming, and catching fish in inland waterways are all important economic activities, with around 80,000 people making their living from fishing. Commercial

MALAYSIA'S GDP

The Malaysian gross domestic product (GDP) was $287 billion in 2005. The figure is adjusted for purchasing power parity (PPP), an exchange rate at which goods in one country cost the same as goods in another. PPP allows a comparison between the living standards in different nations.

MAIN CONTRIBUTORS TO MALAYSIA'S GDP

Agriculture	8 percent
Industry	48 percent
Services	44 percent

Source: CIA, 2005

fishing is concentrated in the Strait of Malacca, which is lined by fishing ports; some deep-sea fishing boats also operate from the west coast of Peninsular Malaysia. More traditional smaller boats operate from the east coast. Fish farming is a growing industry; by 2000, some 20,000 fish farmers supplied around 10 percent of Malaysia's fish. Some disused tin mine pits have been converted into fish farms.

INDUSTRY

The Malaysian economy has witnessed a shift in industry since the 1970s. In the early 1970s, Malaysian industries were predominantly labor intensive and resource-based in products such as food, wood, and rubber. These sectors alone accounted for one-half of industrial output in the early 1970s. By the mid-1980s, however, electronics and electrical products had become the most dynamic sector; double-digit percentage growth was registered for the electronics and electrical products sector in the 1980s and 1990s and into the twenty-first century. The industry is a key employer, and in the early years of the twenty-first

Fish farming is a growing industry along the Malaysian coast. On this fish farm at Langkawi Island, fish are raised in tanks that are constantly replenished with seawater.

century, exports of electronic goods alone accounted for more than one-half of all Malaysian exports. However, up to 80 percent of the turnover in the sector comes from imported components; Malaysia remains largely an assembler of electronic and electrical goods—many of the parts come from Japan and South Korea—rather than a manufacturer of the constituent parts. The textile and clothing industries also saw significant growth in the last quarter of the twentieth century. In addition, rubber and oil processing and the processing of agricultural products remain important industries in Malaysia, along with the key electronics and light manufacturing industries. Malaysian industry is diverse, avoiding reliance on any single industry. Industrial development remains concentrated in and around Kuala Lumpur (for example, in Shah Alam, the new city that is home to the Proton automobile works), Kelang, Johor Baharu, and other larger cities.

Government policies have played a significant role in industrial development under various initiatives. The 1970s saw a switch in focus from import-substitution (producing goods that would otherwise be imported) to industries that produce goods for export. Heavy industries were also promoted in the early 1980s, and there was direct government intervention in various sectors. Government intervention was replaced in the mid-1980s with a liberalization of investment rules and a focus on boosting privatization and private-sector growth.

SERVICES

Services have accounted for a significant proportion of GDP since the mid-1980s. In 2005, services supplied 44 percent of Malaysia's GDP. However, the variety of services has changed since the 1980s, and the key drivers of the service sector in the twenty-first century include finance, real estate, transportation, storage, and communication. Change was shaped by government programs, including the Technology Master Plan and the Human Resource Development Plan.

Islamic finance has rapidly expanded, and moves have been made toward the establishment of Malaysia as a hub for Islamic finance (Islamic banking is fee-based and banks neither charge nor pay interest, which is forbidden by Islam). By the early twenty-first century, the assets of Islamic banks accounted for about 10 percent of the Malaysian banking system.

The tourist industry has great potential; people in countries in the region, such as China, have rising standards of living and more disposable income for vacations. Tourist receipts rose 39 percent in 2003, and the industry is now one of the largest contributors to Malaysia's earnings of foreign currency. The tourist sector attracts visitors from Europe and Australia as well as from other nations in the region; more than one-half of tourists visiting Malaysia enter the country from Singapore.

Deforestation is rapid in Malaysia, where 1.2 percent of forest cover is felled annually. Some logging licenses have not been renewed in Sabah in an attempt to allow the forests to regenerate.

TRADE

Because of a rapid increase in the value of exports, partly led by the high prices of crude petroleum, Malaysia had a trade surplus in the 1990s and into the twenty-first century. Exports achieved double-digit percentage growth in the 1990s, with growth reaching 27.3 percent in the third quarter of 2004. Export growth slowed from 2004, however, due to a slowdown in exports of manufactured goods.

Electrical and electronic products continue to be Malaysia's largest export earner, accounting for up to 50 percent of total export revenue. Other key exports include palm oil and related products, timber, chemicals, and other petroleum products. Major imports include raw materials used in export-based industries, capital goods (manufactured goods, such as electronic components, used in the production of other goods), and other consumer goods. In 2005, Malaysia exported goods and services valued at $147.1 billion; in the same year, the nation imported goods and services worth $118.7 billion.

The United States is Malaysia's largest trading partner, taking 20 percent of Malaysia's exports and supplying 13 percent of Malaysia's imports. Other markets for Malaysian exports include Singapore (which received 16 percent of Malaysian exports in 2004), China including Hong Kong (16 percent), Japan (9 percent), Thailand, and the countries of the European Union (EU), particularly Great Britain and Germany. Malaysia imports goods and services from Japan (which supplied 15 percent of imports into Malaysia in 2004), the United States (13 percent),

Singapore (12 percent), China including Hong Kong (12 percent), Thailand, Taiwan, South Korea, Germany, and Indonesia. With a proliferation of free trade agreements (FTAs), along with relatively low tariffs and nontariff barriers, Malaysia's economy is finding ways to reap benefits from international trade despite rising competition from China, particularly in electronic goods. Malaysia conducts a considerable amount of trade with China and is currently the sixth-largest exporter of goods to China, ahead of all other Southeast Asian countries.

TRANSPORTATION AND COMMUNICATION

The move from an agriculture-based economy to one based on manufacturing brought with it key developments in the provision of transportation infrastructure. In 2006, Malaysia had 1,175 miles (1,890 km) of railroad track, of which 1,139 miles (1,833 km) was narrow gauge. In modern times, the emphasis in railroad development has been on light railroad systems for commuters; the Kuala Lumpur metropolitan area suffers heavy traffic, and light railroad systems have been constructed for its commuters. Highways transport most raw materials and manufactured goods. In 2006, there was a total of 44,633 miles (71,814 km) of highways, including 34,769 miles (55,943 km) that were paved.

With a coastline of 2,905 miles (4,675 km), Malaysia has 19 main ports and harbors. The main seaport is Port Kelang, which has three harbors, including Westport, one of the region's principal container ports. Malaysia's other major ports are

Sungai Besi open-cast mine is one of the remaining working tin mines in western Peninsular Malaysia. Production has declined since the 1980s as many Malaysian mines have become uneconomic.

George Town and Johor Baharu. There are 4,475 miles (7,200 km) of navigable waterways. Malaysia has 118 airports, of which 38 have paved runways. The principal international airport is Kuala Lumpur International Airport; Penang International, Ismail International (at Johor Baharu), Langkawi International, and the airports at Kuching in Sarawak and Kota Kinabalu in Sabah also receive international flights. Economists predict an expansion of secondary airports in Malaysia as a result of the rapid increase in budget air travel in Asia in the early twenty-first century.

By 2003, there were 8.7 million Internet users in Malaysia and more than 100,000 Internet hosts. More Malaysians rely on mobile cellular phones than land lines: in 2003, 11.1 million Malaysians had mobile cellular phones and there were 4.6 million telephone lines. Demand for telecommunication services suggests that the communication sector will experience further strong growth. Malaysia's program for the development of the information sector includes Vision 2020, the creation of a 9-mile (15 km) wide and 31-mile (50 km) long "information corridor" called the Multimedia Super Corridor, where global information and communication companies and research and development facilities are concentrated. The corridor is centered on the new city of Cyberjaya, which adjoins Putrajaya, the administrative capital of Malaysia. The final phase of the construction of the project is scheduled for completion in 2020.

CHANG CHIOU YI

The Philippines

The Philippines consists of more than 7,000 islands, of which the two largest, Luzon and Mindanao, account for two-thirds of the nation's total area. The archipelago was named for Prince Philip of Spain, later king (reigned 1556–1598), in 1543 when a Spanish navigator explored the islands. The first Spanish settlement was established in 1565. Under Spanish rule, Roman Catholicism and Spanish culture took root. Nationalist unrest grew in the late nineteenth century, and in 1898 a revolt nearly ousted the Spanish. However, when Spain and the United States went to war in Cuba in 1898, U.S. forces occupied the Philippines, which Spain ceded to them. Philippine nationalists declared independence, but U.S. rule was secured by the Philippine-American War (1898–1901), although some nationalists continued fighting until 1913. The islands gained internal self-government in 1935. After occupation by Japanese forces from 1942 through 1945, the islands gained full independence in 1946. Under President Ferdinand Marcos (in office 1965–1986), corruption grew, and in 1972, citing communist insurgency, Marcos took emergency powers. The Marcos dictatorship ended in a revolution in 1986.

GEOGRAPHY

Location	Southeastern Asia, an archipelago between the South China Sea and the Pacific Ocean
Climate	Tropical maritime climate; the southwest monsoon blows from May through October and the cooler northeast monsoon from November through April
Area	115,860 sq. miles (300,076 sq. km)
Coastline	22,554 miles (36,289 km)
Highest point	Mount Apo 9,692 feet (2,954 m)
Lowest point	South China Sea 0 ft.
Terrain	Mountainous, with limited coastal plains and a few more extensive lowlands
Natural resources	Petroleum, nickel, cobalt, gold, silver, salt, timber
Land use	
Arable land	19.0 percent
Permanent crops	16.8 percent
Other	64.2 percent
Major rivers	Cagayan, Chico, Mindanao, Abra, Pampanga, Agusan
Major lakes	Laguna de Bay, Lanao
Natural hazards	Typhoons, landslides, volcanoes, earthquakes, tsunamis

FLAG

The flag of the Philippines has two stripes (blue over red) with a white equilateral triangle in the hoist (the part of the flag next to the flagpost). The eight-rayed sun symbol represents the dawn of a new era that was hoped for when the ill-fated declaration of independence was made in 1898. The three stars represent the three main physical regions of the country. Blue symbolizes noble ideas; red represents courage.

METROPOLITAN AREAS, 2000 POPULATIONS

Urban population	60 percent
Manila	9,933,000
Manila (city)	1,581,000
Quezon City	2,174,000
Caloocan	1,178,000
Pasig City	505,000
Valenzuela	485,000

★ Capital city
★ Regional capital
● Other city
━━ National border
── Regional border

Note: Cotabato is the regional capital of both the Autonomous Region in Muslim Mindanao and SOCCSKSARGEN.

National Capital Region

CALOOCAN CITY(NORTH)
VALENZUELA CITY
MALABON CITY
NAVOTAS
QUEZON CITY
CALOOCAN CITY(SOUTH)
MARIKINA CITY
SAN JUAN
CITY OF MANILA
MANDALUYONG CITY
PASIG CITY
MAKATI CITY
PATERAS
Manila Bay
PASAY CITY
TAGUIG
PARAÑAQUE CITY
LAS PIÑAS CITY
Laguna de Bay
MUNTINLUPA CITY

0 ___ 5 miles
0 ___ 8 km

PACIFIC OCEAN

ILOCOS REGION
CORDILLERA ADMINISTRATIVE REGION
CAGAYAN VALLEY
★ Tuguegarao
San Fernando ★
Baguio ★
Luzon
Angeles ●
CENTRAL LUZON
San Fernando ★
NATIONAL CAPITAL REGION
★ Quezon City
★ Manila
● Dasmariñas
CALABARZON

South China Sea

Calapan ★
Mindoro
BICOL REGION ★ Legaspi

PHILIPPINES

MIMAROPA
Samar
EASTERN VISAYAS
Panay WESTERN VISAYAS
Leyte
★ Tacloban
Iloilo ★
Bacolod ●
Cebu
● Mandaue
Cebu ★
Negros CENTRAL VISAYAS

Philippine Sea

Puerto Princesa ● *Palawan*

Sulu Sea

CARAGA
★ Butuan
NORTHERN MINDANAO
★ Cagayan de Oro
ZAMBOANGA PENINSULA
Mindanao DAVAO REGION
★ Cotabato
★ Davao
Zamboanga ★
Isabela ●
Basilan
AUTONOMOUS REGION IN MUSLIM MINDANAO
SOCCSKSARGEN
● General Santos
Sulu Archipelago

MALAYSIA

INDONESIA

N

0 100 100 150 200 miles
0 80 160 240 320 km

1241

Las Piñas	473,000
Tagig	467,000
Parañaque	450,000
Makati	445,000
Marikina	391,000
Muntinglupa	379,000
Pasay City	355,000
Malabon	339,000
Mandaluyong	304,000
Davao	1,200,000
Cebu	1,080,000
Bacolod	735,000
Zamboanga	602,000
Antipolo	471,000
Cagayan de Oro	462,000
Dasmariñas	380,000
loilo City	366,000
San Jose del Monte	316,000
Bacoor	306,000

Source: Philippine census, 2000

NEIGHBORS AND LENGTH OF BORDERS

There are no land borders.

POPULATION

Population	76,499,000 (2000 census)
Population density	660.3 per sq. mile (254.9 per sq. km)
Population growth	1.8 percent a year
Birthrate	24.9 births per 1,000 of the population
Death rate	5.4 deaths per 1,000 of the population
Population under age 15	35 percent
Population over age 65	4.1 percent
Sex ratio	105 males for 100 females
Fertility rate	3.1 children per woman
Infant mortality rate	22.8 deaths per 1,000 live births
Life expectancy at birth	
Total population	70.2 years
Female	73.2 years
Male	67.3 years

ECONOMY

Currency	Philippine Peso (PHP)
Exchange rate (2006)	$1 = PHP 49.42
Gross domestic product (2005)	$412.5 billion
GDP per capita (2005)	$4,700
Unemployment rate (2005)	8.7 percent
Population under poverty line (2001)	40 percent
Exports	$41.3 billion (2005 CIA estimate)
Imports	$42.7 billion (2005 CIA estimate)

GOVERNMENT

Official country name	Republic of the Philippines
Conventional short form	The Philippines
Nationality	
noun	Filipino
adjective	Filipino
Official languages	Filipino (Tagalog) and English
Capital city	Manila
Type of government	Republic
Voting rights	18 years and over, universal
National anthem	"Lupang Hinirang" (Beloved land)
National day	Independence Day, June 12, 1898 (the original unsuccessful declaration of independence)

TRANSPORTATION

Railroads	557 miles (897 km); only 55 percent operational in 2005
Highways	124,324 miles (200,037 km)
Paved roads	12,308 miles (19,804 km)
Unpaved roads	112,016 miles (180,233 km)
Navigable waterways	2,001 miles (3,219 km)
Airports	
International airports	4
Paved runways	83

POPULATION PROFILE, 2005 ESTIMATES

Ethnic groups	
Tagalog	28 percent
Cebuano	13 percent
Ilocano	9 percent
Bisaya/Binisaya	8 percent
Hiligaynon Ilonggo	8 percent
Bikol	6 percent
Others	28 percent
Religions	
Roman Catholics	81 percent
Other Christians	11 percent
Sunni Muslims	5 percent
Others and traditional religions	3 percent
Languages	
Filipino (Tagalog)	around 28 percent
English as a first language	1 percent but spoken by 52 percent
Cebuano	24 percent
Ilocano	10 percent
Hiligaynon	9 percent
Bikol, Waray-Waray, Pampango, and other minority languages	28 percent
Adult literacy	92.6 percent

CHRONOLOGY

around 3000 BCE	Malays from present-day Indonesia and Malaysia enter the region.
after 3rd century CE	The islands fall under the influence of the Hindu-Malay empires of Sumatra and of states in Indochina, but the archipelago remains a patchwork of many small local states.
15th century	Traders from Brunei spread Islam into the southern Philippines. By the mid-sixteenth century, Islamic sultanates develop in the southern island of Mindanao and the Sulu Archipelago.
1521	Spanish explorers land in the Philippines, naming the archipelago for their crown prince, the future King Philip II of Spain (reigned 1556–1598).
1565	The first permanent Spanish settlement is established on the island of Cebu. The Spanish, who introduce Roman Catholicism, face numerous rebellions during their 333-year rule in the islands.
late 19th century	Philippine nationalism grows, led by the Propaganda Movement under José Rizal (1861–1896).
1896–1898	The Philippine Revolution: after the execution of Rizal by the Spanish, Philippine nationalists unite in an uprising against colonial rule. The nationalists nearly oust the Spanish by 1898.
1898	The United States, at war with Spain, intervenes in the Philippines and occupies the islands. Spain cedes the Philippines to the United States at the end of the Spanish-American War.
1898–1901	Philippine nationalists, who declare an independent republic, fight against U.S. rule.
1935	The islands become an internally self-governing U.S. commonwealth with Manuel Luis Quezon (1878–1944) becoming the first president.
1942	Japan invades the Philippines during World War II (1939–1945).
1945	U.S. rule is restored and reconstruction of the war-damaged infrastructure begins.
1946	The Philippines gains full independence as a republic.
1953–1957	President Ramon Magsaysay (1907–1957) crushes a rebellion by Communist-dominated Hukbalahap guerillas.
1965–1986	President Ferdinand Marcos (1917–1989) inaugurates major development programs but his regime presides over large-scale corruption. He uses continuing guerrilla activity by Muslim separatists in the south as justification for repressive rule.
1986	Marcos declares himself winner of a flawed presidential election, but Corazon Aquino (born 1933), who ran against him, disputes the result. Mass protests follow, and Marcos flees the country.
1989	The Philippine government reaches an agreement with Muslim separatist groups leading to the establishment of the Autonomous Region in Mulsim Mindanao. This region is enlarged in 1996 and now comprises five provinces and one city.
1998	Former film star Joseph Estrada (born 1937) is elected president. In 2001, accused of coruption, he stands down and is replaced by his vice-president, Gloria Macapagal-Arroyo (born 1947).
2002	Islamic militants explode bombs in Manila and other Philippine cities.

GOVERNMENT

The Philippines has a democratically elected government that is headed by a president, who is elected by the people. The president serves a single term of six years. Philippine politics is characterized by a large number of political parties, some of which are populist or regional.

The first Philippine constitution in 1935 was based on that of the United States. Under the dictatorship of Ferdinand Marcos (1917–1989; in office 1965–1986), a new constitution abandoned presidential government in favor of a parliamentary system. The change had little impact as Marcos ruled by decree and, until 1981, served as both president and prime minister. The present constitution was ratified in 1987 and approved by the electorate in a national referendum. The 1987 constitution reestablished a presidential system, but it limits the president to a single term, a reform intended to prevent another dictatorship.

THE PRESIDENT

The chief of state of the Philippines is a president who is elected for six years by universal adult suffrage. The voting age is 18. A vice president is also elected at the same time but on a separate ticket for a maximum of two six-year terms. As a result, the chief of state and the vice-president may be from different parties. The president appoints a cabinet of ministers, but most presidential appointments are subject to approval by the Commission of Appointments, whose members are drawn from both houses of Congress.

THE LEGISLATURE

The Philippine Congress has two chambers: the Kapulungan Mga Kinatawan, or House of Representatives, the lower house, and the Senado, or Senate, the upper house. The House of Representatives, which is elected for three years, has a maximum of 260 seats. There are 208 constituencies, each of which elects a single member, and up to 52 other seats are reserved for underrepresented groups and parties; the additional seats are allocated to parties that are not adequately represented by constituencies. The Senate has 24 members, who are elected for a six-year term by a system of proportional representation; one-half of the senators stand down every three years.

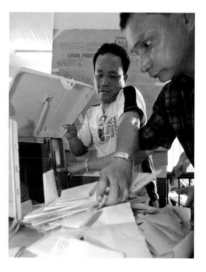

Election officials open a ballot box at a polling center to count votes in the 2004 Philippine legislative election. Voters were able to choose between several dozen political parties.

POLITICAL PARTIES

The largest Filipino political party is (Catholic conservative) Lakas ñg Edsa–Christian and Muslim Democrats (known as LAKAS). Other major parties include the (conservative) Nationalist People's Coalition (NPC), the Liberal Party (LP), the (populist) Kabataan ñg Masang Pilipino (KAMPIL), the (conservative) Struggle for Democratic Filipinos/Laban ñg Demokratikong Pilipino (LDP), and the Nationalist Party (NP). After legislative elections in 2004, another 25 parties were represented in Congress. It is estimated that around 70 political parties and groups are active in the Philippines.

LOCAL GOVERNMENT

The republic is divided into 80 provinces—including one province of regional status (Manila, the national capital)—and 116 chartered cities that are administratively independent from the provinces. A governor, who is directly elected for a maximum of three three-year terms, administers each province. Each province has a provincial board of eight or ten members, who represent the different districts and municipalities into which the provinces are divided. A directly elected deputy governor presides over the provincial board. Each municipality (*bayan*) elects a mayor, deputy mayor, and eight councillors for three years; no elected municipal official may serve more than three terms. The larger municipalities are chartered cities. Municipalities are divided into *barangay*s, small units that cover either a village or a neighborhood.

For administrative convenience, the provinces and chartered cities are grouped into 17 regions, whose boundaries reflect major geographical and cultural-linguistic divisions. Except for the division known as the Autonomous Region in Muslim Mindanao, the regions do not have elected officials. The national government has offices in each regional capital to coordinate its activities.

C. CARPENTER

MODERN HISTORY

After the Philippines gained full independence in 1946, a series of corrupt leaders left the country's economy in ruins and seriously undermined the belief of Filipinos in their own government. This resulted in a number of public uprisings against the administration, popularly called "people power" revolutions.

The Philippines celebrated its independence from the United States on July 4, 1946. However, economic and military ties between the two countries made becoming independent problematic. In economic terms, the currency of the Philippines, the Philippine peso, was tied to the U.S. dollar, and the passage of the parity amendment to the Philippine constitution in 1947 gave U.S. citizens and Filipinos equal rights in the ownership and exploitation of Philippine natural resources. The United States also kept two military bases in the Philippines: Clark Air Base near Manila, the Philippine national capital, and the important naval base in Subic Bay, around 63 miles (100 km) northwest of Manila.

Almost immediately after independence, the United States intervened in Philippine politics when six candidates of the Democratic Alliance, who had been elected to the Philippine Congress, were unseated because they were perceived to be against the parity amendment.

The United States was also militarily involved in the Philippines after independence. In the 1950s, the U.S. Central Intelligence Agency (CIA) was involved in the suppression of the Communist (Huk) rebellion in central Luzon; the Huk guerrillas originally formed to fight the Japanese occupation of the islands during World War II (1939–1945).

The first president of the independent nation was Manuel Roxas (1892–1948), who died in office. The presidency of his successor, Elpidio Quirino (1890–1956; in office 1948–1953), was threatened by the Huk insurgency and tainted by corruption. One persistent theme in Philippine postwar political history has been the continuous charges of corruption against successive presidents and members of the government. Political families and their associates rose and fell at different elections. For much of the history of the independent Philippines, kinship politics or the use of political power to benefit the ruling family has been the norm.

Ramon Magsaysay (1907–1957) defeated Quirino in the 1953 presidential election. Magsaysay, whose presidential campaign received substantial CIA support, was a strong U.S. ally. After Magsaysay's death in an air crash in 1957, Carlos P. Garcia (1896–1971; in office 1957–1961) became chief of state. Garcia's successor, Diosdado Macapagal (1910–1997; in office 1961–1965), focused on fighting corruption; his economic reforms, including allowing the Philippine peso to find its own level on the world market, were not very successful.

THE MARCOS PRESIDENCY

In 1966, Ferdinand Marcos (1917–1989) became president. Claiming in 1972 that Communist forces were threatening to overthrow the government, Marcos declared martial law, leaving only one center of power, the alliance of the Marcos family and Romualdez family (his wife's kin), effectively to dominate national politics. Marcos pursued a program for a so-called New Society (Bagong Lipunan). He confiscated businesses owned by powerful families and distributed them to his associates; as a result, corruption increased. Marcos abolished Congress and closed the free press, and although he periodically held referendums, there were widespread allegations of vote rigging. Opposition figures were allowed to leave for exile, and Marcos did not permit congressional elections again until 1978.

Through the early years of his presidency, Marcos received U.S. support. In 1972, worried U.S. businesspeople protested a ruling that Americans were no longer allowed to hold farmland in the Philippines. In order continue to attract U.S. investors, Marcos overturned the decision. He also allowed U.S. military bases to remain. By the 1970s, the U.S. bases had become a contentious issue; many Filipinos were concerned by

Ferdinand (center left) and Imelda Marcos (right) meet with U.S. president Lyndon Johnson (center right; in office 1963–1969) and Lady Bird Johnson (left) in 1966. Marcos received U.S. support through most of his presidency.

Demonstrators carry signs denouncing vigilantes during the 1986 Philippine presidential election. The election was flawed in favor of the incumbent President Marcos.

prostitution in the bases and by incidents in which Filipinos, straying near the bases, were shot and killed. The incidents provoked demonstrations against the U.S. military presence.

CORRUPTION AND DICTATORSHIP

Following incidents such as the 1971 bombing of Plaza Miranda in Manila during a rally of the Liberal Party, Marcos sought to justify martial law with the claim that he was restoring order. He also claimed that martial rule was essential to destroy the old ruling class and the Communist Party and to create his New Society. However, although he did attack the old ruling class, Marcos created a new oligarchy composed of his relatives, cronies, and the military. Kinship politics, dubbed "crony capitalism," was endemic, and Marcos handed profitable government contracts to his friends and to family members. Many of the companies established by his allies failed, and Marcos used government funds to keep them afloat, seriously damaging the country's economy. His close ties to the United States meant that Marcos received continuous U.S. financial support during his time in office; he also received rent for the U.S. military bases. Some historians argue that U.S. endorsement of the Marcos regime helped legitimize it in the eyes of the world.

Opposition to the Marcos regime was not tolerated. He increasingly imprisoned members of the opposition; the human rights organization Amnesty International documented up to 70,000 political detainees who were arrested, tortured, and killed during his presidency. Political repression forced opposition groups underground. These conditions provided fertile ground for the Communist Party (CPP) to thrive. The CPP gained supporters in its guerrilla war against the military, and by 1985, it was the biggest challenge to the Marcos regime.

When opposition senator Benigno Aquino (1932–1983) was assassinated at Manila International Airport in 1983, his death unleashed the anger of those who felt victimized by the regime's excessive corruption and repression. The idea that members of the Marcos family were involved in such a blatant act of murder fueled the opposition to begin a series of demonstrations. Many of those who spoke out or demonstrated had for a long time been involved in the underground opposition or had been in exile overseas. In these rallies, Aquino's widow, Corazon (known as Cory; born 1933), became a symbol for all those who felt suppressed by the regime. In 1986, while on a visit to the United States, Marcos was pressured to call a snap election. In the election, Aquino stood as an opposition candidate, but the CPP boycotted the poll because it did not believe the proceedings would be fair. Independent observers reported widespread cheating; Marcos was declared the winner, but Corazon Aquino refused to accept the result.

PEOPLE POWER

On February 22, 1986, Reform the Armed Forces Movement (RAM), a faction of the army, staged a coup against the Marcos regime. Led by Marcos's defense minister, Juan Ponce Enrile (born 1924), and army officer Gregorio "Gringo" Honasan (born

1948), the plan was to capture Malacañang Palace (the presidential palace) in Manila, kidnap the president's family, and institute a military junta. However, Marcos discovered the plan, and the 300 men involved barricaded themselves in Camp Aguinaldo military base in Manila. General Fidel Ramos (born 1928) joined the leaders of the coup, but for a while it looked as if the plotters would be defeated by troops loyal to Marcos and that civil war would break out. In the crisis, the military sought the aid of the influential cardinal Jaime Sin (1928–2005), the head of the Roman Catholic Church in the Philippines, who used Catholic radio stations to persuade Filipino Catholics to surround the base and protect the military from any attack by forces loyal to Marcos. Around 2 million people responded in an event that was dubbed the "People Power 1" revolt. Although Marcos sent armored personnel carriers to confront the plotters, soldiers refused to fire into a crowd of unarmed civilians surrounding the camp, who carried rosaries, flowers, and images of the Virgin Mary. Soon after the military refused to obey orders, the air force defected, leaving Marcos powerless. He fled the country to seek refuge in Hawaii.

PRESIDENT AQUINO

Corazon Aquino reluctantly became president and inherited a country facing enormous problems. Although her victory signaled the beginning of the restoration of democratic institutions, the military felt that she had hijacked their coup, and in the first few years of her six-year term in office, she resisted seven attempts by the military to topple her regime. During her presidency, she succeeded in restoring democratic institutions; a new constitution was written and passed, elections were held, and the free press was restored. Since the CPP had abstained from the revolution that toppled Marcos, it was not rewarded with leadership positions in the new regime.

In 1986, the Philippine economy was in crisis; the plundering of the government's coffers and the lack of job opportunities for Filipinos compelled many to seek work around the world as sailors, construction workers, and domestic helpers. Aquino was perceived to have not supplied strong leadership nor a vision for her fellow Filipinos. Her presidency was marked by a series of natural disasters, including the 1991 eruption of Mount Pinatubo, northwest of Manila. Although the fallout from the eruption resulted in little loss of life, lava flows from the volcano caused widespread damage in the area and forced the closure of the two U.S. bases.

RAMOS AND ESTRADA

In 1992, Fidel Ramos (born 1928) was elected to replace Aquino as president. During his presidency from 1992 through 1998, Ramos focused on the economy, and his Philippines 2000 Plan sought to develop industry and the national infrastructure. Ramos was succeeded by movie star Joseph Estrada (born 1937;

in office 1998–2001), who was soon perceived to be inefficient, incompetent, and corrupt. In September 2000, a provincial governor confessed that he gave the president 400 million pesos (then worth around $7 million) as his payoff from an illegal gambling operation. The revelation led to calls for Estrada's impeachment and resignation. The House of Representatives (the lower house of the Philippine Congress) voted for impeachment on November 13, 2001, and the case was transmitted to the Senate (the upper house), where an impeachment court was established. However, the majority of members of the court were allies of Estrada, and the prosecutors walked out in protest when it soon became clear that corruption would lead to Estrada's acquittal. In response, Filipinos again took to the streets, proclaiming a "People Power 2" revolt, calling for Estrada's resignation. The army supported the movement, and Estrada was forced to step down to face charges of corruption.

PRESIDENT MACAPAGAL-ARROYO

The vice president, Gloria Macapagal-Arroyo (born 1947), who was the daughter of Diosdado Macapagal, was sworn in as president and immediately had to face a "People Power 3" revolt when a smaller band of pro-Estrada demonstrators took to the streets, questioning the legitimacy of the Arroyo succession. In July 2003, a faction of the army instigated an unsuccessful coup against President Macapagal-Arroyo.

Although the coup failed, it highlighted the problems the army was facing in the fight against terrorism following the terrorist attacks in the United States on September 11, 2001. Since 2001, U.S. Special Forces have collaborated with the Philippine military to combat radical Islamic groups in the archipelago, including the Philippine Muslim radical terrorist group Abu Sayyaf (literally, "the swordbearer"), which has links with Al-Qaeda. Muslim separatism has been a recurring issue in the southern Philippines, particularly in the island of Mindanao. In 1989, some Muslim separatists agreed to the formation of a Muslim region with limited self-government: the so-called Autonomous Region in Muslim Mindanao. Not all separatist groups were satisfied, however, and in 1996, an agreement was made that allowed for the enlargement of the autonomous region and an increase in the region's powers of self-government. The region now comprises five provinces and a city.

Although the 1987 Philippine constitution stipulates that an incoming president may only serve one term of six years, Arroyo began her presidency by serving out Estrada's term and so was eligible to run again. In 2004, Arroyo won another term. However, in 2005 she was accused of interfering in the 2004 election results, and a call to impeach her was instigated. The Philippine "People Power" revolts have made presidents of the Philippines accountable to the public. Although they might send the message that Philippine political life is unstable, the threat of such revolutions seems to have checked the dominance of kinship politics and corruption in the Philippines.

M. ROCES

CULTURAL EXPRESSION

Literature

There is great richness and diversity in Philippine culture, deriving from more than 50 different ethnic groups that live in the islands. Philippine literature has also been shaped by the Spanish colonial era in the islands (from the sixteenth through the late nineteenth centuries) as well as by the later period of U.S. rule.

In the late twentieth century, the contribution of regional and ethnic Philippine literatures that had been overlooked in favor of Spanish and later literatures in English and Tagalog (the national language) was rediscovered by literary scholars. These works include bodies of writing by Chinese Filipinos, Muslim Filipinos, and Filipinos living abroad. However, the literary use of minority languages greatly declined in the twentieth century. Since the 1970s, Tagalog has challenged English as the language of literature in the Philippines, although Filipino Americans have contributed to literature in English.

PRECOLONIAL LITERATURE

Early forms of indigenous Philippine literature included songs (*awit, kanta*), lullabies (*uyayi*), love songs (*kundiman*), riddles (*bugtong*), proverbs (*salawikain*), everyday lyrics or verses (*laji, ambahan, tanaga*), courtship songs (*subli*), harvest songs (*bagbag-to*), ritual chants, and dirges (*dung-aw*). Although early Filipinos used different alphabets—including a Tagalog script that was called *baybayin*—most early forms of literature were transmitted orally and only in later centuries were transcribed by scholars into Spanish, other local languages, and later into English.

The most important early narrative forms are the ethno-epics, produced by almost all major ethnic groups in the Philippines. Most of them remain unwritten. Among those that have been transcribed and translated into English are the *Aliguyon* or *Hudhud* of the Ifugao people, which is thought to have originated before the seventh century; the Ilocano *Biag ni Lam-Ang* (The life of Lam-Ang), which was first recorded in written form around 1640, the Panay *Hinilawod*; and the Muslim *Darangan*. All Philippine ethno-epics detail exploits of their heroes and supernatural and animistic elements, as well as tribal life and change in the societies that produced them. The earliest poets in precolonial times were priestesses variously called *babaylan* (in the Visayas), *catalonan* (among the Tagalog people), or *mambunong* (in the northern Cordillera region of Luzon).

THE EARLY SPANISH PERIOD

Many of the literary forms introduced in the Spanish period were religious in nature, including prayers, confession manuals, novenas to the saints, and devotional poems or religious epics (passion plays) on the life and passion of Christ (in Tagalog passion plays are known as *pasyon*). The introduction of passion plays was at the expense of folk epics as Roman Catholic missionaries attempted to eliminate non-Christian literature and lore. Romantic dramas in poetic meter (*corridos*) also became popular. Printing was introduced in 1593, and Tagalog poetry written specifically for printing in the Roman alphabet made its appearance at this time.

Bilingual Filipino poets were called *ladinos*; the foremost example is the poet Fernando Bagongbanta (dates unknown), whose poetry translations appeared in *Memorial de la vida cristiana en lengua tagala* (An account of Christian life in the Tagalog language), published in 1605. *Ladino* poets translated Spanish texts into the local languages, and owing to the nature of translation, the works were able to gain elements of folk sensibility and imagery. There were also Spanish missionary poets who began to accommodate folk techniques in their work, demonstrating the exchange of influences in the period. Christian themes of human suffering, sin, guilt, and divine retribution permeated literary works, despite the trend toward more secular literature in the late 1700s and 1800s.

The *awit* (song or verse), *komedya* (play), and *sarswela* (a dramatic play set to music) were popular from the middle to late Spanish colonial period. The *sarswela* became especially popular in the twentieth century. Spanish ballads and romances about courtly love, knights, chivalry, and the battle between Christian and Moorish states in the age of the crusades were adapted by Filipino poets and playwrights such as José de la Cruz (more widely known as Huseng Sisiw; 1746–1829) and Francisco Baltazar (known as Balagtas; 1788–1862). The most popular romance by Balagtas, who is considered the most important poet of the Spanish period, is *Pinagdaanang Buhay ni Florante at Laura sa Cahariang Albania* (The history of Florante and Laura in the kingdom of Albania), which combined social commentary on colonial conditions with refined poetic references to European, Greek, and Roman cultures.

THE LATE SPANISH PERIOD

Toward the end of the Spanish period in the Philippines, a growing number of children of middle- and upper-class families were able to travel to Europe to attend universities. They freely discussed the oppressiveness of colonial rule in the islands and found sympathy with liberal Spaniards who supported their demand for reforms. Marcelo H. del Pilar (1850–1896) founded a newspaper called *Diariong Tagalog* (Tagalog newspaper) in 1882, fanning the growing nationalist movement.

The most famous works from the period from 1882 through 1896 are the novels of José Rizal (1861–1896), a member of a landed Tagalog family who is now regarded as a national hero. His novels *Noli Me Tangere* (1887; Touch me not; also translated as The lost Eden; 1961) and *El Filibusterismo* (1891; Subversion; 1962) were originally written in Spanish and translated into Tagalog and English later. Rizal wished to expose the sufferings afflicting the Philippines under Spanish rule. The Spanish so feared his effect upon the growing revolutionary movement that Rizal was arrested in 1892 after returning from studies in Europe and exiled to Dapitan in Mindanao. In 1896, he was wrongly accused of leading a rebellion and was executed by a firing squad. Although Tagalog was the language of some members in the Katipunan (revolutionary) movement against Spanish rule, other nationalists wrote in Spanish or their own languages, such as Cebuano.

The first Filipino women writers were published late in the nineteenth century. Leona

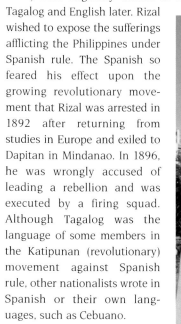

The poem "Mi Ultimo Adios" (My last farewell) was written in Spanish by national hero José Rizal on the eve of his public execution by Spanish colonial authorities in December 1896. The poem was smuggled from his prison cell and disseminated by the nationalist movement.

Florentino (1849–1884), who gained international recognition, is credited with being the first Filipino woman to have poetry published.

THE AMERICAN PERIOD

Despite the declaration of independence by the Philippine revolutionary government in 1898, Spain ceded the Philippines to the United States in the Treaty of Paris that concluded the Spanish-American War that same year. However, an armed struggle for independence continued long after 1901.

Although English became the language of instruction in the public school system established by the Americans, the use of Spanish by educated society, by teachers, and by writers continued for many years. There was also a great outburst of writing in vernacular languages, as well as in Spanish, from 1900 through 1940. The adoption of English by Filipinos was only gradual, and English was not a significant influence upon Filipino literature until the 1920s. American schoolteachers and professors arrived in the Philippines, bringing Anglo-American prose and poetry models to the attention of Filipino students,

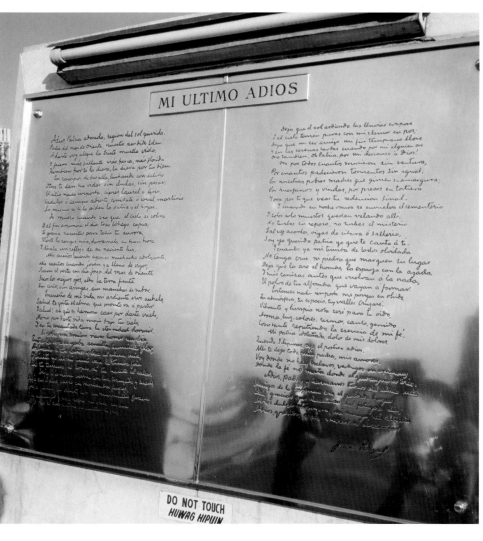

who were at first encouraged to copy the imported styles, although there was inevitably some variation through the introduction of local color.

Early English-language fiction writers included Paz Marquez Benitez (1894–1983), who in 1927 published "Dead Stars," the first published short story in English by a Filipino writer. The first Philippine novel in English was *A Child of Sorrow* (1921) by Zoilo Galang (1895–1959), which demonstrates some of the sentimental and romantic tendencies of eighteenth- and nineteenth-century Tagalog prose narratives. Vernacular writing still flourished, and the Hiligaynon writer Magdalena Jalandoni (1891–1978) was the first published Filipino woman novelist. At age 16, she wrote the novel *Ang Mga Tunok Sang Isa Ka Bulak* (A flower's thorns); she went on to write 24 other novels and 70 books of poems.

DRAMA

In the early twentieth century, Philippine drama comprised religious plays in the vernacular, verse plays based on romances, stories of courtly love (*komedya* and *moro-moro*), and comedies of manners set to music (*sarswela*s). In the first decade of the twentieth-century, there were also so-called "seditious plays," dramas in local languages that carried a nationalist message to their audiences. Despite the passing in 1901 of the Anti-Sedition Act by the U.S. authorities (which stipulated that Filipinos gathering in groups of more than three could be suspected of subversive, anticolonial activity), theater groups found ingenious ways to express their nationalist sentiments; using costumes and assembling themselves quickly, they were able to act and to display the Philippine flag in public.

After the 1950s, drama moved to the legitimate stage and saw Filipino performers appear in a varied international theatrical repertoire as well as in original works by Filipino playwrights writing in both Tagalog and English. Major Filipino playwrights in English include Nick Joaquin (1917–2004), Wilfrido Ma. Guerrero (1917–1995), and Alberto S. Florentino (born 1931), who wrote the play *The World Is an Apple*, one of the most widely performed plays in the Philippines.

POETRY

Early Filipino poets writing in English, such as Rafael Zulueta da Costa (1915–1990), who is best known for his poem "Like the Molave," were influenced by nineteenth-century European verse models. From the 1950s onward, with the influence of new genres, writers were concerned with image and metaphor, although there was an equal concern for the search for an original voice and the embodiment of a Filipino sensibility in the poem. Poets that rose to prominence during the American period included Angela Manalang-Gloria (1907–1995), Trinidad L. Tarrosa-Subido (1912–1994), and Luis G. Dato (1906–1997). Of this generation of poets, José Garcia Villa (1907–1997) is

considered one of the most original and flamboyant, for having achieved a distinct poetic idiom and for being the first to break taboos on writing about sex. He left the Philippines in 1929 and lived in exile in New York until his death. The poet Edith L. Tiempo (born 1919) cofounded the Silliman Writers Workshop.

MODERN LITERATURE

Notable twentieth-century Filipino writers include the poets Ricaredo Demetillo (1920–1998), Manuel Viray (1917–1997), Carlos A. Angeles (1921–2002), Tita Lacambra Ayala (born 1931), Bienvenido Lumbera (born 1932), Federico Licsi Espino (born 1939), and Cirilo Bautista (born 1941), and the poet and dramatist Rolando S. Tinio (1937–1997). Novelists writing in English included N. V. M. Gonzalez (1915–1999), who is best known for *The Bamboo Dancers*, and Nick Joaquin, who wrote *The Woman Who Had Two Navels* (1961).

Martial law was declared in the Philippines in September 1972, ostensibly to check the eruption of political violence. Writers in the martial law years found themselves censored and silenced. Works produced in a realist modern mode displayed a disdain for the romantic or sentimental or anything that could be deemed escapist. A more insistent literary style of discontent and realism emerged in the wake of the assassination of opposition leader Benigno Aquino (1932–1983), an articulate statesman who was also a writer and a serious threat to the dictatorship of President Ferdinand Marcos (in office 1965–1986). Literature also emerged from the underground (the dissident Communist Party of the Philippines), as well as from nontraditional and nonacademic sources, such as the urban poor and peasant communities. José Ma. Sison (born 1939) began as an academic and scholar, but his writings were closely associated with the politicized left-wing underground movement. In 1983, a group of poets writing in English published *In Memoriam* through the underground press; their collected poems protested the Aquino assassination and the corruption in Philippine government.

Tagalog became the national language after independence in 1946 but was not effectively spread by the educational system until the 1970s. Since then, it has become the national literary language alongside English.

Since the 1980s, Filipino writers in all genres have become more conscious of language and the multiple realities that can be constructed through it. Modern Filipino writers acknowledge the complex background of inherited traditions and cross-cultural influences, recognizing the legitimacy of indigenous, ethnic, colonial Spanish, and other contributions at the same time that they continue to explore new ideas. Literary competitions play an important role in the Philippines, and the National Commission for Culture and the Arts, together with literary organizations and telecommunication companies, have sponsored "text" poetry contests, in which young people submit short poems by text on cellular phones.

L. IGLORIA

Art and Architecture

The artistic heritage of the Philippines is rich and varied, encompassing indigenous cultures and Islamic influences alongside the colonial traditions established by Spain, which ruled the country from the late sixteenth century, and the United States, which held power during the first half of the twentieth century.

Before the arrival of the Spanish, buildings in the Philippines were impermanent structures made of wood, bamboo, palm fronds, and rattan. Similar dwellings are still built in rural regions and are known as nipa huts, after the leaf of the nipa palm, which is often used to thatch them. They have a single square or rectangular room and are raised on stilts to improve air circulation and avoid monsoon floodwaters.

Another grander type of traditional dwelling, called a *torogan*, is still made by the Maranaos people on the southern island of Mindanao. Built by village communities to house their leaders, *torogan*s stand on heavy posts fashioned from tree trunks and are topped with thatched roofs with two or three tiers, which show the influence of Javanese architecture. They are extensively decorated with brightly painted wood carvings, including highly distinctive *panolongs*—large, triangular, decorative elements that project from the front and rear of the building.

In the southern islands of Mindanao and Sulu, where from the late fourteenth century many people embraced Islam, mosques were the focal point of local communities. Early mosques were made from wood and typically had multitiered roofs; later, as building technology improved, they were topped by domes. In the second half of the twentieth century, western Asian–style designs were increasingly adopted, as at the King Faisal Mosque at Marawi State University in Mindanao.

SPANISH COLONIAL ARCHITECTURE

The arrival of Spanish colonists in the sixteenth century brought radical changes to the architecture of the Philippines. Friars from missionary orders converted the majority of the population to Roman Catholicism and led the construction of many churches and monasteries. They used stone, mortar, and tiles as building materials and brought with them the classical and baroque styles of architecture fashionable in Spain at the time. The church of Saint Augustín (1618) in Manila, one of the oldest surviving churches in the country, is typical of the classical style, with its regular facade and paired columns.

Frequently, European styles were modified by influences from colonial architecture in Mexico—a Spanish colony from which many of the friars came—as well as by the embellishments of local craftsworkers. The design of Philippine churches was also affected by the need to make them resistant to earthquakes. The church at Paoay, Luzon (built around 1710), is shored up with massive buttresses with undulating, scroll-like profiles in a style known as "earthquake baroque." Its bell tower is set apart to further minimize earthquake damage. The unusual fortress church of Saint Tomás de Villanueva (completed about 1797) in Miagao, Panay, is a similarly flamboyant local variation of the baroque style. Its facade is covered with a profusion of carvings of Biblical themes and luxuriant tropical vegetation.

Spanish power was centered on Manila, where the colonists founded a fortified walled city known as Intramuros in 1571. Like much of Manila, Intramuros was flattened after 1942 by bombing during World War II (1939–1945), and today one of the best places to see colonial urban architecture is the once-thriving port of Vigan in northern Luzon. Vigan has many substantial townhouses, built by the city's merchants, combining features from Spanish and Asian architecture. The houses typically have classical-style decoration, such as pilasters, square columns, and entablatures (features, such as friezes, above columns in classical temples), together with Asian features, such as large sliding windows comprising an inner screen covered with translucent capiz (oyster) shell and an outer wooden storm shutter.

AMERICAN URBANISM

When Spain ceded the Philippines to the United States in 1898, at the end of the Spanish-American War, a major new cultural influence arrived. In architectural terms, this influence was most clearly expressed in the new master plan for Manila commissioned from U.S. architect Daniel H. Burnham (1846–1912). Burnham's plan provided new civic and government buildings designed in a monumental classical style and set along wide, tree-lined avenues. The program was partly implemented by another American architect, William E. Parsons (1872–1939), although it was never completed.

American influence was further consolidated as Filipino architects began training in the United States, among them Juan F. Nakpil (1899–1986), who is regarded as the father of modern architecture in the Philippines. In the 1960s, Leandro V. Locsin (1928–1994) came to prominence with his modernist-style buildings. The closing decades of the twentieth century were marked by the construction of large numbers of high-rise apartments and office towers in the nation's cities.

The Ifugao people of Luzon carve guardian figures (bululs) to stand in the fields to protect their crops.

SCULPTURE

Some traditions of carving are practiced by peoples in remote regions that have remained largely untouched by Western culture. The Ifugao people of Luzon carve sacred wooden guardian figures called *bulul*s (or *bulol*s), which they place in rice granaries and fields to protect crops. Similar carvings protect villages and, on a smaller scale, decorate containers and spoon handles. In modern times, Ifugao carving is produced for tourists.

In the southern islands, Muslim peoples practice *okir*, a design tradition with Indian and Islamic influences. Some of the most accomplished examples of *okir* are wood carvings made by the Maranaos in Mindanao and the Taosugs of Sulu. They are highly decorative works with sinuous, curvilinear lines, and designs based on motifs such as the *sarimanok* (a bird with a fish in its beak or talons), the *niaga* (a serpent), and *pako-rabong* (a fern), of derive from ancient epics. The carvings are often polished or brightly painted, and are either freestanding or used to decorate buildings, prows of boats, and musical instruments.

From the sixteenth century, the Spanish transformed local sculptural traditions. The Roman Catholic Church became the main patron of artworks, which it used to instruct and inspire worshippers. Workshops overseen by friars produced carved statues of saints for churches and cathedrals. These sculptures were usually carved from locally available hardwoods and were painted and gilded. Like colonial architecture, the sculptures were made in the classical and baroque styles fashionable in Spain. Alongside sculptors who produced work for churches, other untrained artists made cruder figures for people's homes.

During the U.S. colonial period, artists produced a growing number of sculptures with nonreligious subject matter. The classically inspired styles taught in European and American academies also shaped the approach of many artists, including Guillermo Tolentino (1890–1976), the leading sculptor of the day. In the mid-twentieth century, sculptors were influenced by trends in modern European art. Tolentino's pupil Napoleon Abueva (born 1930) created stylized works that bordered on abstraction and used a variety of materials, including stone, wood, and metal. Other pioneering sculptors who explored abstraction and new materials and techniques included Arturo Luz (born 1926) and Eduardo Castrillo (born 1942).

PAINTING

Religious patronage and subjects dominated painting during the Spanish era. However, the rise of a prosperous merchant class created a demand for other paintings, such as portraits, landscapes, and scenes of everyday life, which became popular in the 1800s. The formal style taught in Western academies became influential in the second half of the nineteenth century and is seen in the grand paintings of Juan Luna y Novicio (1857–1899) and Felix Resurrección Hidalgo (1853–1913), both of whom spent time in Europe and earned international reputations. In the 1900s, a few artists, such as Fernando C. Amorsolo (1892–1972), painted idyllic, brightly colored local scenes inspired by Impressionism. In the late 1920s, Victorio Edades (1895–1985) championed a more radically modern style and, in his later work, also created a specifically Filipino style.

DECORATIVE ARTS

Decorative arts include metalwork, wood carving, furniture making, textile weaving, and basketry. The techniques, types, and styles of the objects made vary widely, reflecting the differing indigenous peoples as well as the influence of Islamic and Spanish cultures. In metalwork, Filipinos have established traditions of making gold jewelry using techniques such as filigree and repoussé. From the late sixteenth century, Spanish colonists oversaw the production of gold and silver vessels and objects for church use, from chalices and candlesticks to crucifixes and statues. Smiths working in Ilocos and Batangas provinces in Luzon produced fine metalwork of this type. In the Islamic south, brass was widely used, often inlaid with silver and decorated with *okir* designs. Typical objects included *gadur* and *kabul* (types of lidded containers), betel sets (for the custom of betel chewing), and ceremonial weapons such as the *barong* and *keris*. Similar variations are seen in basketwork produced throughout the country, ranging from the plain baskets and headgear made by the Ifugaos in Luzon to mats decorated with geometric designs and brightly colored, stylized bird-shaped containers made by the Maranaos in Mindanao.

R. BEAN

Music and Performing Arts

The colonial history of the Philippines shaped much of its modern culture. Although traditional music is popular with communities around the archipelago who have avoided much contact with Westerners, modern Filipino musicians are heavily influenced by Western cultural trends.

Spanish rule from the sixteenth century through 1898, followed by U.S. administration until 1946, added layers of Western cultural influence over local traditions. In the large southern island of Mindanao, many people follow Islam, and Muslim and west Asian influences affect the music of the region. The uplands of northern Luzon and several islands in the south, especially the interior of Mindanao, are home to numerous non-Christian, non-Muslim ethnic groups, whose cultures show little or no Western or west Asian influence.

MODERN MUSIC

Mainstream Philippine music is largely Westernized, showing virtually no affinity with the rest of Southeast Asia. There is, for example, Western classical music supported by conservatories and indigenous composers. The best-known Filipino composers are Felipe de Leon (1861–1944), who brought a Philippine dimension to Western classical music in his sonatas and concertos, and Antonio Molina (1894–1980), who wrote orchestral, chamber, and vocal music, including the popular "Hatinggabi," a serenade for violin and piano.

Secular vocal music includes *sarswelas* (musical dramas), lullabies, courtship songs, musical debates, and other types associated with seasonal festivals and life cycle events. Many songs are associated with religious feasts and festivals, including songs for Christmas, Lent, Holy Week, and Easter, but songs celebrating the month of May are also important.

Instrumental music includes, besides bands and orchestras, the *rondalla*, a Spanish-derived ensemble of plucked instruments similar to guitars. These include the *bandurria*, *laud*, *octavina*, *gitara*, and bass guitar. Ensembles vary in size from about eight to thirty musicians, and many groups of musicians are supported by schools or companies. Western-style popular music is also quite prominent.

MUSIC IN THE SOUTHERN PHILIPPINES

In the Muslim areas of the south, especially Mindanao and the Sulu Archipelago, Islamic vocal practices, such as a call to prayer (*adhan*) five times a day and reading the Koran, are typical parts of daily life. The most prominent secular music is the *kulingtang* ensemble, whose lead melodic instrument (the *kulingtang*) consists of eight bronze gongs that are suspended horizontally on ropes along a straight wooden frame and beaten with sticks. Two styles predominate, one called Maguindanao in the province of the same name, the other called Maranao from Lanao del Sur province. Several instruments provide the rhythm and meter of the music, including a pair of large suspended bronze gongs called *agung*, a single gong called *babandir*, a drum called *dabakan*, and *gandingan* gongs. The ensemble provides music for entertainment, including the possibility of audience members taking turns playing the *kulingtang* itself. Other instruments include a small, flat xylophone (*gabbang*), a long, narrow lute (*kutyapi*), and a vertical log or bamboo xylophone (*kwintangan kayu*).

TRADITIONAL ENSEMBLES

The ancient cultures of the upland peoples who live in northern Luzon, Mindanao, Sulu, Palawan, and Mindoro have more in common with similar groups elsewhere in Southeast Asia. The most distinctive form of music making is the gong ensemble: some groups use flat gongs, others bossed (gongs with a raised center). In some groups, each player has a single gong, a style similar to the music of upland peoples of Vietnam, Laos, and Cambodia. In other ensembles, a series of gongs are strung for a single player. In addition, there are many bamboo instruments, including ensembles of flutes, clappers, and bowed instruments. While some music is connected to life rituals and the agricultural cycle, other kinds are connected to rites associated with various forms of animism.

R. A. SUTTON

The **kulingtang** *gong is the most prominent traditional instrument in the music of the Muslim peoples of the southern Philippine island of Mindanao.*

Festivals and Ceremonies

Filipinos enjoy many public holidays. While some festivals commemorate national heroes and the struggle for independence, others are religious holidays. The Philippines is a largely Roman Catholic nation, and its citizens celebrate Easter as one of the main holidays of the year.

The Philippine year begins with New Year's celebrations in which families gather for a meal of *lechon* (roast suckling pig). The large number of Filipinos working abroad gather in hotels and restaurants to celebrate; in the Philippines people welcome the New Year with loud firecrackers. Over a month later, the Chinese community holds its own New Year festival.

NATIONAL HOLIDAYS

There are two public holidays in early summer: Labor Day (May 1) and Independence Day (June 12), the anniversary of the proclamation of independence from Spain. Independence Day is marked by parades at Cavite, where independence was proclaimed, and there are reenactments elsewhere in the Philippines. Two of the Philippines' national heroes are commemorated by public holidays. José Rizal (1861–1896), the

A boy wipes the face of the Black Nazarene, a 400-year-old statue of Christ that is carried through the streets of the Quiapo district of Manila every January in one of many local religious festivals that are celebrated in the Philippines.

leading figure of the Philippine nationalist movement in the nineteenth century, who was executed by the Spanish colonial authorities on December 30, 1896; the anniversary of his death is a public holiday. Andres Bonifacio (1863–1897), the leader of the Philippine Revolution against Spanish rule, is remembered annually by a public holiday on the date of his birth, November 30. The other national heroes whose efforts secured independence are remembered by a holiday on the last Sunday in August.

People Power Day, in late February (the date varies from year to year), commemorates the revolution in 1986 that overthrew the dictatorship of President Ferdinand Marcos (1917–1989). Rallies are held at the public places in Manila where protesters gathered in February 1986. April 9 is the Day of Valor, or Bataan Day, which is a solemn commemoration of the tens of thousands of Philippine and U.S. soldiers who surrendered to the Japanese on April 9, 1942, during World War II (1939–1945) and were then forcibly marched to prison camps; thousands did not survive even the journey to the camps.

RELIGIOUS AND LOCAL HOLIDAYS

Christmas Day (December 25) is a public holiday, but Easter is the major religious festival in the Philippines. Beginning on Palm Sunday, for one week through Easter Sunday, almost the entire country shuts down, although only Maundy Thursday and Good Friday are official public holidays. Processions of church congregations holding palms are common on Palm Sunday. On Good Friday, reenactments of the Crucifixion are performed; in a few communities, young men volunteer to be nailed to crosses. Religious processions, in which crosses and statues are carried, are held throughout the Philippines. The day after Good Friday resembles a day of mourning, but on Easter Sunday, the mood changes and festivals, fiestas, and float parades are held and Easter egg hunts for children are popular. In Muslim areas, Eid al-Fitr, the festival that marks the end of Ramadan (the month of the Islamic calendar during which Muslims fast during daylight hours) is a public holiday.

Many local festivals and ceremonies take place around the Philippines, including municipality and village fiestas, which have long and rich traditions. Among the largest are Ati-Atihan in Calibo and Sinulog in Cebu.

K. ROMANO-YOUNG

Food and Drink

Once a colony of Spain and later a U.S. possession, the Philippines is a sprawling archipelago comprising more than seven thousand islands, whose inhabitants have absorbed Spanish and American influences in their cuisine as well as elements of the cooking of other countries in the region, particularly the countries of Southeast Asia, India, and China.

In almost all Philippine meals, rice is the main ingredient. Other ingredients are added depending on availability and cost. For many Filipinos, rice is served for breakfast, lunch, and dinner, and other foods are merely side dishes or toppings. While every Filipino cook does things his or her own way, certain practices prevail. It is common, for example, to include different kinds of seafood or meats in one dish. Often fish is served uncooked; one popular way to serve raw fish is to stuff it with onions and wrap it in banana leaves. Other ingredients are boiled in soups or served *ihaw* (grilled). Lightly cooked seafood, meat, fruits, and vegetables that have been briefly steamed, blanched, or roasted are infused with salt and vinegar.

Whole pig carcasses are spit roasted over a fire for a Philippine feast.

PHILIPPINE TASTES

The salty taste found in most Philippine dishes comes from sauces or pastes made from fermented fish and shrimp, including *patis*, or fish sauce, and *bagoong*, or shrimp paste, as well as from plain salt. Fish sauce and vegetables may be brewed together to make a sour stock in which seafood may be soaked or simmered. *Sinigang* is a typical dish made in this way; the chief ingredient is fish. Another sour fish dish, *kinilaw*, is fresh fish soaked in vinegar, salt, ginger, onions, and red peppers. Sour tastes come from a variety of sources, including the *wee kalamansi*, a citrus fruit known for its tartness. Other fruits that are sour when unripe, including guava, mango, and tamarinds, also go into recipes.

Food from other lands, such as noodles and soy sauce from China, as well as the practice of stir-frying, have added nuance to Philippine cuisine, but they are often found colored in Philippine tones: *pancit* noodles originally from China, for example, are served with *wee kalamansi* in the Philippines, and spring rolls come not with sweet duck sauce or pungent mustard as they are traditionally served in China, but with garlic and vinegar.

Another major element in Philippine cooking comes from coconut milk, used in *guinatan*, a class of dishes originally from Malaysia that includes a variety of meat and vegetables.

Adobo, one of the Philippines' national dishes but originally a Spanish dish, is a pickling sauce for chicken or pork (or sometimes both), made from vinegar and salt, along with garlic, bay, and peppercorns. Influences from the United States are seen in the proliferation of fast food. Fried chicken, hamburgers, and soft drinks are widely available in the capital Manila and beyond; however, all are cooked Philippine-style, with garlic, soy sauce, and vinegar.

SNACKS AND DESSERTS

In addition to main meals, *meriendas* or snacks are served in the middle of the morning or the middle of the afternoon and include coconut, *ginataan*, fruit cooked in coconut milk, and rice cakes.

Popular desserts include *bibingka*, baked rice and coconut puddings topped with salted duck eggs, ripe mangoes, rolls and a heavy jam called *macapuno*. Ice cream is popular, as are milk shakes. Other favorite beverages include fruit juice, especially sour hot and cold drinks made from *kalamansi*, green lemons.

K. ROMANO-YOUNG

DAILY LIFE

Religion

Apart from the small nation of East Timor, the Philippines is the only Christian nation in Asia. Around 81 percent of Filipinos are Roman Catholics and another 11 percent belong to other Christian churches, including two endemic Philippine churches, Iglesia ni Cristo and the Aglipayans. Sunni Muslims, most of whom live in Mindanao and the Sulu Archipelago, account for another 5 percent of the population.

Although the Portuguese explorer Ferdinand Magellan (c. 1480–1521) raised a cross at Cebu when he landed with the first Spanish expedition in 1521, the conversion of the Filipinos did not begin until 1565, when Miguel López de Legaspi (c. 1510–1572) conquered the Philippine Archipelago for the Spanish crown.

ROMAN CATHOLICISM

Roman Catholics account for the overwhelming majority of Filipinos, and most practice their faith. Church attendance is the norm, and the church has much political and social authority. Under the 1986 constitution, the church pays no taxes. Although the church owns property, its portfolio is nowhere as extensive as it was in Spanish colonial times because the U.S. administration that ruled the archipelago from 1898 through 1946 confiscated large areas of church property. There are around 2,000 Roman Catholic schools, attended by a total of 1.6 million Filipinos. Church schools have a reputation for providing a high standard of education, and the church also runs a number of universities as well as hospitals and other facilities.

The permanent council of the Catholic Bishops' Conference is influential, and the council and the head of the church in the Philippines are sometimes accused of meddling in politics by some politicians. Cardinal Jaime Sin (1928–2005), archbishop of Manila for nearly three decades until his retirement in 2003, played a leading role in helping to topple the dictatorship of President Ferdinand Marcos (1917–1989; in office 1965–1986) and the corrupt regime of President Joseph Estrada (born 1937; in office 1998–2001). Under Cardinal Sin and his successor, the influence of the church has shaped many government decisions, for example slowing the introduction of birth-control policies.

In the countryside, Roman Catholicism exists alongside a lingering belief in spirits and other traditions. Folk healers use Christian symbolism that barely disguises older practices.

The Roman Catholic Church seeks to reinvigorate more orthodox beliefs and practices among the rural poor but suffers a shortage of priests.

IGLESIA NI CRISTO

Iglesia ni Cristo (literally, "the Church of Christ") is a dynamic Philippine "national" church founded by Felix Manalo (1886–1963), a former Seventh-day Adventist, in 1914—the church claims that Manalo did not found Iglesia ni Cristo but reestablished the church of the Apostles of biblical times. The number of adherents is secret but is thought to be around 7 percent of the Philippine population, and the church is generally said to be the second-largest religion in the Philippines. Most of the church's members are former Roman Catholics.

The church is conservative and disciplined; followers attend services twice weekly and give a percentage of their income to the church as a tithe. Iglesia ni Cristo's churches have a distinctive well-lit appearance and a central spire. Filipinos have taken Iglesia ni Cristo to more than 60 other countries in the community of Philippine citizens working abroad, and almost the entire international membership of the church is Filipino. Within the Philippines, Iglesia ni Cristo has considerable political influence, and the church can usually rely upon its members to cast a block vote in elections.

THE AGLIPAYAN CHURCH

The Aglipayan Church, another "national" Philippine religious organization, was founded by Gregorio Aglipay (1860–1940) during the Philippine revolt against Spanish colonial rule in the 1890s. Aglipay was a Roman Catholic priest who supported the revolt and was excommunicated. As a result, he established a breakaway church that severed all ties with the Roman

Catholics. Catholicism became identified with the colonial power, and many Filipinos joined the new "national" church, which in the early part of the twentieth century attracted between one-quarter and one-third of the nation's population. However, the majority of converts eventually returned to Catholicism, and by 2000, only around 4 percent of Filipinos were Aglipayans. In modern times, the Aglipayans are associated with the Episcopalians in the United States.

THE RIZALISTS

José Rizal (1861–1896), the nationalist hero of the revolt against Spanish rule in the Philippines, inspired a number of sects that are usually described as Rizalist. Rizalists claim that Rizal was a second incarnation of Christ, and some founders of various sects have claimed to be reincarnations of Rizal. Rizalist sects are generally millenarian, that is, they believe in

The church of the Iglesia ni Cristo (Church of Christ) sect in Quezon City, Manila, is a confident expression of the group's growing number of followers. The sect is thought to be the second-largest Christian church in the Philippines, although the number of adherents is kept secret.

an imminent second coming of Christ and a final judgment. The most prominent Rizalist sects have included the Colorums in the early twentieth century and, in modern times, the Philippine Benevolent Missionary Association. Rizalists tend to be from among the poorest and most deprived sections of society.

ISLAM IN THE PHILIPPINES

Islam arrived in the Philippines from the East Indies (modern Indonesia) after 1350. By the time the Spanish began to convert Filipinos to Christianity in the sixteenth century, Muslims controlled Mindanao, Palawan, and the Sulu Archipelago, and had a presence in the Visayan Islands and Luzon. Legazpi drove the Muslims from Luzon and the central islands of the archipelago, confining most of the Filipino Muslim population to the south of the country.

In modern times, Filipino Muslims (popularly known as Moros) in Mindanao and the Sulu Archipelago are somewhat set apart by their religion from the mainstream of Philippine life. Muslims now account for around 17 percent of the population of Mindanao, where they once formed the majority. Throughout the twentieth century, large-scale migration of Filipinos from other islands has reduced the influence of Mindanao's Muslims. By contrast, Muslims dominate the Sulu Archipelago, where 98 percent of the population are Moros.

Centralization of government and neglect of the southern regions occurred under President Marcos. As a result, the resentment of the Moros toward the Philippine government increased and a Muslim insurgency grew. Many Muslim Filipinos came to identify with the broader Islamic community worldwide rather than with other Filipinos.

There are some differences within the Filipino Muslim population, with some groups being stricter in their adherence to Islam and its practices than others. At the same time, certain pre-Islamic practices, including folk beliefs and culture, survive among Mindanao's Muslims. However, some Filipino Muslims now follow fundamentalist beliefs.

Since the 1970s, around 120,000 people have been killed in violence associated with the revolt by the Moro National Liberation Front in Mindanao. The Philippine government tried to reach an accommodation with Moro separatists through the creation of a Muslim region with limited self-government, the Autonomous Region in Muslim Mindanao, which includes parts of southwestern and central Mindanao as well as the Sulu Archipelago, including Tawi-Tawi. Autonomy brought a cease-fire agreement with moderate Moros, although occasional violence still occurs. There is also a low level of terrorist activity centered on the island of Jolo, where the Abu Sayyaf group, which has sympathies with Al-Qaeda, has a history of taking Western hostages.

V. MORRES

Family and Society

Filipinos have strong ties with the members of their extended families, including grandparents and cousins. Each family member has obligations that extend to the family of a person's marriage partner. In return, relatives provide support and offer preferential treatment to extended family members in business and employment.

Filipino men are still generally regarded as the head of the household and have responsibility for the family finances. However, in modern times, many women are in full-time employment and work away from home in the cities; others have joined the large numbers of Filipinos who work abroad in domestic service. As a result, the traditional patriarchal society has been diluted, particularly in cities, where increasing numbers of people now live in smaller nuclear families (parents and their children) or live alone.

Farm workers in Mindanao fill baskets with split coconuts. Philippine rural society is still divided between wealthy landowners and poor tenants and workers.

THE FAMILY AND RELIGION

Muslim families in the southern islands have a different society and culture from other Filipinos. In modern times, increasing numbers of Muslims follow Islamic customs. Marriages are still arranged among some Moro (Filipino Muslim) communities.

The overwhelming majority of Filipinos are Roman Catholics, and religious practices also have an impact on their family lives. Whereas in Western Catholic society the godparents of a child may have little influence upon the life of a girl or boy, in the Philippines the role of a godparent is far more important. The two godparents, the *comadre* (literally, "co-mother") and *compadre* ("co-father"), have a major role in the upbringing of a child and are regarded as an integral part of the family, even if they are not blood relations. In Philippine Catholic society, godparents have the same obligations to their godchildren that they have to their own natural children. Children play an important part in family relationships and the child-parent bond is strong; an unmarried son or daughter is not generally regarded as a full member of adult society until he or she has a spouse and child.

RICH AND POOR

Philippine society is unequal. Historically, a group of elite families have controlled much of the economy, initially as landowners and later as owners of corporations. In 2001, 40 percent of the population lived below the official poverty line. The gap between a small wealthy class and most of society is huge and appears to be widening. Tax avoidance among the rich is commonplace, and corruption remains a problem. The provision of education, health care, housing, a safe water supply, and transportation for the poor is inadequate.

Filipinos are increasingly organizing themselves into self-help and other groups that echo the traditional practice of *bayanihan* (mutual exchange) that was once common among country people. Neighborhood associations, church groups, business foundations, private voluntary organizations, and other bodies cater to the needs of the elderly, the sick, working groups, children, and others. A Filipino civil society is emerging that reflects growing concern for and obligations toward the less privileged.

V. MORRES

Welfare and Education

The disparate geography of the Philippines, combined with historical social inequality, presents the Philippines government with challenges in its provision of health care, education, and social welfare. Ambitious programs are trying to address various inequities.

In theory, health care in the Philippines is universal, but in practice, access to a doctor or to hospital treatment is restricted, partly by geography and partly by income. The nation comprises more than seven thousand islands, and many of the more remote smaller islands have few doctors and no hospitals. Consultations, vaccinations, and other public health services are provided by the state for free. Private medicine is also available, but poorer Filipinos are unable to afford the better health care offered by the private sector. The resulting two-tiered system favors the wealthy and those employed in the cities and often leaves the poor with inferior facilities and treatment. Many disadvantaged Filipinos still use traditional remedies for common ailments.

In 1999, two initiatives were launched in an effort to redress the imbalances between the two health care systems. The introduction of the state-run Philippines Health Sector Reform Agenda has had limited success, but a second initiative, the FriendlyCare Foundation, Inc., has yielded better results. This joint venture by government and business leaders with funding from the U.S. Agency for International Development (USAID) has encouraged private-sector investment in reproductive and family health care and has created a range of new facilities that have reduced some of the overcrowding in state-run hospitals and health centers.

The government has also introduced awareness and treatment programs to combat the growing problems of HIV/AIDS infection and drug abuse. The other main health threats include malnutrition and a range of communicable diseases. However, health and living standards are slowly improving, and life expectancy for Filipino women has increased to 73.2 years, although it remains largely unchanged for men at only 67.3 years. Infant mortality fell from 30 to 22.8 per 1,000 live births between 2000 and 2006.

Maintaining staff numbers is a major problem for the Philippine health care system. Many medical professionals leave the Philippines for better paid jobs abroad. Around 2,000 doctors currently leave the Philippines every year, while only 1,000 medical students qualify to replace them. Large numbers of Filipino nurses work in hospitals in North America and Europe.

WELFARE

Medical care is partly financed by employee contributions; 1.25 percent of a person's monthly salary is paid into the state health care fund. Other forms of social welfare are paid for by contributions from employees (3.33 percent of earnings) and from employers (5 percent of earnings). These payments are compulsory for all private-sector workers up to age 60 who earn more than the low-pay threshold that is periodically adjusted with inflation. The self-employed must pay 8.4 percent of their earnings into the state social welfare fund. In most cases, retirement pensions are based on total contributions over the beneficiary's working life, although exceptions are made for people on low income for whom a safety net is provided.

In addition to health care and pensions, social welfare contributions finance sickness and maternity benefits as well as funeral expenses. Payments for temporary and permanent disability are also made. A person who becomes disabled while employed receives a lump sum equal to their monthly pension entitlement multiplied by the number of monthly contributions he or she has made.

EDUCATION

School education in the Philippines is state-funded and free, although there are also some private schools, most of which are run by the Roman Catholic Church or by Protestant churches. Children start primary school at age seven for a six-year course. In 2005, over 96 percent of children of primary school age were enrolled; most of those who do not attend school live in the remote rural areas of outlying islands. Despite the high percentage of children in primary school, only 56 percent of those eligible complete the four-year course in high school.

Teaching is conducted in Filipino, the national language of the Philippines, which is based on the Tagalog dialect of the capital, Manila, and in English. More Filipinos read and speak English than the citizens of any other Asian nation. About 92.6 percent of Filipinos are literate. The use of Spanish, which ceased to be the country's third compulsory language in schools in 1987, has gradually diminished since the end of Spanish colonial rule in 1898.

The Philippines has several world-ranked further education establishments, among the most distinguished of which are the University of Santo Tomas in Manila (the oldest university in Asia); the University of the Philippines, which has seven constituent universities located in 12 campuses throughout the Philippine Archipelago; Ateneo de Manila University in Manila;

and De La Salle University, also in Manila. Some universities, such as De La Salle University, are maintained by the Roman Catholic church. The Asia Institute of Management (AIM) is an internationally renowned business school modeled on the business school at Harvard. The nation's largest university, the Polytechnic University of the Philippines, has around 30,000 students. Its campuses are spread throughout Manila and on some of the larger islands.

Government spending on education increases every year, but it varies considerably as a proportion of GDP (gross domestic product, the total value of the goods and services produced in a nation over a fixed period of time, usually one year). In the early twenty-first century, spending on education was the equivalent of only 3.2 percent of GDP. The Philippine government spends a lower percentage of its GDP on education than most of its neighbors, and the education system is widely perceived to be in crisis as a result of underfunding. One in eight schools has a teacher-to-student ratio of 1:50 or more, and more than one-third of students do not have textbooks. There is a shortage of classrooms and equipment, and in tests Filipino students scored lower in science and math than students in neighboring countries.

The availability and quality of facilities and equipment for students varies greatly among institutions in the Philippines. These cadets at the national military academy enjoy greater access to computers than their peers at many Philippine colleges.

HOUSING

As a result of migration to the cities in the second half of the twentieth century, about 60 percent of Filipinos now live in cities, where more than 40 percent of migrant families subsist in shantytowns in which housing is often unsanitary and sometimes illegally constructed. Many steps have been taken to combat this urgent problem. One of the most ambitious programs, begun in 2003, is a $48.8 million project to create new affordable housing. The program, which is due for completion in 2009, is spearheaded by the Housing and Urban Development Coordinating Council (HUDCC), an arm of local government, which has contributed $6.3 million of the total fund. The rest of the funding has come from the national government (mainly in the form of a gift of unoccupied land), the Asian Development Bank (ADB), which has lent $30.5 million to be repaid over 25 years, the Development Bank of the Philippines (DBP), and numerous other backers, including the governments of Germany and Finland. Although the initiative has so far resulted in the creation of 20,000 new homes in the Manila metropolitan area, demand still outstrips supply. The Urban Poor Colloquium (UPC) and the Philippines Homeless People's Federation—nongovernmental organizations (NGOs) that provide short-term relief while lobbying for a long-term political solution—are also involved in efforts to provide adequate housing for poor people in Philippine cities.

H. RUSSELL

Manila

Manila, the national capital of the Philippines, owes its development in part to its site along Manila Bay, a large inlet that forms one of the finest natural harbors in Southeast Asia. Although the city site is constricted in the narrow Pasig Valley, the largest agricultural lowlands in the Philippines are nearby.

Metropolitan Manila, which is popularly known as Metro Manila, is the largest urban area in the Philippines. At the 2000 national census, Manila City had 1,581,000 inhabitants. However, the National Capital Region comprises Manila, the larger contiguous city Quezon City (which had 2,174,000 inhabitants in 2000), two other cities, and 13 municipalities. It forms one large sprawling built-up area that was home to 9,933,000 people in 2000. Since 1975, the National Capital Region has had a single administrative body over the councils of its cities and municipalities. The capital contains more than one-half of Philippine industrial capacity and it is the center of the nation's commerce, finance, administration, and education systems.

THE DEVELOPMENT OF MANILA

When the Spanish arrived at Manila Bay in 1570, they discovered a small Muslim settlement called May Nilad on the site of modern downtown Manila along the Pasig River. The Spanish quickly conquered the settlement, renaming it Manila, and built a walled city that is now known as Intramuros. In 1595, Manila became the capital of the Spanish Philippine Islands. The city grew as a trading center, spreading unplanned beyond the walled city of Intramuros. Development of Manila was not planned until U.S. rule replaced Spanish rule in 1898. The designs of U.S. architect Daniel H. Burnham (1846–1912) brought straight avenues and public buildings in the neoclassical style to downtown Manila south of the Pasig River.

During World War II (1939–1945), U.S. troops left the city on December 31, 1941; on January 2, 1942, Japanese forces entered Manila, which they occupied until 1945. In the final days of the war, the Japanese systematically destroyed most of the historic buildings in the Intramuros district and killed more than 110,000 citizens. The Intramuros quarter was not fully restored until the 1980s.

In 1946, Manila became the capital of an independent nation when the Commonwealth of the Philippines gained full sovereignty. However, two years later the city lost its status when the capital was transferred to Quezon City, which adjoins Manila's northern border. Quezon City, named for President Manuel Quezon (1878–1944), was founded in 1939 as a new capital for the Philippines. Covering about one-quarter of metropolitan Manila, Quezon City is still home to some government buildings, the headquarters of the national police

force and of the principal broadcasting networks, and the University of the Philippines. The capital did not transfer back to Manila until 1976.

AN INDUSTRIAL CITY

The metropolitan region is home to the greater part of Philippine industry. Many of the city's industries are based on processing local agricultural products, including making rope and other items from Manila hemp, making coconut oil and soap, food processing, furniture manufacture and timber preparation, and making paper. Other industries include textiles and garments, electronic and electrical engineering, printing, optical goods, pharmaceuticals, and metalworking (particularly aluminum). Manila's factories are typically small and many are crowded into a few city districts, particularly Tondo, the poorest area.

The city is the major retail center for the nation and the country's largest port. Manila is also the center for Philippine banking and insurance and is home to the only stock exchange in the Philippines. Administration and government agencies are major employers, and the city also has a number of universities and other institutions of higher education.

Manila is one of the world's most crowded cities, with 52,223 inhabitants per square mile (20,164 per sq. km); by comparison, Tokyo, another of the world's most crowded cities, has a population density of 26,124 inhabitants per square mile (10,087 per sq. km). Manila suffers traffic gridlock and pollution and has few parks and open spaces in or near the downtown area. More than one million people, both workers and students, commute into Manila every day.

THE CITY SIGHTS

The historic center of Manila is the Intramuros area, the original Spanish colonial city along the southern bank of the Pasig River. Severely damaged during World War II, the walls have been rebuilt and the city gates have been reconstructed. The moat outside the walls has been replaced by a narrow golf course. Inside the walls, cobblestone streets have been restored and some of the historic buildings faithfully rebuilt; the district's street furniture, such as its lampposts, has an antique appearance, but like almost everything else within the walls, it

Set within the walled city of Intramuros in Manila, Fort Santiago is a sixteenth-century fortress that was built by the Spanish conqueror Miguel López de Legazpi (1510–1572).

is a reconstruction or a rebuilding that gives the illusion of age. Manila Cathedral, originally founded in 1581, has been rebuilt six times after damage by typhoons, earthquakes, fires, and war. The present building, dating from the 1950s, follows the style of the fourth and fifth churches that were built on the site. Fort Santiago, the restored Spanish colonial fort, also lies within Intramuros. The fort's ornate 131-foot (40 m) high main gate was been rebuilt and the 26-foot (8 m) thick walls repaired; the historic complex is now a museum devoted to objects from the Spanish period.

South of Intramuros is Rizal Park, the scene of the execution of national hero José Rizal (1861–1896). The park, which is also known as Luneta (Spanish for "crescent" or "moon") and previously as Bagumbayan, is the city's main open space and focuses around a monument to Rizal. It contains Japanese and Chinese gardens, a relief map of the Philippines, the National Museum of the Filipino People, and the National Library. The only other major open space is Manila Baywalk, a 1.25-mile (2 km) boulevard and narrow garden along the bay; lined by tall coconut trees, the promenade has many bars and cafés and is a popular place for people to meet.

Malacañang Palace, the official residence of the chief of state, was originally built in 1802 as the summer home of a wealthy Spanish merchant. The palace complex also comprises the smaller Bonifacio Hall (originally a state guesthouse but preferred as a residence by the most recent presidents), the New Executive Building, Kalayaan Hall (the former executive building), Mabini Hall (the administration building), and other government buildings. Along with Malacañang Park on the opposite bank of the river, where the presidential guard is based, the Malacañang area forms a government district.

Each city district in Manila has its own character and a busy market. The district of Binondo is Manila's Chinatown. Established in 1594, when the Spanish gave the land to the Catholic Chinese, Binondo has become a popular area with tourists for its restaurants and shops. Tourists are also drawn to the sights, luxury hotels, shopping malls, restaurants, cafés, and nightlife found in the Malate and Ermita districts, which are also host to a lively student scene.

C. CARPENTER

Cebu City

With a population of 1,080,000 in its metropolitan area, Cebu City, on the east coast of the island of Cebu, is the third-largest urban area in the Philippines. At the 2000 national census, 719,000 inhabitants lived within the city limits.

When Portuguese explorer Ferdinand Magellan (c. 1480–1521) landed at the site of Cebu City in 1521, it was already a busy fishing port and trading center. Magellan concluded an agreement with the chief of Cebu, securing his conversion to Christianity, but was later killed by the chief of the neighboring small island of Mactan. In modern times, Cebu City's most famous monument is Magellan's Cross. Legend states that the cross was erected by the explorer when he arrived at Cebu. The city played an important role in the early history of the Philippines, and it boasts of being the nation's oldest city.

CEBU IN THE PAST

Spanish forces under Miguel López de Legazpi (1510–1572) returned to Cebu in 1565 to found a colonial settlement and a Roman Catholic mission. The settlement, originally named San Miguel and later La Villa del Santissimo Nombre de Jesus, was the center of Spanish rule in the Philippines until Legazpi moved north to found Manila in 1570. The city grew along a sheltered strait that is protected by Mactan Island, and it became the main port and commercial center for the Visayan Islands. In 1860, the Spanish colonial authorities opened the port to the shipping of other nations, and Cebu City increased in importance as a center for the collection and export of produce from the Visayan Islands, including sugar, timber, copra (dried coconut flesh from which oil can be extracted), and fish. Cebu grew under U.S. rule after 1898, but Japanese forces destroyed much of the city in May 1942 during World War II (1939–1945).

Magellan's Cross, now housed in a chapel, is said to have been raised by the explorer Ferdinand Magellan when he landed at the site of Cebu City in 1521.

PRESENT-DAY CEBU

The port is a center for ferry routes from other Visayan Islands and the city's airport on Mactan Island receives international flights and scheduled flights from Philippine cities. A second airport at nearby Lahug also serves Cebu City. A road bridge connects Cebu City with Mactan, where a large industrial park, the Mactan Export Processing Zone, has been established. The industrial park is a tax-free zone where Philippine and foreign corporations have established factories, many of which assemble electrical goods and other consumer goods. Cebu City's industries include textiles and clothing, food processing and vegetable oil, footwear, chemicals, and making musical instruments. A flourishing decorative arts sector includes making pearl jewelry and items of polished Mactan stone, brass and bronze ware, shell craft, and basketry. The city is also one of the world's main centers for the manufacture of rattan furniture.

The city is an educational center with five universities, including San Carlos University, which was founded in 1595. Cebu City is a commercial center and attracts tourists, mainly Filipinos, to its beaches, coral reefs, and historic sites, including its sixteenth-century cathedral. Cebu City grew rapidly in the second half of the twentieth century, when many people settled in the city from rural areas on Cebu Island and from neighboring islands. City suburbs spread north and south along the coastal plain of Cebu Island, but Cebu City still has a housing shortage. The city is an administrative center, a provincial capital, and the capital of the Central Visayas region.

C. CARPENTER

Davao City

Davao City is the second-largest metropolitan area in the Philippines, with a population of 1,200,000 at the 2000 census. However, the city is the nation's largest by area, covering 854 square miles (2,212 sq. km) and including large stretches of countryside within the city limits.

Situated on the north coast of the island of Mindanao, Davao City is a meeting point for different cultures in the island. These diverse vibrant cultures come together in a colorful festival, the Kadayawan Festival, each August to celebrate the fertility of the local region and its harvest of fruits, flowers, and vegetables.

A REGIONAL CENTER

Davao City is at the center of an important agricultural region that produces rice, coconuts and copra, flowers, corn, and fruits. The region is particularly known for its production of abaca, a plant related to the banana whose leaf stalks are the source of the fiber known as Manila hemp. The city's industries were originally based on processing these products, then shipping abaca, copra, corn, and timber to other islands and abroad. Davao City has two ports along Pakiputan Strait, which is sheltered by Samal Island. The smaller port, Santa Ana, receives interisland shipping and ferries, while the deepwater port at Sasa, which is 5 miles (8 km) from the city, handles international shipping. Between them, the two ports make Davao City the leading hub for cargo transshipment in the southern Philippines.

Davao City lies close to Mount Apo (background, left), an active volcano and the highest peak in the Philippines.

In modern times, Davao City has a wide range of industries, including manufacturing consumer goods, textiles and clothing, electrical goods, and cement and building materials. Processing abaca fiber is still a major industry. The city dominates southeastern Mindanao and it is a route hub with an international airport. Davao City is now a university city, and it is the capital of a province and of Davao Region, which covers much of southeastern Mindanao.

THE DEVELOPMENT OF THE CITY

Davao City is much younger than most other major cities in the Philippines. Spanish colonial rule was less intrusive in Mindanao than in many other Philippine islands, owing to the strong influence of Islam in the area. Davao City was not founded until 1847, when a Roman Catholic mission was established close to the site of the present city. Despite becoming a local center of administration and the center of a diocese—Davao City's San Pedro Cathedral dates from 1847—the settlement grew slowly under Spanish rule. After U.S. forces established control of the region in 1900, transportation links improved, and agriculture began to prosper as large farms were established in the surrounding countryside.

The main boost to the economy of the area, however, was the arrival of Japanese entrepreneurs after 1903. The Japanese established plantations for growing abaca and coconuts. The Japanese community expanded, becoming known locally as Little Japan, and soon had its own businesses, schools, and newspapers as well as a Shinto shrine. The settlers developed interests in forestry, fishing, and commerce, and before long, the local Filipinos learned new agricultural techniques from the Japanese. The port developed and in 1937, Davao City received city status, independent of its province.

Although the city had a substantial Japanese community, it did not escape destruction during World War II (1939–1945) at the hands of Japanese forces, when most of the downtown area was razed. In the late 1940s, downtown Davao City was rebuilt in a mixture of Spanish, Western, and Moorish styles—Davao City is close to the region that contains the majority of the Philippines' Muslim population. The city grew rapidly in the second half of the twentieth century as people settled to work in Davao City's factories.

C. CARPENTER

Zamboanga City

Zamboanga City, in western Mindanao, is one of the oldest cities in the Philippines. The capital of Zamboanga Peninsula region, the city had a population of 602,000 at the 2000 Philippine census.

Zamboanga City is situated on the southern tip of the Zamboanga Peninsula along the Basilan Strait. Its port, which is sheltered by Basilan Island, dominates trade from the Philippine islands that surround the southern part of the Sulu Sea.

A HISTORIC CITY

Spanish colonists in the Philippines founded Zamboanga City in 1635, but the site was already inhabited by Moro (Muslim) seafarers, many of whom were pirates. The city's name derives from the Malay *jambangan* (literally, "the place of flowers"), which gave rise to its modern nickname, "the City of Flowers." Tropical flowers, such as bougainvilleas and orchids, are still common in the city's gardens and along its streets.

Zamboanga City was the scene of several battles between Spanish troops and the Moro people until 1718, when the fort that the Spanish had begun in 1635 was strengthened. Under U.S. rule after 1898, Zamboanga City was the seat of a regional governor, one of whom was General John J. Pershing (1860–1948), later a famous military commander. The United States made Zamboanga City one of its principal military bases in the Philippines, and today the city is still an important center for the Philippine army. Japanese forces took the city in March 1942 during World War II (1939–1945) and made the base their defense headquarters for the region. U.S. troops recaptured Zamboanga City in 1945, but there was widespread damage to the city's historic buildings during the campaign.

In modern times, the coastlands of the Moro Gulf to the east have been a center of unrest among the Moro people. In 2003, the city suffered isolated terror activities by fundamentalist Muslim Moro separatists, and Zamboanga City's Southern Command base has been host to U.S. military advisers in the Philippine army campaign against the separatists.

A DIVERSE CITY

Zamboanga is home to diverse peoples and languages; the local dialect Chabacano acts as a common language. The city retains many Spanish-style colonial buildings, and there are also "water villages," communities of houses built on stilts above the sea, that are home to some of the local Muslim population. Zamboanga City's Bajau people live on sailing boats and fish the waters of the Basilan Strait.

A member of Zamboanga City's Muslim community prays in a city mosque.

The city also has modern commercial, industrial, and residential quarters. Many of its industries are based on the port, which is a maritime route hub, importing rice and other food stuffs and exporting fish and fish products, shells, timber, abaca fiber (Manila hemp), and other products of Mindanao and neighboring islands. Zamboanga City processes food, fish, and timber, makes items in brass and bronze, and manufactures buttons from shells. The city also has a range of consumer goods industries. Tourism is a major employer; Zamboanga City has good beaches and a pleasant climate that is less humid and hot than that of Manila, the Philippine national capital, from where many of Zamboanga's visitors come. The city's airport receives both domestic and international flights.

C. CARPENTER

ECONOMY

Most Filipinos live in one of the 11 largest islands that contain the bulk of the nation's cultivable lowland and resources. The Philippines was one of the more economically advanced countries in the region at the beginning of the last quarter of the twentieth century, but a combination of problems and challenges has held the republic back while other economies in the region have prospered.

Some of the nations of Southeast Asia developed rapidly toward the end of the twentieth century; called the "tiger economies" for their powerful growth, they benefited from investment from Japan, Taiwan, South Korea, and other countries to develop industries that were competitive because the cost of labor was cheaper than in developed nations. These vibrant economies experienced great industrial growth that included rapidly expanding electric and electronic engineering (including computers), the manufacture of domestic consumer goods, and the assembly of transportation equipment and parts. The Philippines has shared to a lesser extent in this economic boom, but the nation also fared better in the financial crisis that hit so many countries in eastern and southeastern Asia in 1997 and 1998. However, in the twenty-first century, the Philippine economy has been dramatically overtaken by neighbors, such as Malaysia and Thailand.

ECONOMIC CHALLENGES

Poverty is more widespread in the Philippines than in Malaysia or Thailand. In 2001, 40 percent of Filipinos lived below the official poverty line; in Malaysia the corresponding figure was 8 percent, and in Thailand it was 10 percent. There is huge inequality in the distribution of wealth, and the government is unable to afford the education programs that would provide the better qualified workforce that Philippine industry and services demand.

Standard of Living

The Philippines has a lower standard of living than neighbors such as Thailand and Malaysia. Around 40 percent of Filipinos live below the poverty line, according to official estimates from 2001. There are great differences between the rural and urban population in income, and the rural poor have a much lower standard of living than many city dwellers. The per capita GDP (gross domestic product) was $4,700 in 2004; this figure is adjusted for purchasing power parity (PPP), a formula that allows comparison between living standards in different countries.

A rapidly increasing population is another challenge: in 2006, the birthrate was 24.9 live births per 1,000 of the population, one of the highest rates in Asia. It has been calculated that the population of the Philippines—76.5 million at the 2000 national census—could double by 2030. The provision of education, health care, and housing for so many more people, and finding employment for them, would be beyond the current resources of the Philippine authorities. However, the government avoids taking measures to slow the population growth rate, such as promoting birth control programs, for fear of offending the Roman Catholic Church (which opposes artificial methods of contraception); around 81 percent of Filipinos are Catholics, most of them practicing.

The Philippines cannot offer enough well-paid employment for its people. Many of the graduates from Philippine universities and colleges emigrate for better-paying jobs in North America, western Asia, or Europe. Annually, twice as many doctors leave the Philippines as the number that qualify. Emigration is not confined to the qualified: large numbers of Filipinos work abroad as cooks, cleaners, domestic staff, and laborers. The disadvantage of emigration is that it leaves the Philippines lacking qualified staff to develop its own industries and services more fully, and many of those who are left to fill positions are among the less enterprising. The advantage of large-scale emigration is that the country receives huge remittances (money sent back home by workers employed abroad) every year. The millions of Filipinos abroad send back an average of some $8 billion annually, and without this injection of foreign capital, the economy could collapse. The scale of the remittances helped the Philippines weather the Asian financial crisis in the late 1990s, and the Philippine economy was less severely affected than those of its neighbors. After a decline in 1998, the Philippine economy grew by 2.4 percent in 1999 and had recovered to a healthy 4.4 percent growth rate by 2000. By 2005, the growth rate stood at nearly 5 percent per annum.

The major problem facing the Philippine government is the nation's debt. The demands upon the government are great and there is a large budget deficit. International financial institutions are increasingly worried concerning the Philippines' ability to sustain such a large national debt. The Philippine national debt is over 75 percent of the nation's GDP (gross domestic product; the total value of all the goods and services produced in a

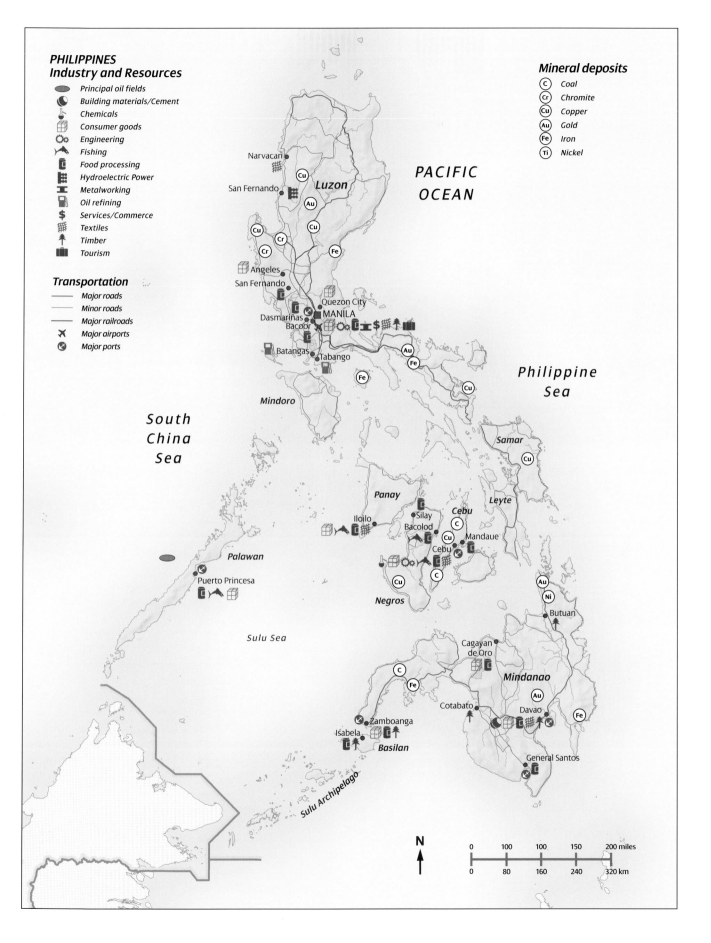

PHILIPPINES
Industry and Resources

- Principal oil fields
- Building materials/Cement
- Chemicals
- Consumer goods
- Engineering
- Fishing
- Food processing
- Hydroelectric Power
- Metalworking
- Oil refining
- Services/Commerce
- Textiles
- Timber
- Tourism

Transportation

- Major roads
- Minor roads
- Major railroads
- Major airports
- Major ports

Mineral deposits

- C Coal
- Cr Chromite
- Cu Copper
- Au Gold
- Fe Iron
- Ti Nickel

PACIFIC OCEAN

Philippine Sea

South China Sea

Narvacan

Luzon

San Fernando

Angeles
San Fernando
Quezon City
Dasmariñas MANILA
Bacoor
Batangas Tabango

Mindoro

Samar

Panay

Leyte

Cebu

Iloilo
Silay
Bacolod
Mandaue
Cebu

Palawan

Puerto Princesa

Negros

Sulu Sea

Cagayan de Oro

Butuan

Mindanao

Cotabato
Davao

General Santos

Zamboanga
Isabela
Basilan

Sulu Archipelago

N

| 0 | 100 | 100 | 150 | 200 miles |
| 0 | 80 | 160 | 240 | 320 km |

Sugarcane processing is a major industry in the Visayan Islands. Large processing plants, such as this one in Negros, are operated throughout the island group.

country in a fixed period of time, usually one year). The cost to central government of servicing the debt is greater than the annual budget of the education and defense ministries combined.

The state supports a number of public enterprises that are unprofitable and inefficient, particularly in the energy sector. However, these enterprises remain in public ownership on

THE PHILIPPINE GDP

The Philippine gross domestic product (GDP) was $412.5 billion in 2005. The figure is adjusted for purchasing power parity (PPP), an exchange rate at which goods in one country cost the same as goods in another. PPP allows a comparison between the living standards in different nations.

MAIN CONTRIBUTORS TO THE PHILIPPINE GDP

Agriculture	14.4 percent
Industry	32.6 percent
Services	48.0 percent

Source: CIA, 2005

grounds of national security. At the same time, there is concern about the nation's political stability. Two recent presidents have been forced from office after public demonstrations—Ferdinand Marcos (1917–1989; in office 1966–1986) and Joseph Estrada (born 1937; in office 1998–2001)—while a separatist Muslim movement in the southern island of Mindanao and adjoining smaller islands has resorted to violence and terror. Some 120,000 people died in the violence between 1970 and 2005. Perceived instability discourages some foreign investors from supporting projects in the southern islands.

The Philippines is subject to a variety of natural hazards. Not only does the nation experience earthquakes but it is also home to around 20 active volcanoes. Earthquakes, eruptions, floods, landslips, and mud slides have resulted in loss of life and have also severely damaged the infrastructure. Aspects of the nation's geography also hinder development; much of the country is mountainous and unsuitable for cultivation or settlement, and many of the smaller islands are too remote to be successfully integrated into the Philippine economy.

Government programs to reform the economy include privatization, the improvement of the infrastructure, and a revised and more efficient taxation system to increase revenue. The Philippines has traditionally had two major trading partners, the United States and Japan, and the health of the Philippine economy depends in part on the performance of the economies of these two nations. The recent growth of China (including Hong Kong) as an important trading partner has reduced this dependence on the United States and Japan.

RESOURCES

The Philippines has many mineral resources and lays claim to areas of the South China Sea that are potentially rich in reserves of oil and natural gas. An oil field off the north coast of the southern island of Palawan currently produces around 26,000 barrels of crude oil a day, and the nation has reserves of 152 million barrels of crude oil. One barrel is the equivalent of 42 gallons and is usually given in metric measurement as 0.16 cubic meter. The sector of the Spratly Islands claimed by the Philippines is thought to contain substantial reserves of oil.

Apart from copper, which is found in western central Luzon, none of the mineral deposits in the Philippines is large enough to provide major exports. However, there are important deposits of gold in Luzon, iron ore in Mindanao and Luzon, lead in western Mindanao, coal in Cebu and Palawan, and chromite (chromium ore) in several islands. Other mineral deposits, including silver, mercury, nickel, cadmium, and manganese, occur in several other places. Limestone (for cement) and marble are found in several islands and are useful resources for the Philippine building industry. There are also commercially important deposits of asphalt and salt.

Relatively few of the rivers of the Philippines have been harnessed to provide hydroelectric power; the nation has instead relied upon thermal power stations that use imported oil and local coal. However, the construction of several large dams in Luzon and Mindanao has increased the percentage of electricity produced by hydroelectric plants.

AGRICULTURE

Farming (including forestry and fishing) supplies nearly 15 percent of the nation's GDP and provides employment for 36 percent of the labor force. However, the nation is largely mountainous, and land that can be cultivated is restricted. About 19 percent of the land is arable and another 16.8 percent is permanently cropped. Where land is suitable for farming, the soils are generally fertile, and a hot wet climate provides ideal conditions for crops to grow all year.

Philippine farming faces a variety of problems, including the small scale of many farms that rely upon family labor to plant, tend, and harvest crops. Many farms are so small that family members must take other jobs to provide an additional source of income. Poorer farmers are unable to afford fertilizers, herbicides, or machinery, and Philippine farming is among the least mechanized in the region. Rural poverty is a problem, and enterprising people from country areas have joined the drift to the cities to find work; large numbers have also emigrated.

The principal crops are sugarcane, rice, corn, coconuts, bananas, casava, pineapples, mangoes, and other fruits (including citrus fruits and papayas), and a wide variety of vegetables. Abaca (Manila hemp) is grown for its fiber. Filipino farmers also raise hogs, cattle, and poultry. The principal cereal crop is rice, which is particularly important in Luzon, Mindanao,

Panay, and Negros. Rice farmers cultivate small plots under irrigation; in areas where irrigation is not available, the rice crop is vulnerable, and in some years the failure of the crop causes economic hardship. Rice is typically grown on small family farms, and farmers are unable to afford the mechanization that now characterizes rice cultivation in some other countries of Southeast Asia. However, rice production improved dramatically in the last quarter of the twentieth century with the introduction of new varieties of higher-yielding rice and the greater use of chemical fertilizers. The authorities have also extended irrigation systems. As a result, the Philippines sometimes has excess rice for export. Chemical fertilizers are expensive, however, and most have to be imported; many small farms cannot afford fertilizers, and where chemicals are used, the pollution of waterways has increased.

Sugar was a major export until the 1980s and 1990s, when the United States and Europe grew more sugar beets. As a result, sugar is no longer exported in large quantities, and the economy of islands such as Negros, which is the center of the Philippine sugar industry, has suffered; all of the sugar crop from Negros is now used within the Philippines. Philippine sugar is traditionally grown on large plantations (haciendas) that employ large numbers of poorly paid workers who do most of the work by hand. Since the downturn in the sugar industry, many of the haciendas have been broken up into smaller farms.

In most years, the Philippines is the world's largest producer of coconuts and provides about one-third of the world's copra (the dried, oil-yielding coconut kernel). Coconuts are used for a variety of food products, oils, fibers, and cosmetics. Nearly one-third of the nation's arable land grows coconuts, and more farmers depend upon the crop than any other. Coconuts are usually grown as a monoculture (the continuous growing of one crop) and diversification is being encouraged; at the same time, various agencies are promoting local coconut processing units to allow small-scale farmers to add value to their crops and to earn extra income.

In the early twentieth century, as much as one-half of the Philippines was covered by forests. The amount of forest cover has been dramatically reduced by heavy logging and little reforestation. Some high-quality woods are still exported and used locally, but the industry is no longer as important.

EMPLOYMENT IN THE PHILIPPINES

Sector	Percentage of labor force
Agriculture	36 percent
Industry	16 percent
Services	48 percent

Source: Philippine government. 2004

In 2005, the official unemployment rate was nearly 8.7 percent.

Fishing is a major industry, and fish forms a large part of the diet of Filipinos. The seas that surround the islands are rich in fish, both in numbers and variety; the waterways and lakes are also sources of fish, and fish farming in ponds is widespread in parts of Luzon. The principal fishing ports are Zamboanga and Iloilo. Canned tuna is a major export, and the Philippines also exports pearls, mother-of-pearl, tortoiseshell, and shells. The authorities are promoting the fishing industry, which currently suffers from poor equipment and inadequate boats and a lack of refrigeration and processing plants. At the same time, overfishing, pollution, and the destruction of coral reefs are growing problems.

INDUSTRY

Philippine industry was characterized by mining, processing farming products, and light industry to supply the needs of the local population until the 1970s and 1980s. A program to establish industries to achieve self-sufficiency in some fields and wide-scale foreign investment to fund plants to assemble goods for export diversified the nation's industries. Under the presidency of Ferdinand Marcos, ambitious industrial development programs established plants to smelt copper, produce iron and steel, make phosphate fertilizers, and produce chemicals from coconut oil. However, although much industrial development has been achieved, Philippine industry has not grown at the same rate as industries in either Malaysia or Thailand.

More than one-half of Philippine industrial production comes from the Manila metropolitan area, and another 20 to 25 percent comes from industries in central Luzon. The Philippine authorities have introduced programs to spread industrial development to other major cities but with mixed results. There

Although fishing is an important industry in the Philippines, many fishers lack modern boats or equipment. These outrigger canoes in Luzon are typical of small-scale Philippine fishing.

has been some success in promoting medium-sized factories, such as textile and consumer goods plants, in Cebu City and Davao City. However, the structure of Philippine industry impedes development.

Although some factories are licensees of foreign corporations, for example assembling electronic goods and other products for export, most industrial output is in the hands of a small number of corporations. At the same time, small- and medium-sized Philippine firms employ about 80 percent of the industrial workforce but produce only one-quarter of the nation's industrial goods by value. Philippine industry is inefficient and is unable to compete with the more modern industries of some other countries in the region.

The principal industries include assembling electronic goods, textiles and garments, footwear, pharmaceuticals and chemicals, food processing and making beverages, wood products, petroleum products, and optical instruments. Electronic goods, clothing, and optical instruments are major exports.

SERVICES

Service industries employ 48 percent of the Philippine workforce and supply 53 percent of the national GDP. While Manila, the national capital, is the center of the nation's commerce, retail industry, and banking, and is the home of the Central Bank of the Philippines and the Philippine National Bank, there are also many local savings banks and rural banks. The Philippine service sector is resilient and recovered quickly after the Asian financial crisis in the late 1990s.

With beaches, sunshine, dramatic scenery, vibrant culture, and historic sites, the Philippines has the potential to develop an important tourist industry, but instability and the activities of Muslim separatists in Mindanao have held back its growth. Most visitors arrive in the country through Manila, but the city is perceived as being less interesting, and less safe, than other major Southeast Asian national capitals, such as Bangkok and Singapore. The majority of tourists staying at Philippine resorts are Filipinos, and many of the tourists arriving in the country are Filipinos living abroad.

TRADE

The Philippines exported goods worth an estimated $41.3 billion in 2005 and imported goods and services worth an estimated $42.7 billion in the same year. The largest export from the Philippines in terms of revenue is electronic equipment. Other major exports include machinery and transportation equipment, garments, optical instruments, coconut products, fruits and nuts, copper and copper products, shrimp, and chemicals. The largest markets for Philippine goods are China including Hong Kong (which took 18 percent of the Philippines' exports in 2005), the United States (18 percent), Japan (18 percent), Singapore (8 percent), Malaysia, Taiwan, the Netherlands, and Germany.

The Philippines' major imports are raw materials for industry, machinery and transportation equipment, refined mineral oils, vehicles and vehicle parts, plastics, chemicals, and foodstuff, particularly grains. Imports are mainly from the United States (which provided 19 percent of imports to the Philippines in 2005), Japan (17 percent), China including Hong Kong (10 percent), Singapore (8 percent), Taiwan (8 percent), South Korea, Saudi Arabia, and Malaysia.

TRANSPORTATION AND COMMUNICATION

Railroads play little part in the transportation system of a nation that comprises around seven thousand islands. The Philippines has only 557 miles (897 km) of railroad track, 55 percent of which was operational in 2006. Most of the operational track is in Luzon; the only other sections of railroad in the Philippines are in Mindanao, Negros, Cebu, and Panay, but not all these railroads are working. Philippine railroads suffer from lack of investment and the inability to travel more than short distances by train. Some railroads, such as the track on Negros, have been primarily used to transport goods rather than passengers, but in the Manila metropolitan area, where traffic gridlock is a major problem, the government focuses on improving the railroad system for commuters.

This gold and copper strip mine is in Benguet in northern Luzon, one of the leading gold-producing areas in the Philippines. Miners in the Philippines also quarry pyrite and limestone.

There are 124,324 miles (200,037 km) of highways in the Philippines, but only 12,308 miles (19,804 km) of paved roads. The principal highways are those between the major cities on the larger islands; elsewhere, the main routes between the main Philippine cities are by air or by sea from one island to another. The main seaports are Manila, Cebu City, Iloilo City, Zamboanga, Subic Bay, Davao City, and Cagayan de Oro, and there are regular ferry services between the principal cities and neighboring islands. There are four international airports. Manila's Ninoy Aquino International Airport, 4 miles (7 km) south of downtown Manila, handles most international flights to and from the Philippines; Mactan-Cebu International Airport receives a much smaller amount of international traffic. The airports at Davao and Laoag also handle some scheduled international flights.

International telephone lines and the service between the major islands is more reliable than communication with the smaller islands. In 2004, there were more than 3.4 million telephone lines in the Philippines, but the greater number of mobile cellular telephones (32.8 million) indicated the better service provided by that technology. In the same year, 7.8 million Filipinos had Internet access.

C. CARPENTER

Singapore

At the beginning of the nineteenth century, Singapore was a sparsely populated island belonging to the Malay state of Johor. In 1819, the British East India Company established a trading post on the island, which was ceded to the company in 1824. In 1867, Singapore became a British colony. Singapore rapidly grew as a port along a busy shipping route between Europe and China. Japanese forces occupied the island from 1942 to 1945. In 1959, Singapore gained complete internal self-government, and in 1963, the state joined with Malaya, Sabah (formerly British North Borneo), and Sarawak to form Malaysia. Difficult relations between the state government in Singapore and the federal government in Kuala Lumpur led to an agreement for Singapore's secession in 1965. Since then the city-state has flourished economically. The port has become the world's largest in terms of tonnage handled, and Singapore has developed an advanced economy based on manufacturing, finance, digital technology, biotechnology, and tourism.

GEOGRAPHY

Location	Southeastern Asia; one main island and many smaller islands south of the Malay Peninsula
Climate	Tropical wet climate with two monsoon seasons; the northeast monsoon blows from December to March and the southwest monsoon from June to September
Area	269 sq. miles (697 sq. km)
Coastline	120 miles (193 km)
Highest point	Bukit Timah 545 ft (166 m)
Lowest point	Singapore Strait 0 ft
Terrain	Undulating lowland rising to a central plateau
Natural resources	Deepwater anchorages
Land use	
Arable land	1.6 percent
Permanent crops	0 percent
Other	98.4 percent
Major rivers	None
Major lakes	None
Natural hazards	Occasional flash floods

FLAG

The flag of Singapore consists of two horizontal bars, red over white. White symbolizes virtue; red, a traditional lucky Chinese color, represents equality. There are a white crescent moon and five white five-pointed stars in the canton (the upper quarter next to the flagpost). The crescent moon (an Islamic symbol) was originally intended to assure the island's Muslim Malay citizens that Singapore was not a Chinese state. In modern times, the moon is usually said to represent a young nation rising. The five stars represent justice, peace, progress, democracy, and equality.

METROPOLITAN AREAS, 2002 POPULATIONS

Urban population	100 percent
Singapore	4,064,000

Source: Singaporean census department estimate, 2002

NEIGHBORS AND LENGTH OF BORDERS

There is a short land border with Malaysia along an artificial causeway that links the two nations.

POPULATION

Population	4,064,000 (2002 Singaporean census department estimate)
Population density	15,937.3 per sq. mile (6,157.6 per sq. km)
Population growth	1.4 percent a year
Birthrate	9.3 births per 1,000 of the population
Death rate	4.3 deaths per 1,000 of the population
Population under age 15	15.6 percent
Population over age 65	8.3 percent
Sex ratio	108 males for 100 females
Fertility rate	1.1 children per woman
Infant mortality rate	2.3 deaths per 1,000 live births
Life expectancy at birth	
Total population	81.7 years
Female	84.5 years
Male	79.1 years

ECONOMY

Currency	Singapore Dollar (SGD)
Exchange rate (2006)	$1 = SGD 1.54
Gross domestic product (2005)	$126.5 billion
GDP per capita (2005)	$28,600
Unemployment rate (2005)	3.1 percent
Population under poverty line	N/A
Exports	$204.8 billion (2005 CIA estimate)
Imports	$188.3 billion (2005 CIA estimate)

GOVERNMENT

Official country name	Republic of Singapore
Conventional short form	Singapore
Nationality	
noun	Singaporean
adjective	Singaporean
Official languages	Chinese (Mandarin), Malay, English, Tamil
Capital city	Singapore
Type of government	Republic
Voting rights	21 years and over; compulsory
National anthem	"Majulah Singapura" (May Singapore progress)
National day	Independence Day, August 9, 1965

POPULATION PROFILE, 2005 ESTIMATES

Ethnic groups	
Chinese	77 percent
Malayan	14 percent
Indian (mainly Tamil)	8 percent

Eurasians, Europeans, and others	1 percent	Malay	14 percent
		Hokkien Chinese	11 percent
Religions		Cantonese	6 percent
Buddhist	43 percent	Tamil	3 percent
Sunni Muslim	15 percent	Other minorities	8 percent
Protestant Christians	10 percent		
Chinese folk religions (including Taoism)	9 percent	Adult literacy	92.5 percent
Roman Catholic	5 percent		
Hindu	4 percent		
Others and nonreligious	14 percent		

TRANSPORTATION

Railroads	24 miles (39 km)
Highways (all paved)	2,010 miles (3,234 km)
Expressways	93 miles (150 km)
Navigable waterways	None
Airports	
International airports	1
Paved runways	10

Languages

Chinese (Mandarin)	35 percent
English	23 percent

Singapore Strait, the narrow passage that separates Singapore from Indonesia, is one of the world's busiest shipping routes.

CHRONOLOGY

7th–13th centuries CE	The island of Singapore is an outpost of the Srivijayan Empire, which is centered in Sumatra; a walled city called Temasek develops on the site of present-day Singapore.
15th century	Temasek is taken by the sultanate of Malacca (modern Melaka).
16th century	Temasek becomes part of the sultanate of Johor on the Malay Peninsula after Malacca falls to the Portuguese.
1617	Portuguese forces set fire to Temasek, after which the city declines and disappears.
1819	Thomas Stamford Raffles (1781–1826), an administrator for the British East India Company, signs a treaty with the sultan of Johor to establish a trading post in Singapore.
1824	Johor cedes the island of Singapore to Great Britain.
1826	Great Britain forms the Straits Settlements territory, which includes Singapore, Malacca, and Penang. Singapore becomes the center of administration of the territory in 1832.
1867	The Straits Settlements become a British crown colony.
late 19th century	The British develop Singapore as a major port and trading settlement along a strategic strait on the sea route between Europe and China. Large numbers of Chinese and later Indians are attracted to settle on the island.
1941	Japanese forces bomb Singapore during World War II (1939–1945).
1942	Japan occupies Singapore, renaming it Syonan ("Light of the South").
1945	Great Britain retakes control of Singapore.
1946	The British abolish the Straits Settlements, making Singapore a separate colony.
1959	Singapore gains complete internal self-government and Lee Kuan Yew (born 1923) becomes the first prime minister of Singapore. The People's Action Party (PAP) wins a landslide in the elections; it has retained power ever since.
1959–1990	Under Lee Kuan Yew, Singapore develops a prosperous modern economy and attains a high standard of living, progressing from developing nation status to developed nation status.
1963	Singapore joins the Federation of Malaysia, which also includes Malaya, Sabah, and Sarawak.
1965	After a dispute between the PAP and the Malaysian federal government, Singapore separates from Malaysia to become an independent republic.
1971	Great Britain withdraws its military forces from Singapore.
1990	Goh Chok Tong becomes prime minister when Lee Kwan Yew steps down.
1998	Singapore enters a recession following the 1997 Asian financial crisis.
2004	The eldest son of former prime minister Lee Kuan Yew, Lee Hsien Loong (born 1952), becomes prime minister.

GOVERNMENT

Singapore has a parliamentary system of government. Since before independence in 1965, the People's Action Party, generally known as the PAP, has dominated Singapore's political life. Other parties include the Singapore People's Party, the Workers' Party of Singapore, and the Singapore Democratic Alliance.

Singapore is a republic with a democratic constitution that was adopted in 1959, when the British colony of Singapore gained full internal self-government. In 1963, Singapore joined with Malaya, Sabah (formerly British North Borneo), and Sarawak to form Malaysia, but tensions within the new federation led to the withdrawal of Singapore in 1965. The island-state amended its constitution and became an independent republic.

THE PRESIDENT AND THE GOVERNMENT

The chief of state of Singapore is a president who, since 1999, is directly elected for a six-year term. Previously, the president was elected by parliament. Candidates for the presidency are assessed by the (appointed) Presidential Election Commission, which can debar candidates on the grounds of insufficient competence or integrity. The commission disqualified all the opposition candidates from running for office in 1999 and 2005, and the PAP presidential candidate was elected by default.

The presidency is largely ceremonial, but constitutional amendments in 1999 gave the chief of state additional powers, including the right to appoint many key public officials and responsibilities for national security. However, power is concentrated in the hands of the prime minister. The leader of

Old Parliament House in Singapore was built in 1827 and was replaced by a larger building in 1999. It is now an arts center.

the largest party in parliament, which has always been the PAP, forms a government and chooses other ministers to form a cabinet. The government is responsible to parliament.

THE PARLIAMENT AND ELECTIONS

Singapore has a unicameral parliament with 93 members. The president appoints nine members; the remaining 84 members are elected for a five-year term by compulsory universal adult suffrage (from age 21). There are two types of constituencies: nine single-member constituencies each elect one member to parliament, while 14 group representation constituencies (GRCs) each elect three, four, five, or six members to parliament. This system is perceived as favoring the PAP because the winners in GRCs take all the seats rather than seats being awarded in proportion to the number of votes cast, which is the general practice in electoral systems with multimember constituencies.

A party must contest all the seats in a GRC, and one of the candidates must be from an ethnic minority. Smaller opposition parties have difficulty raising enough money for the deposit that candidates submit to stand for election—only the winners keep their deposits. The PAP has been known to resort to defamation laws to silence criticism from opposition candidates and to debar them from participation. As a result of these obstacles, many PAP seats in parliament are not contested in elections. PAP officials claim that the small number of opposition candidates reflects a lack of opposition; the opposition cites measures taken to discourage them. A constitutional amendment allows the government to appoint additional members of parliament to represent the opposition to ensure that it has at least three representatives. Although opposition parties obtain more than one-fifth of the vote, they usually have only a few seats.

LOCAL GOVERNMENT

Singapore is divided into five districts, which are subdivided into smaller areas administered by town councils. Each town council is headed by an appointed mayor, who is concurrently the member of parliament for one of the constituencies within the town council area.

C. CARPENTER

MODERN HISTORY

Singapore achieved internal self-government in 1957, and, after briefly forming part of Malaysia, the city-state gained full independence in 1965. Since 1957, Singapore has been ruled by the People's Action Party (PAP), which for more than 30 years was headed by Lee Kuan Yew (born 1923).

Thomas Stamford Raffles (1781–1826), an administrator for the British East India Company, signed a treaty with the sultan of Johor to set up a trading post on the southern tip of Singapore in 1819. In 1824, Johor ceded the island to Great Britain. In 1826, the British established the Straits Settlement territory, which included not only Singapore but also Malacca (now Melaka) and the island of Penang. In 1832, Singapore became the capital of the Straits Settlements, which at the time was the only British colonial interest in the Malay region. In 1867, after the British East India Company lost its administrative role, Singapore became a British crown colony.

ECONOMIC DEVELOPMENT

The importance of Singapore increased enormously with the advent of the steamship in the 1860s and the opening in 1869 of the Suez Canal, linking the Mediterranean Sea with the Indian Ocean. These developments reduced the time and the distance required to travel by sea between Europe and Asia; traffic increased, and Singapore became a major international port. By 1880, 1.5 million tons (1.4 million metric tons) of goods passed through Singapore port annually. With the development of rubber planting in neighboring Malaya, Singapore also became a major export center. The city's prosperity attracted immigrants from many parts of Asia, principally from China, the Malay Peninsula, and India. As a result, Singapore's population soared.

WAR AND ITS AFTERMATH

Singapore's long period of economic growth, during which it became one of the largest ports in the world, came to an end on December 8, 1941, when Japanese forces bombed Singapore. Japanese troops invaded in January 1942, and the British governor of Singapore surrendered on February 15, 1942. The island remained under Japanese occupation until the end of World War II in 1945. The Japanese claimed to be liberating the island from colonialism, but their rule was harsh and Japanese forces committed many atrocities, particularly against Singapore's majority ethnic Chinese community.

When the British returned in September 1945, they expected to be able to restore Singapore to its former status, but they soon discovered that the war had changed the popular mindset: the commercial classes, in particular, were no longer content with colonial status and demanded self-government. The British authorities were forced to make concessions. In 1946, Great Britain abolished the Straits Settlements, transferring Malacca and Penang to a federal British-ruled Malaya and establishing Singapore as a separate colony. Singapore was then granted limited internal self-government and the island's first free election—with participation restricted to British subjects—was held in March 1948. Shortly afterward, a Communist insurgency in mainland Malaya threatened to take over Singapore by force. The British responded in June 1948 by declaring a state of emergency, which lasted for 12 years.

Although the British were determined to prevent the spread of communism through the Malay Peninsula, they recognized that it would be impossible to retain power in Singapore without introducing some reforms. As a result, the British made plans to increase the political involvement of the city's population while retaining control over internal security and foreign affairs as well as a veto over legislation. When elections were held in 1955, the 300,000 registered voters (four times as many as in 1948) returned a coalition headed by the two largest parties, the Labor Front led by David Marshall (1908–1995) and the People's Action Party (PAP).

Marshall became chief minister, but he remained in office only a year, resigning when talks with the British government about independence broke down. He was succeeded by his deputy, Lim Yew Hock (1914–1984), who cracked down on communism and negotiated a new constitution, which was signed in London on May 28, 1958. There were further elections, and Singapore gained complete internal self-government (but not full independence) from Great Britain on June 5, 1959. The first prime minister of the self-governing state was PAP leader Lee Kuan Yew.

THE MALAYSIAN INTERLUDE

Shortly after gaining autonomy, and faced with a stagnating domestic economy and rising unemployment, Lee entered talks with his Malayan counterpart, Tunku Abdul Rahman Putra (1895–1960), about a merger between their two countries. The controversial initiative caused a split in the PAP, and a faction led by Lim Chin Siong (1933–1996) left to form the Barisan Sosialis (Socialist Front). Great Britain was eager to

Lee Kuan Yew, who dominated Singaporean political life for more than three decades, speaks at a meeting of the Association of Southeast Asian Nations (ASEAN) in 1987.

decolonize in the region and promoted the idea of a federation that would also include Brunei, British North Borneo (now Sabah), and Sarawak. Lee held a referendum in which his proposal to unite with Malaya (independent since 1957) received overwhelming support. However, the option of separate independence for the city-state was not put to the Singaporean electorate.

In September 1963, Singapore joined Malaya, Sarawak, and British North Borneo to form the Federation of Malaysia; Brunei declined to join the new nation. Although Singapore retained considerable autonomy within Malaysia, the federation exacerbated racial tensions in Singapore as the island's majority ethnic Chinese community became increasingly concerned that Malays were receiving preferential treatment from the Malay-dominated federal government in Kuala Lumpur. At the same time, President Sukarno of Indonesia (1901–1970) tried to destabilize the federation by inciting Malayan hostility toward the Chinese.

The federation proved unworkable. UMNO (the United Malays National Organization), the ruling Malay party, practiced discrimination in favor of ethnic Malays, a policy it perceived as affirmative action for Malays who were underrepresented in business, industry, and higher education. The PAP saw pro-Malay favoritism as unjustified and racist. Chinese Singaporeans faced growing economic and political discrimination and the relationship between the federal government and the Singapore state government broke down. On August 7, 1965, Tunku

Abdul Rahman Putra, the federal prime minister, proposed that the national parliament should vote to "sever all ties" with the Singapore state government. The separation became law on August 9, when Singapore gained independence as a sovereign republic and, although Singapore was technically expelled from Malaysia, legally the island-state is regarded as having withdrawn because of the actions of its government.

INDEPENDENCE

Lee Kuan Yew remained in office as prime minister of independent Singapore. The priorities for his government were to achieve economic stability and to create a sense of national identity among the ethnically disparate groups that had been alienated from each other by the events of the previous three years. The government began an ambitious industrialization program, including the construction of several industrial parks and the transformation of the British air base at Changi into an international airport. Labor law was reformed to reduce unrest in the work force, and the government offered new investors "tax holidays" of between 5 and 10 years. English was made the language of instruction in all schools and colleges. A vigorous public housing policy created new towns with low-cost private residences. In 1967, Singapore joined Indonesia, Malaysia, the Philippines, and Thailand in a regional trade agreement, the Association of Southeast Asian Nations (ASEAN). When Great Britain withdrew the last of its forces from Singapore in 1971, the city-state established its own army, navy, and air forces.

PROSPERITY AND RESTRICTIONS

By the 1970s, Singapore had become an important trading nation with a high rate of economic growth. Its prosperity consolidated the power of the PAP, which won all the seats in the elections of 1972, 1976, and 1980. Although the country went into recession after the 1973 global oil crisis, the ruling party responded by encouraging domestic industry to move into the emerging computer technology market. The PAP's effective policies helped keep it in government; the party lost only six seats in both the elections of the 1980s. Although the PAP is not perceived as corrupt and has presided over growth that has seen Singapore progress from developing nation status to developed nation status, electoral technicalities and restrictive laws became obstacles to any real opposition.

On November 28, 1990, after more than 30 years as prime minister, Lee Kuan Yew finally stepped down. He remained, however, a senior minister until 2004, when he took on a new government role as minister mentor. Lee was replaced as prime minister by Goh Chok Tong (born 1941) who successfully steered the republic through the Asian economic crisis of 1997. Goh stepped down in 2004 to be replaced as prime minister by Lee Hsien Loong (born 1952), the eldest son of Lee Kuan Yew.

H. RUSSELL

CULTURAL EXPRESSION

Literature

The different peoples of Singapore each draw on their own literary heritage—Chinese, Malay, or Indian. Until the second half of the twentieth century, few writers worked in Singapore, and the poems, stories, and other writings of the first Singaporean literary figures are generally considered to belong to the tradition of the literature of their own language.

Around 35 percent of Singaporeans speak Mandarin Chinese as a first language, while another 11 percent speak Hokkien Chinese, and 6 percent Cantonese. The remaining Singaporeans speak English (23 percent), Malay (14 percent), Tamil (3 percent), and other languages. Many Singaporeans are also bilingual or trilingual. As a result, the peoples of Singapore read many different literatures.

A NATIONAL LITERATURE

The first significant writers in Singapore wrote in English, the language of commerce and administration, as well as the language of the colonial power until 1959, when Great Britain granted Singapore full internal self-government. However, although writers in Singapore wrote in Mandarin, English, Malay, or Tamil, their work came to be recognizable as Singaporean because their subject matter reflected the distinct society of Singapore and the shared experience of the island's history and culture. At the same time, the city-state's different cultures have influenced each other, and cultural crossover gives a characteristic style to its literature.

THE FIRST SINGAPOREAN WRITERS

Some poets and novelists write in more than one language. Since his first collection of poetry, *The Giant*, appeared in 1968, Tan Swie Hian (born 1943) has published poems, essays, and

An elderly Singaporean reads a Malay-language newspaper. Chinese-, English-, and Tamil-language newspapers are also published in the city-state.

stories in English and Malay. Edwin Thumboo (born 1933) is widely regarded as the pioneer of poetry in Singapore. Writing in Engish, he has published a relatively small body of work, but his poems have a distinctive Singaporean identity that distinguishes them as major contributions to the foundation of a national literature. *If Gods Can Die*, a collection of 48 poems that appeared in 1977, is his most characteristic work. Robert Yeo (born 1949) is both a poet and a dramatist, whose English-language plays, including *Are You There, Singapore?* (1974), *One Year Back Home* (1980), *The Adventures of Holden Heng* (1986), and *Changi* (1996), have been successfully staged in Singapore and abroad. Yeo's best-known poetry collections are *Coming Home, Baby* (1971) and *Leaving Home, Mother* (1999).

Wang Gungwu (born 1930) published English- and Chinese-language poetry from the 1950s. His poems achieved the first distinctly local voice in English. Although writers in Chinese and Malay followed the examples of the pioneers, since the early 1990s many writers in Singapore have returned to English as their medium. The novelist and dramatist Su-Chen Christine Lim (born 1948) draws on the different cultures in Singapore in her novels. In 1992, she was the first winner of the Singapore Literature Prize, for her third novel, *Fistful of Colours* (1992). The Singapore Literature Prize was established by Singapore's National Book Development Council to promote literature by local writers in the English language.

K. ROMANO-YOUNG

Art and Architecture

The art and architecture of Singapore reflect the city-state's rapid growth and its diverse population. Nineteenth-century colonial buildings, Chinese and Hindu temples, and Islamic mosques stand next to high-density housing and the soaring skyscrapers that today dominate the city's skyline.

Many of Singapore's finest colonial buildings were constructed between the 1850s and the 1930s in architectural styles that were then fashionable in Europe. The British favored the classical style for their new municipal buildings, including the Court House (now Empress Place Exhibition Hall; 1865), the Istana (originally Government House, now the president's residence; 1867), the National Museum of Singapore (1887), and the Supreme Court (1939). One of the country's best-known classical-style structures is the Raffles Hotel (1887). Other historic buildings include Chinese-style terraces of shop-houses with commercial premises at the front of the first floor and living quarters behind and upstairs. Some of the best preserved examples are in the Tanjong Conservation Area. Colonial settlers also introduced single-story houses, or bungalows, such as the black-and-white buildings along Scotts Road.

RELIGIOUS ARCHITECTURE

Singapore's places of worship reflect the diversity of the population. Chinese temples are among the most colorful buildings in the city. Typically they have multitiered roofs with upturned corners and sculpted dragons on their ridges; carved timber beams and stone columns; and interiors decorated with lacquer, gilding, calligraphy, paintings, and sculptures of various gods. A fine example is Thian Hock Keng temple (1842), the oldest and largest Chinese temple in Singapore. Hindu temples, such as Sri Mariamman temple built in 1843, are also distinctive and are based on examples from southern India. The Hindu temples are notable for their *gopura*, tower gateways covered in a profusion of painted sculptures of Hindu deities. Mosque architecture varies considerably and reflects various Southeast Asian and Indian influences. Sultan Mosque, Singapore's principal mosque (founded 1824, rebuilt 1928), fuses Mogul, Persian, and Turkish features and is capped by a magnificent gold dome. Colonial architects also designed a number of Christian churches, such as the classical-style Cathedral of the Good Shepherd (1844) and the Gothic-style Saint Andrew's Cathedral (1862).

HIGH-RISE SINGAPORE

During the 1950s, the colonial government oversaw the construction of thousands of concrete apartment buildings to house Singapore's rapidly growing population. The government of independent Singapore continued the trend toward the end of the twentieth century and developed a number of new satellite towns, such as Jurong and Ang Mo Kio. High-density building is most evident in the skyscrapers of the central business district of downtown Singapore. The 659-feet (201 m) tall OCBC Centre (1976) by the U.S. firm Pei Cobb Freed and Partners was the first major skyscraper in the city. Air traffic control restrictions limit the height of high-rises to a maximum of 919 feet (280 m), and three sleek skyscrapers have been built to this height: OUB Centre (1986), UOB Plaza One (1992), and Republic Plaza (1995).

THE ART MARKET

Singapore's newly flourishing art market is a sign of the nation's vibrant economy. Singapore traditionally did not have a strong culture of visual arts; it had no art schools and few formal organizations for exhibiting art. The situation began to change in the middle of the twentieth century with the creation of the Nanyang Academy of Fine Arts (founded in 1937), the Singapore Art Society (1949), and the Modern Art Society (1964). The Singaporean visual arts scene now encompasses a diverse range of approaches, from Chinese ink painting and Western oil painting to conceptual and installation art.

R. BEAN

The 1930s Supreme Court building was designed in a neoclassical style, with Greek Corinthian pillars, British Georgian windows, and a large Italianate dome.

Music and Performing Arts

Music in Singapore had its roots in the folk music of the city's Chinese, Malay, and Tamil communities. In modern times, contemporary Chinese popular music and Western popular and classical music have become more popular and have influenced composition in Singapore.

Singapore's local folk tradition is Peranakan (so-called Straits Chinese) folk music, a genre that unites Malay tunes with Hokkien Chinese traditions and often an English lyric. In modern times, songwriters in Singapore have continued to compose tunes in the Peranakan style; the song *Bunga Sayang* (1994) is a popular well-known example. *Bunga Sayang* is one of a number of songs that have been adopted by or written for Singapore's National Day Parade (August 9), whch is a colorful celebration. Each year, a theme song is chosen for the ceremony. The songs, some of which are adapted from folk music, receive considerable exposure on radio and television and form a body of modern music that is known by all Singaporeans.

STATE SPONSORSHIP AND THEATER

As well as concert halls and theaters for music, drama, and dance in the downtown district of Singapore, there is a network of smaller arts centers across the island. A state-of-the-art national cultural center, the Esplanade-Theatres on the Bay complex, opened in 2002. The government encourages music and the performing arts and has a program to make Singapore a regional center of the arts. State funding is available not only for buildings and other facilities but also for performers and festivals. Singapore has three principal theater companies: The Necessary Stage (which produces modern, sometimes controversial, plays), the intercultural TheatreWorks company (which blends Asian and Western performance styles), and The Theatre Practice, which is bilingual but is known for Chimese-language productions, including works by Kuo Pao Kun (1939–2002). Although western styles of theater dominate, Chinese theater and opera are also performed. Priority is given to developing major arts companies to nurture new works and talent and to draw new audiences from within the city and from abroad. Principal recipients of funding have included the Singapore Symphony Orchestra and the Singapore Chinese Orchestra, but a program that began in 2000 has spread funding more widely.

POP MUSIC

Singapore is a flourishing center for Chinese-language pop music. Rock music became popular in the city in the 1960s, when Singapore's only real competitor as a base for recording

Singaporean dancer and performance artist George Chua (born 1973) performs an experimental dance during a festival at the avant-garde Plastic Kinetic Worms Gallery in Singapore.

Chinese pop music was Hong Kong. Singapore produced its own pop groups, including The Quests, a 1970s band that came to dominate the music charts in Singapore, Malaysia, and Hong Kong. Through the 1960s and 1970s, Singapore had many local singers who became popular throughout the Chinese-speaking communities of Southeast Asia. The Singapore-based rock band Sweet Charity and its lead singer Ramli Sarip (born 1952) were successful through the 1980s; since then, a number of other Singaporean bands have gained regional popularity. These bands include The Oddfellows, The Observatory, and Electrico.

DANCE

The government supports dance companies, including the Singapore Dance Theatre, the national ballet company whose members are drawn from different nations. The company, which performs modern and neoclassical dance, owes its reputation in part to the choreography of Singaporean dancer Goh Choo San (1948–1987). Folk dance in Singapore draws on the diverse traditions of China, the Malay Peninsula, India, and the Indonesian island of Sumatra.

P. FERGUSSON

Festivals and Ceremonies

Singapore is a multiethnic state whose different peoples follow different religions; Buddhists form 43 percent of the population, Muslims 15 percent, Christians 15 percent, followers of Chinese folk religions 9 percent, and Hindus 4 percent. The principal festivals of Singapore's main religions are public holidays.

Singapore is a prosperous city-state in which the work ethic is a prominent part of national consciousness. As a result, the republic celebrates fewer public holidays than most other Southeast Asian nations.

NATIONAL DAY

There are three secular public holidays in Singapore. As well as New Year's Day (January 1) and Labor Day (May 1), the only public holiday that is neither ethnic nor religious in nature is National Day, August 9. The National Day holiday commemorates the withdrawal of Singapore from Malaysia in 1965, after an unhappy two-year membership in the federation. Following increasingly strained relations between the state government in Singapore and the Malaysian federal government in Kuala Lumpur, the federal parliament voted to sever relations with Singapore on August 7, 1965. Two days later, Singapore assumed national sovereignty, and Malaysia was the first country to recognize its independence. A colorful celebration in the National Stadium is the centerpiece of National Day in Singapore. A parade and various displays (including displays by units of the country's armed forces) are followed by spectacular fireworks. National Day is promoted as the principal celebration for Singaporeans of all ethnicities and religions.

Colorful dragon decorations line the streets of Singapore for the New Year celebrations.

RELIGIOUS HOLIDAYS

Singapore's Christians, two-thirds of whom are Protestant while one-third are Roman Catholic, celebrate Easter and Christmas as the main religious festivals of the year. Both Good Friday and Christmas Day are public holidays.

Vesak Day, in the spring, is the principal Buddhist holiday, commemorating the birth and enlightenment of the Buddha and his entry into nirvana (final release from the cycle of reincarnation). Worshippers attend temples to pray, meditate, and make offerings, while monks chant. Pious Buddhists perform acts of generosity, such as visiting the poor and giving them money or releasing caged birds. Mass blood donation sessions are held. The day ends with a candlelit parade through the streets.

Hari Raya Raji is the celebration of the end of the annual pilgrimage by Muslims to the holy places in Mecca and Medina in Saudi Arabia. Goats or buffaloes are sacrificed and the meat is given to the needy. Hari Raya Puasa marks the end of Ramadan, the month of the Islamic lunar calendar when Muslims fast during the hours of daylight. After prayers at the mosque, Muslims gather with their relatives for a celebratory family meal.

Singapore's Hindus celebrate Deepavali, known in India as Diwali, the festival of lights. Hindus believe that the souls of the departed visit their former earthly homes at this time, and many tiny earthenware lamps are lit to guide them on their journey.

CHINESE NEW YEAR

About 77 percent of the population are ethnic Chinese, and the Chinese New Year is one of the most popular festivals in Singapore. Although the New Year holiday is officially confined to one day, when the sound of firecrackers fills the air and huge firework displays light the night sky, Singaporeans stretch the celebrations over six weeks with events in the evening. The Chinatown district stages the Light Up Festival, during which every building and road is decorated with many colored light bulbs and sidewalk kiosks offer traditional seasonal delicacies, such as waxed duck. Displays and illuminated decorative sets transform the Marina Promenade in the River Hong Bao festival for Chinese New Year, when a so-called cultural village is created, illustrating the diverse customs and traditions of different parts of China.

K. ROMANO-YOUNG

Food and Drink

Singaporean food includes regional influences from China, Malaysia, Java, Sumatra, India, Thailand, Japan, and Korea. Singapore's location at the hub of East-West trade routes enriches its cuisine with a balance of influences from around the world, but Malay influences are particularly strong.

As in other countries in the region, rice is a staple food in Singapore. Freshly grated coconut or coconut milk is added to most rice recipes to give a characteristic flavor. Many Singaporean dishes benefit from the addition of *belacan*, a fermented shrimp paste that is also popular in Malaysia and Indonesia. The paste is often mixed with a sauce of crushed chilies to make *sambal belacan*, which is a national favorite.

REGIONAL INFLUENCES

The Indonesian cooking style *nasi Padang*, originally from the Padang district of western Sumatra, is popular in Singapore, as is *sota ayam*, a dish of chicken, potato, rice, and bean sprouts. Hainanese chicken rice, in which chicken is served with rice and a ginger sauce, is a favorite, originally from the Hainan region of southern China.

The signature dish of Singaporean cuisine is satay, originally from the Malay Peninsula; satay comprises mutton, beef, or chicken grilled over hot coals and served with peanut sauce, cucumber, onions, and rice. Malay dishes are known for their spiciness and for their fragrance, which come from the blend of galangal, ginger, kaffir lime leaves, lemon grass, garlic, and shallots, along with dried leaves of tamarind, turmeric, saffron, cumin, and coriander. *Nasi lemak*, another Malay favorite, is fragrant rice cooked in coconut milk.

Seafood is a mainstay throughout the region, and Singaporean cooks make use of a wide variety of seafood, from sea cucumber to squid. Crab *bee hoon* is a popular dish of crab served with fried vermicelli noodles, garlic, and chili. A classic Singaporean dish is beef *rendang*, chunks of beef served with herbs and spices with a distinctly Malay flair. A typical menu in Singapore may include such delicacies as chicken in a clay pot, *bak ku teh* (pork rib soup), oyster omelets, chili crab, chili shrimp, plum chicken, and orange-carrot soup. *Otak otak*, spicy fish cakes made as fine as a mousse, served on banana leaves, is a favorite. *Chy tow kueh*, fried carrot cakes, made not from carrots, but from a white raddish, are readily available in the markets and on the street. They are served either "black," with sweet black soy sauce, or "white," without the sauce. Other Singaporean fast foods served as snacks and street food include curry puffs, *char kuey teow* (fried noodles), and *popiah* (spring rolls).

The city-state's Indian population introduced curries and a wide range of dishes from the Indian subcontinent, while the British colonial period also left its mark. In modern times, the city has many restaurants that serve French, Japanese, Italian, and other inter-national cuisines.

DRINKS AND DESSERTS

Popular desserts include cakes baked with coconut milk, puddings, fruit, and ice cream. Tea and coffee are usually served with meals, and tea is available at street stalls everywhere. In 1915, Singapore's famous Raffles Hotel was the birthplace of the Singapore Sling cocktail, a mix of gin, Benedictine, cherry brandy, and club soda.

K. ROMANO-YOUNG

Bustling sidewalk cafes along Bugis Street in Singapore serve Chinese food.

DAILY LIFE

Religion

Because Singapore is home to different ethnic groups, many religions are represented. Religious tolerance has become a matter of public policy and national pride, and while the government exercises a number of controls on religion, tolerance and control are perceived as necessary in a nation with so many different faiths.

Buddhists and followers of Chinese folk religions, including Taoism, account for 51 percent of the population, reflecting the Chinese ancestry of the majority of Singaporeans; Buddhists alone form 43 percent of the population. Muslims account for 15 percent of Singaporeans, and while 10 percent of the population are Protestant Christians, another 5 percent are Roman Catholics. Some 4 percent of Singaporeans are Hindus.

BUDDHISM AND TAOISM

Although Chinese settled in the region centuries earlier, the major influx of ethnic Chinese into Singapore began in the middle of the nineteenth century, bringing with them Buddhism and, later, Taoism. In modern times, both religions have experienced reforms and a new vigor in Singapore. Taoists follow the teachings of Chinese philosopher Lao-tzu (c. 604–c. 531 BCE), who advocated a simple life, noninterference in the course of natural events, and continuity in the constantly

A man prays at the Thian Hock Keng Temple, which is dedicated to a traditional sea goddess and is the oldest temple in Singapore.

changing universe. In the 1990s, Taoist associations in Singapore became involved in social services, promoting care and activities for the elderly, young people, and orphans, and organizing study groups and camps. At the same time, Taoists have concentrated on the more philosophical aspects of the faith. Buddhism, too, has experienced a renaissance in Singapore; Buddhism has become more socially engaged, and Buddhist groups have opened new facilities, including clinics and health centers, schools, and meeting places. They have involved more young people and reformed practices to eliminate elements of ancestor worship. The Singapore Buddhist Federation, led by the abbot of one of the city's temples, increasingly promoted reforms.

MUSLIMS, CHRISTIANS, AND HINDUS

Singapore's ethnic Malays are almost all Sunni Muslims. Muslim affairs come under the Singapore Muslim Religious Council, whose members are nominated by Muslim associations. The council standardizes the practice of Islam, administers trusts, collects tithes and obligatory gifts (*zakat*), and organizes the pilgrimage to Mecca. Since the 1990s, increasing numbers of Muslim parents have exercised their right to send their children to religious schools rather than state schools. The trend worries the Singaporean authorities because religious schools are perceived to offer a curriculum that does not prepare students for modern commercial or industrial life, and the city-state's Muslims are thought to be losing out to the majority Chinese as their educational standards decline.

Christian missionaries arrived in Singapore in 1820. Most converts were Chinese, who belonged to the professional classes. In modern times, many wealthy Chinese in Singapore are Protestant Christians; at the beginning of the twenty-first century, one-third of the members of Singapore's parliament were Chinese Christians. Most Indian Singaporeans are Hindus, although there are also Indian Sikhs, Jains, and Muslims.

K. ROMANO-YOUNG

Family and Society

Singapore is largely a patriarchal society. Its guiding principles are based on those of Confucianism, the ancient Chinese way of life named for its founder Confucius (551–479 BCE), which teaches hierarchical respect: for example, that of citizens for the state, staff for employers, pupils for teachers, and the young for the old.

A patriarchal value system permeates Singaporean society, and in 1996, this tradition found expression in a law requiring children to take financial responsibility for their elderly parents should the need arise. Owing to falling birth rates, government policies since the 1980s have also encouraged larger families. The Baby Bonus program, first introduced in 2001, provides cash incentives for a family's first four children. The amount paid increases for each successive child. Policies such as this promote the traditional family, and there is a strong emphasis on filial responsibility and respect for elders.

Singapore has a series of laws that regulate personal conduct and control society. Large fines are imposed for littering, jaywalking, spitting, not flushing the toilet, smoking in any public place, and other antisocial behavior. Chewing gum (except sugarless gum available as a medical prescription), toy guns and currency, obscene publications, personal weapons, and bulletproof clothing are banned. As well as hefty fines, convicted criminals face long-term imprisonment, caning, or the death penalty. As a result, Singapore has little crime.

Many Singaporeans live in high-rise buildings of small apartments. With such little personal space, good neighbor relations become important in maintaining social harmony.

ETHNIC DIVERSITY

Singapore is a multiethnic nation in which ethnic Chinese dominate the population. As a result, Chinese social customs govern the daily lives of the majority of the city-state's citizens and influence the commonly accepted social behavior of Singaporeans in general. The rights and customs of other ethnicities are respected and protected. The other major groups in Singapore include Malays (who account for 14 percent of the population), Indians who are mainly Tamils (8 percent), and Eurasians and Europeans.

The different minorities have their own family structures and societal values. The Malays are mainly Muslim; some Indian Singaporeans are Buddhists and are also attuned to the precepts of Confucianism. In an effort to forestall possible tensions among the disparate communities, the government has made great efforts to foster social cohesion and to encourage citizens to feel Singaporean rather than Chinese, Malay, or Indian. Patriotic flag-raising and pledge-taking ceremonies are compulsory in all the island's primary and high schools and junior colleges. The policy of the Housing Development Board also requires that each housing district has a mix of different races. This is intended to encourage interaction between different racial groups.

GENDER DIVISIONS

In a patriarchy, men have precedence and dominance over women. This is broadly the case in Singapore, although women have the same civil liberties as men and have had the vote since the foundation of the republic. In some ways, Singaporean women are better educated than men—60 percent of Singaporean women have completed high school, while only 50 percent of men have reached that level. However, no more than 4 percent of the 90-seat national parliament has ever been female (the current world average is 10 percent).

The picture of gender differences is complicated by the active participation of women in the workforce (42 percent of Singaporean women have full-time jobs). While women in Singapore currently earn less than their male equivalents, the income gap is steadily diminishing, from a 32 percent difference to a 25 percent difference in the last decade of the twentieth century. Muslim (mainly Malay) women in Singapore are protected by the Women's Charter Act (1961), which gave women a number of rights, including property rights and a right to trade, although there is also a Muslim Law Act, which empowers Sharia (Islamic law) courts to oversee religious marriages.

H. RUSSELL

Welfare and Education

Singapore has an effective welfare system that provides state support for the elderly and the sick, although private alternatives are also available. The government spends a considerable amount of its budget on education and provides housing for the majority of Singaporeans.

Health care in Singapore is mainly financed by compulsory individual savings accounts, into which all working citizens must pay a large portion of their net income (20 percent in 2005). An employer adds a further 13 percent contribution to the savings account. The requirement is different for the self-employed, who, depending on age, must contribute between 6 and 8 percent of their net annual income into their account.

Collectively, the savings accounts raise two-thirds of the funding for the nation's medical services. There is also a state-financed safety net to provide funds to treat victims of chronic illnesses and serious injuries that prevent them from working. The state also finances the health care of the poorest members of society. Within this statutory framework there is some latitude; the government permits citizens to choose between the state plan, known as Medisave, and private equivalents. For people aged 55 and over, part of the monthly payment is invested in a retirement account, the balance of which must be maintained above a certain level (25,000 Singapore dollars in 2003). From age 62, Singaporeans may retire and draw from the account. In 2006, life expectancy in Singapore was 81.7 years, compared with 77.9 years in the United States; retirement accounts therefore would be expected to provide for 20 years on average.

The state welfare system has some advantages, for example, ensuring contributions from all workers to fund their health care and welfare. However, the system spreads its revenue too thinly—typically more than 70 percent of an individual's contributions are withdrawn from their account before they reach retirement age, thereby reducing their own individual pension fund. Consequently, the retirement age was increased in 1999 from 60 to 62, and a further increase has been suggested. Because the state does not finance welfare in the same way as in most developed countries, and since the government actively regulates the supply and price of health care services, general taxation levels are low. Funds raised through worker contributions are paid into a Central Provident Fund (CPF), which finances home purchases, insurance, and education.

EDUCATION

Singapore spends 20 percent of its annual budget on education. Schooling in the city-state is free, apart from small charges for materials and equipment, and is compulsory from age 6 through 15. The language of instruction is English, which is one of the compulsory core subjects, together with the student's mother tongue (Chinese, Malay, or an Indian language), math, and science. Since 1984, the Gifted Education Program (GEP) at the high-school level accelerates the most able pupils. There are six tertiary institutions: the National University of Singapore (NUS) and five polytechnics. In 2004, the NUS came eighteenth in the World University Ranking list compiled annually by the British newspaper *The Times*.

HOUSING

Most domestic residences in Singapore are built and maintained by the state Housing and Development Board (HDB). About 85 percent of Singaporeans live in HDB accommodation. Although HDB homes are built as public housing, around 90 percent of people living in HDB homes purchase them. Most apartments constructed for the program have two, three, or four bedrooms; there are also some HDB executive apartments, which have three bedrooms and separate dining and living rooms in a total area of about 1,600 square feet (150 sq. m).

H. RUSSELL

These secondary school students are following an accelerated course of study called the Gifted Education Program (GEP), which includes advanced studies both in their mother tongue and in English.

Singapore City

Singapore is one of three nations in the world that is both a city and a sovereign state. The city-state is one of the world's greatest ports, and it is among the most prosperous and modern cities in the region.

From the seventh through the thirteenth centuries, a walled city called Temasek flourished on the site of modern Singapore. Temasek was an outpost of the Hindu Srivijayan Empire that was centered in Sumatra, and its fortunes rose and fell with those of Srivijaya. By the fourteenth century, the island was also known as Singapura (Sanskrit for "Lion City"). In the fifteenth century, the powerful sultanate of Malacca (modern Melaka) conquered Temasek, and in the following century, after Malacca fell to the Portuguese, Temasek was taken by the sultanate of Johor on the southern tip of the Malay Peninsula. In 1617, during the Malay-Portuguese wars, the Portuguese burned Temasek, after which the city declined and eventually disappeared, although archaeologial evidence of the ancient city can still be found in Singapore.

THE RISE OF SINGAPORE

In 1819, Thomas Stamford Raffles (1781–1826), an administrator employed by the British East India Company, signed a treaty with the sultan of Johor to establish a trading post on the island that had been known as Temasek, but was by then called Singapore. Raffles saw the potential of the site, with its natural port beside a channel through which shipping between Europe and India in the west and China in the east had to pass. In 1824, Johor ceded the island of Singapore to the East India Company, and two years later, the British authorities organized Singapore, the Malay island of Penang, and Malacca into the Straits Settlements territory. In 1832, Singapore became the capital of the territory, and the rapid growth of the city and port began.

The British developed Singapore—a colony from 1867—into a major port. In 1869, the opening of the Suez Canal linking the the Indian Ocean with the Mediterranean Sea and northern Europe provided a boost to shipping, and the growing tin and rubber trade in the Malay Peninsula led to the construction of miles of wharves in Singapore. Large numbers of migrants from China and India, as well as from the Malay Peninsula and the East Indies (modern Indonesia), settled in Singapore. In 1921, the British naval base in Singapore was also greatly expanded.

The development of the city came to a halt in December 1941, when Japanese forces bombed Singapore during World War II (1939–1945). In February 1942, Japan took Singapore and held the island until September 1945. Postwar Singapore again developed rapidly, and British rule ended in 1963, when Singapore joined the new Federation of Malaysia. In 1965, the city became an independent sovereign state when Singapore withdrew from Malaysia.

One of the world's most famous hotels, the Raffles Hotel was named for the "father of Singapore," Thomas Stamford Raffles (1781–1826). The hotel, which was founded in 1887, was declared a Singaporean national monument in 1987.

MODERN SINGAPORE

The built-up area of the city of Singapore covers the greater part of the island. The downtown area is in the southern part of the island, and the main modern port district and much of Singapore's industry is centered in Jurong district in the southwest. Other industries, such as information technology, have been established in the northeast around Changi International Airport and the Changi Business Park. Residential areas stretch northward, forming a continuous zone of housing, as well as industrial parks and urban amenities, right across the island to the causeway that links Singapore with Johor in Malaysia.

Singapore is a multiethnic city, and different ethnic quarters are popular with visitors. Little India, a focal point for the city's Tamil, Telegu, and Bengali communities, has many small shops that sell spices, textiles and saris, brassware and silverware, and other decorative items. As well as small provision shops, the district has colorful temples.

About 77 percent of Singaporeans are ethnic Chinese, and Chinatown, a district of brightly painted shop-houses with covered sidewalks, is at the center of much of the city's social life. Chinatown has several different areas, including Bukit Pasoh (the Street of Clans), which is known for its cafés. The night market in Bugis Street is a popular tourist attraction, and

Multistory office buildings overlook the government and court buildings along the Singapore River in downtown Singapore.

Singapore is a major shopping center; the principal multistory malls are in the Orchard Road district, which is also home to many hotels. The most famous hotel in Singapore is the Raffles Hotel, an elegant nineteenth-century building.

The downtown area of Singapore centers upon the Boat Quay, along the western bank of the Singapore River, whose skyline of towering skyscrapers is one of the city's most photographed sights. A group of buildings from the British colonial period adjoins the central business district, including the former parliament (now the Arts House; built in 1827), the cricket club (established in 1852), which is dwarfed by multistory office buildings, City Hall (1929), and the Supreme Court (1939). Beyond the downtown area, tall apartment buildings dot the landscape, but some traditional Malay *kampung*s (villages) remain alongside British colonial architecture. The best view of the city is seen from Mount Faber inland.

Singapore's industries include food processing, timber, tin smelting, oil refining, electrical and electronic engineering, rubber processing, and a wide variety of consumer goods industries. The city is also a major banking, insurance, and commercial center, with one of Asia's three most important stock markets. In modern times, Singapore has become the financial capital of Southeast Asia. The city's educational establishments include the National University of Singapore.

The island of Sentosa, a short ride from Singapore Island by ferry or cable car, is a busy, popular resort and amusement theme park that includes a beach, an aquarium, and a replica village. Other tourist attractions on Sentosa include two historical exhibits: Images of Singapore shows the history of the island from the seventeenth to the twentieth centuries, while Fort Siloso gives visitors an insight into life in the British Army during the colonial years. The city zoo, which is famous for its "night safari" of nocturnal animals, and the bird garden at Jurong are also popular destinations.

C. CARPENTER

ECONOMY

With a population of around 4 million, Singapore is a vibrant industrial and financial center. The country's free-trade policies have stimulated high rates of growth since the mid-1960s, and Singaporeans enjoy a standard of living equivalent to that of western European nations.

Singapore comprises a tropical island, along with a number of islets, situated off the southern tip of the Malay Peninsula. In 2005, the city-state covered 269 square miles (697 sq. km), but the state gets bigger almost every year because of a continuing program to reclaim land from the sea. Much of the reclamation activity involves joining some of the small islets together, or to the main island, and reclaiming the land in between.

ECONOMIC CHALLENGES

Singapore grew as a trading post, gathering the raw materials of the region for export, mainly to Europe. The city began to transform itself from a trading post into an industrial center when it was granted self-government by the British in 1959, and the program gained pace after the state achieved full independence in 1965. The basic strategy of the Singaporean government was to create a niche for itself in the world market as a site of cheap and reliable manufacture. The authorities went to great lengths to attract companies, mostly from the United States but also from Japan and Europe. In the early 1960s, Singapore had high unemployment and inner-city slums, but by the middle of the 1970s, it had achieved full employment and shifted most of the population into new high-rise apartment buildings. To make Singapore attractive to foreign investment, the government kept wages low, brought labor unions under strict control, and began teaching adult workers new skills suitable for factory work. As a long-term plan to make Singapore more competitive, the government also required students to learn English.

In the 1980s, the government reformed its economic strategy because it feared the challenge of emerging competition from new competitors, such as China, Malaysia, Indonesia, and Thailand, which could manufacture even more cheaply than Singapore. In what became known as the "second industrial revolution," Singapore set out to become a provider of services and upscale products to the region and to the world; it developed knowledge-intensive activities, such as research and development, engineering design, and computer software services.

Since the early 1990s, Singapore has developed what it calls an "external wing" to overcome the limitations of Singapore's small physical size and small domestic market by deriving a larger share of the country's income from overseas enterprises that are owned by Singaporean companies. As a result, Singapore has invested capital and personnel overseas, especially in the Asia-Pacific region, looking for higher returns. Examples include investment in the Suzhou Industrial Estate in China, a joint development with Indonesia of the Indonesian islands of Bintan and Batam as industrial and tourist estates, and the purchase of telecommunication companies, such as Optus in Australia.

Singapore has worked to position itself as a knowledge-based economy with emphasis on services such as research and development, biotechnology, health and medical services, and higher education. The local education system was upgraded to produce computer-literate graduates to help facilitate this development. The city-state is also moving to become less reliant upon traditional domestic manufacturing and processing by developing manufacturing abroad.

Singapore survived the Asian financial crisis of 1997 and 1998 with minor damage to its economy, but since then it has struggled to maintain its edge. Malaysia and China have begun to rival Singapore in many fields, giving the transition away from traditional industries a greater sense of urgency. The Singaporean authorities have now prioritized development programs that will make the city-state less vulnerable to cycles in international business and to offer high-tech and financial services for which demand is constant in the world market.

RESOURCES

Singapore has only two natural resources, its strategic position and its deep harbor. The port lies astride one of the busiest waterways in the world through which passes one-third of the world's global trade and one-half of the world's oil supply.

Standard of Living

Singapore has a high standard of living, with most people earning an income comparable to their counterparts in the biggest Western economies. The per capita gross domestic product (GDP) was $28,600 in 2005; this figure is adjusted for purchasing power parity (PPP), a formula that allows comparison between living standards in different countries.

Singapore is, therefore, ideally positioned for shipping, ship-building, and oil refining industries. The city is also well placed as a stopover for long-distance flights, particularly those between Australia and Europe.

AGRICULTURE

Singapore has had virtually no agricultural output since the 1970s, when the Singaporean government wound up most of the small agricultural sector in favor of developing the country's manufacturing base. The state leases small plots of between 5 and 75 acres (2–30 hectares) to farming companies to produce vegetables and flowers, eggs, or milk on biotechnology parks

EMPLOYMENT IN SINGAPORE

Sector	Percentage of labor force
Manufacturing	18
Construction	6
Transportation and communication	11
Financial, business, and other services	49
Other	16

Source: Government of Singapore, 2003

In 2005, government figures showed that 3.1 percent of the labor force was unemployed.

using advanced mechanization and hydroponics. A small fishing industry is centered on the port of Jurong, in southwestern Singapore, but fishing has been in decline since the 1960s, and the city-state imports fish.

INDUSTRY

In the first period of industrial expansion between the 1950s and the 1970s, the government set up statutory boards and government-owned companies (government-linked companies or GLCs). The industries that were the key to Singapore's success in this period were the petroleum industry, shipbuilding, textiles, and finance and banking. Other industries that grew in the period include tourism, transportation (both airlines and shipping lines and the port), and defense technologies.

Major new industries developed through the 1980s including electronics and precision equipment, engineering and environmental services, communications, chemicals, aeronautics, and logistics and transportation engineering. At the same time, the city took a leading role in the data storage market. Singapore has consolidated its position in the world electronics market by heavily investing in electronic goods used for data storage and is the market leader in the manufacturing of such goods.

Companies in Singapore now produce hard-disk drives and other storage devices that generate more than 30 percent of total global output. The data storage industry represents the biggest sector in Singapore's electronics industry, and the country's annual output in 2004 was 50 million units. In order to achieve this position, Singapore introduced initial

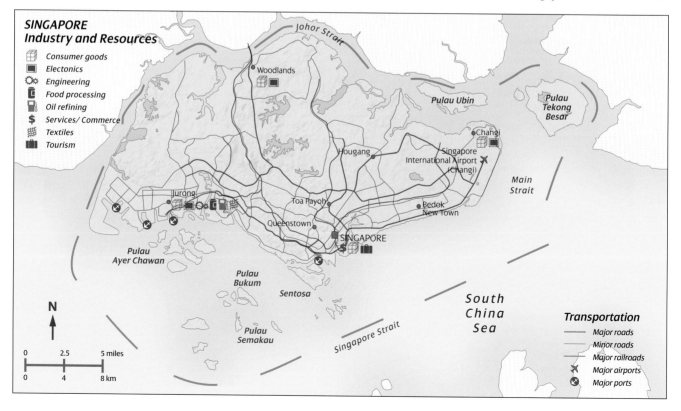

economic and tax incentives for electronics companies, as well as providing general industrial support and training and research facilities.

In 1992, Singapore opened a technology center called the Magnetics Technology Centre, which, in 1996, became the Data Storage Institute (DSI). The center's research has since expanded to include optical storage technology. Rated among the top research-and-development centers in the world, the DSI has attracted international attention and made Singapore a world leader in electronics innovation and development.

SERVICES

Through the last quarter of the twentieth century, the government steered the economy to become increasingly dependent on providing services to the region and the world. Since the 1990s, Singapore has become the key regional hub for biomedical sciences and services, education services, infocommunications and media, professional services, and so-called "shared services," which are infrastructure facilities designed to entice multinational corporations to set up their regional headquarters in Singapore.

The Economic Development Board, a statutory authority operating since 1961, initiates new local industries and attracts international corporations to set up factories and bases in Singapore. The program has earned Singaporeans the highest standard of living in the region (and the highest in Asia outside Japan), but it is a strategy fraught with risk. Should Singapore lose its competitive advantages over its neighbors, then both its neighbors and the multinationals will stop using its services. Singapore's most obvious local competitor is Malaysia, which has developed airport and seaport facilities to rival those of Singapore, but threats are also emerging from Thailand and Dubai (in the United Arab Emirates), which are challenging Singapore's dominance as an air route hub.

SINGAPORE'S GDP

Singapore's gross domestic product (GDP) was $126.5 billion in 2005. The figure is adjusted for purchasing power parity (PPP), an exchange rate at which goods in one country cost the same as goods in another. PPP allows a comparison between the living standards in different nations.

Main contributors to Singapore's GDP

Agriculture	0 percent
Industry	33.9 percent
Services	66.1 percent

Source: CIA, 2005

Tourism is a major industry, relying in part upon long-haul air travelers making stopovers. Shopping is an important attraction, and the retail sector has rapidly expanded. In an attempt to attract additional visitors, the government reversed its longstanding opposition to gambling and established two casino complexes in 2005. Commerce and banking are major employers, and Singapore has one of Asia's three principal stock markets.

TRADE

Singapore's major exports are oil and petrochemicals, chemicals, electronics, precision engineering, transport engineering, food, beverages, pharmaceuticals and other medical products, and printing. Corporations in Singapore export large numbers of components that are sold to manufacturers in other countries, particularly in neighboring countries in Southeast Asia. In 2005, Singapore exported goods and services worth $204.8 billion. The leading recipients of its exports are China including Hong Kong (which imports 20 percent of Singapore's exports), Malaysia (15 percent), the United States (12 percent), Indonesia (11 percent), Japan, Thailand, and Australia. Singapore imported goods and services worth $188.3 billion in 2005, with most imports coming from Malaysia (14 percent), the United States (12 percent), China including Hong Kong (11 percent), Japan (10 percent), Indonesia, Saudi Arabia, South Korea, and Taiwan. The principal imports include machinery and equipment, mineral fuels, chemicals, and foodstuffs. Singapore relies upon the free and unhindered flow of trade; the city-state has been a champion of free trade agreements (FTAs) and has signed FTAs with many trading partners, including New Zealand, Australia, Japan, the United States, Jordan, Brunei, Chile, India, and South Korea.

TRANSPORTATION AND COMMUNICATION

Singapore has a comprehensive public transportation system of buses and a light railroad system called the Mass Rapid Transit. The only freight train service in Singapore is the service into Malaysia. The high-quality road system of 2,010 miles (3,234 km) of roads includes 94 miles (150 km) of expressway. Government policy ensures that private cars are expensive to own and run, so most of the population relies on public transportation. Changi International Airport is an important air route hub, and the national carrier, Singapore Airlines, is commercially successful. In 2004, Changi handled 28.6 million passengers. The port, the largest part of which is at Jurong, in southwestern Singapore, is the second-largest in the world in terms of freight handled and is also the world's largest container port.

Singapore is serviced by high-quality telephone and Internet providers. Mobile cellular phones are ubiquitous; in 2005, there were some 4.4 million cellular phones (more than one phone per person). In the same year, there were 1.9 million telephone lines, and 2.4 million Singaporeans had Internet access.

M. BARR

Further Research

WORLD GEOGRAPHY

Brown, James H., and Mark V. Lomolino. *Biogeography*. Sunderland, MA: Sinauer Associates Publishers, 1998.

Butzer, Karl W. *Geomorphology from the Earth*. Reading, MA: Addison-Wesley Educational Publishers, 1976.

Clark, Audrey N. *Longman Dictionary of Geography: Human and Physical*. New York: Longman, 1985.

Lydolph, Paul E. *Weather and Climate*. Lanham, MD: Rowman and Littlefield, 1985.

National Geographic Family Reference Atlas. Washington, DC: National Geographic Society, 2004.

Strahler, Arthur N., and Alan H. Strahler. *Modern Physical Geography*. 3rd ed. Hoboken, NJ: John Wiley and Sons, 1987.

Times Atlas of the World: Comprehensive Edition. New York: Crown Publishers, 1999.

Trewartha, Glenn T., and Lyle H. Horn. *An Introduction to Climate*. 5th ed. New York: McGraw-Hill, 1980.

REGIONAL GEOGRAPHY, HISTORY, AND CULTURAL EXPRESSION

Goda, Toh. *Postcolonialism and Local Politics in Southeast Asia*. Quezon City, Philippines: New Day Publishers, 2003.

Hutchison, Charles S. *Geology of North West Borneo: Sarawak, Brunei, and Sabah*. Boston: Elsevier, 2005.

Major, John S. *The Land and People of Malaysia and Brunei*. New York: HarperCollins, 1991.

Peoples of Eastern Asia. New York: Marshall Cavendish, 2004.

Tong, Cheu Hock, ed. *Chinese Beliefs and Practices in Southeast Asia: Studies on the Chinese Religion in Malaysia, Singapore, and Indonesia*. Selangor Darul Ehsan, Malaysia: Pelanduk Publications, 1993.

Turnbull, C. M. *A History of Malaysia, Singapore, and Brunei*. Boston: Allen and Unwin, 1989.

TRAVEL LITERATURE

Craig, JoAnn. *Culture Shock! Singapore*. Portland, OR: Graphic Arts Center Publishing, 1996.

Hamilton-Paterson, James. *Playing with Water: Passion and Solitude on a Philippine Island*. New York: New Amsterdam, 1987.

Malaysia, Singapore, and Brunei. New York: Rough Guides, 2003.

Rutledge, Len. *Maverick Guide to Malaysia and Singapore*. Gretna, LA: Pelican Publishing, 1992.

Welcome to Brunei Darussalam: The Complete Traveller's Guide. Bandar Seri Begawan, Brunei Darussalam: Brunei Press, 2000.

BRUNEI

Al-Sufri, Jamil, Haji Awang Mohamed, and Haji Mohamed Amin Hasan, trans., eds. *History of Brunei in Brief*. Bandar Seri Begawan: Brunei History Centre, Ministry of Culture, Youth and Sports, 2000.

Arief, Sritua. *The Brunei Economy*. East Balmain, NSW, Australia: Rosecons, 1986.

Chalfont, Arthur Gwynne Jones. *By God's Will: A Portrait of the Sultan of Brunei*. New York: Weidenfeld and Nicolson, 1989.

Hock, Khoo Soo. *Brunei in Transition: Aspects of Its Human Geography in the Sixties*. Kuala Lumpur: Department of Geography, University of Malaya, 1976.

Hussainmiya, B. A. *Sultan Omar Ali Saifuddin III and Britain: The Making of Brunei Darussalam*. New York: Oxford University Press, 1995.

Kaloko, Franklyn R. *Longhouse Communities in Ulu Belait in Brunei Darussalam*. Bandar Seri Begawan, Brunei Darussalam: Department of Geography, Faculty of Arts and Social Sciences, Universiti Brunei Darussalam, 1998.

Saunders, Graham E. *A History of Brunei*. New York: RoutledgeCurzon, 2002.

Singh, Ranjit. *Brunei, 1839–1983: The Problems of Political Survival*. New York: Oxford University Press, 1984.

MALAYSIA

Doolittle, Amity Appell. *Property and Politics in Sabah, Malaysia: Native Struggles over Land Rights*. Seattle: University of Washington Press, 2005.

Drabble, John H. *An Economic History of Malaysia, c. 1800–1990: The Transition to Modern Economic Growth*. New York: St. Martin's Press, 2000.

Guile, Melanie. *Culture in Malaysia*. Chicago, IL: Raintree, 2005.

Hill, R. D. *Agriculture in the Malaysian Region*. Budapest: Akadémiai Kiadó, 1982.

Ibrahim, Ahmad. *The Administration of Islamic Law in Malaysia*. Kuala Lumpur, Malaysia: Institute of Islamic Understanding Malaysia, 2000.

Judith, A. *Malaysian Mosaic: Perspectives from a Polyethnic Society*. Vancouver: University of British Columbia Press, 1979.

Ling, Alex. *Twilight of the White Rajahs*. Kuching, Sarawak, Malaysia: A. Ling, 1997.

Pringle, Robert. *Rajahs and Rebels: The Ibans of Sarawak under Brooke Rule, 1841–1941*. Ithaca, NY: Cornell University Press, 1970.

Roff, William R. *The Origins of Malay Nationalism*. New Haven, CT: Yale University Press, 1967.

Vincent, Jeffrey R., and Rozali Mohamed Ali. *Managing Natural Wealth: Environment and Development in Malaysia*. Washington, DC: RFF Press, 2005.

SINGAPORE

Chen, Peter S. J., ed. *Singapore Development Policies and Trends*. New York: Oxford University Press, 1983.

Chew, Ernest C. T., and Edwin Lee, eds. *A History of Singapore*. New York: Oxford University Press, 1991.

Clammer, J. R. *The Sociology of Singapore Religion: Studies in Christianity and Chinese Culture*. Singapore: Chopmen Publishers, 1991.

Doshi, Tilak. *Houston of Asia: The Singapore Petroleum Industry*. Singapore: ASEAN Economic Research Unit, Institute of Southeast Asian Studies, 1989.

Li, Tania. *Malays in Singapore: Culture, Economy, and Ideology*. New York: Oxford University Press, 1989.

Lim, Linda, and Pang Eng Fong. *Trade, Employment, and Industrialisation in Singapore*. Geneva: International Labour Office, 1986.

Moore, Donald, and Joanna Moore. *The First 150 Years of Singapore*. Singapore: Donald Moore Press (distributed in North America by Cellar Book Shop, Detroit, MI), 1969.

Murfett, Malcolm. *Between Two Oceans: A Military History of Singapore from First Settlement to Final British Withdrawal*. Singapore: Marshall Cavendish Academic, 2004.

Peterson, William. *Theater and the Politics of Culture in Contemporary Singapore*. Middletown, CT: Wesleyan University Press, 2001.

Régnier, Philippe. *Singapore, City-state in South-East Asia*. Translated by Christopher Hurst. Honolulu: University of Hawaii Press, 1991.

Sandhu, Kernial Singh, and Paul Wheatley, eds. *Management of Success: The Molding of Modern Singapore*. Boulder, CO: Westview Press, 1990.

Yen, Ching-huang. *A Social History of the Chinese in Singapore and Malaya, 1800–1911*. New York: Oxford University Press, 1986.

THE PHILIPPINES

Broad, Robin, and John Cavanagh. *Plundering Paradise: The Struggle for the Environment in the Philippines*. Berkeley, CA: University of California Press, 1993.

Constantino, Renato. *A History of the Philippines: From the Spanish Colonization to the Second World War*. New York: Monthly Review Press, 1975.

Davis, Leonard. *The Philippines: People, Poverty, and Politics*. New York: St. Martin's Press, 1987.

Phelan, John Leddy. *The Hispanization of the Philippines: Spanish Aims and Filipino Responses, 1565–1700*. Madison: University of Wisconsin Press, 1959.

Sakili, Abraham P. *Space and Identity: Expressions in the Culture, Arts, and Society of the Muslims in the Philippines*. Quezon City: Asian Center, University of the Philippines, 2003.

Salita, Domingo C., and Dominador Z. Rosell. *Economic Geography of the Philippines*. Bicutan: National Research Council of the Philippines, 1980.

Shirley, Steven. *Guided by God: The Legacy of the Catholic Church in Philippine Politics*. Singapore: Marshall Cavendish Academic, 2004.

Wernstedt, Frederick L., and J. E. Spencer. *The Philippine Island World: A Physical, Cultural, and Regional Geography*. Berkeley: University of California Press, 1967.

PERIODICALS AND OTHER MEDIA

Federspiel, Howard M. "Islam and Muslims in the Southern Territories of the Philippine Islands during the American Colonial Period (1898 to 1946)." *Journal of Southeast Asian Studies* 29 (1998): 340–356.

Rahim, Lily Zubaidah. "Singapore-Malaysia Relations: Deep-Seated Tensions and Self-Fulfilling Prophecies." *Journal of Contemporary Asia* 29 (1999): 38–55.

Yusop, Mohamad. "Historical Dictionary of Brunei Darussalam: Asian/Oceanian Historical Dictionaries, no. 25." *Pacific Affairs* 72 (1999): 288–289.

ELECTRONIC RESOURCES

Asian Governments on the WWW.
www.gksoft.com/govt/en/asia.html

Asia Society.
Asiasociety.org (for Asian educational resources).

The World Factbook. CIA.
http://www.odci.gov/cia/publications/factbook/index.html (for facts about Brunei, Malaysia, Singapore, and the Philippines).

Index

WORLD AND ITS PEOPLES

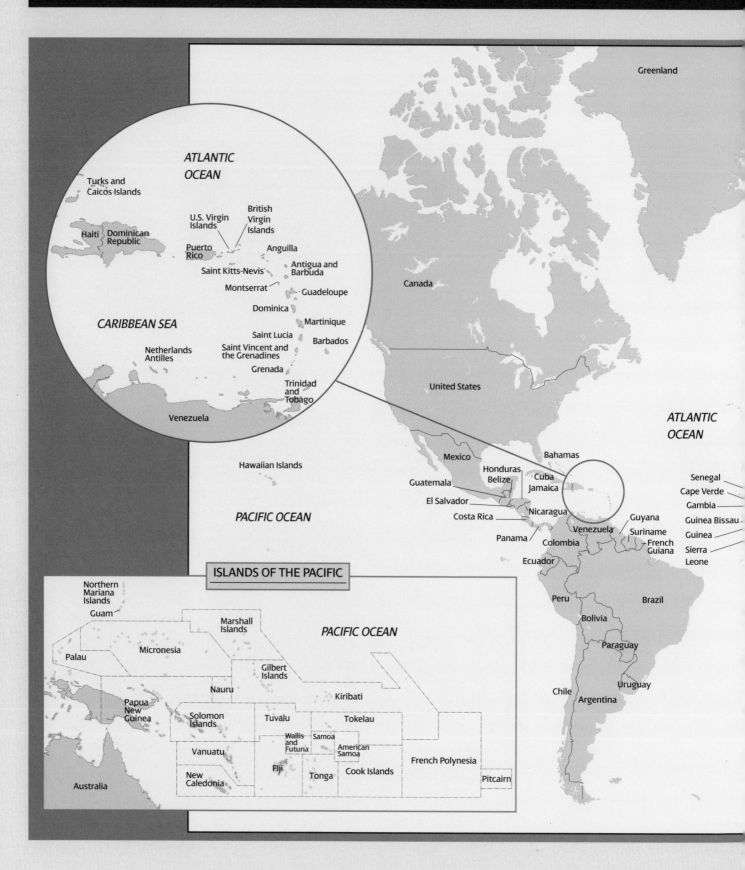

ATLANTIC OCEAN

Turks and Caicos Islands

Haiti | Dominican Republic

U.S. Virgin Islands

British Virgin Islands

Puerto Rico

Anguilla

Saint Kitts-Nevis

Antigua and Barbuda

Montserrat

Guadeloupe

Dominica

Martinique

CARIBBEAN SEA

Saint Lucia

Barbados

Netherlands Antilles

Saint Vincent and the Grenadines

Grenada

Trinidad and Tobago

Venezuela

Greenland

Canada

United States

ATLANTIC OCEAN

Hawaiian Islands

Mexico

Bahamas

Honduras

Cuba

Belize

Jamaica

Guatemala

El Salvador

Costa Rica

Nicaragua

Panama

Venezuela

Colombia

Ecuador

Guyana

Suriname

French Guiana

Senegal

Cape Verde

Gambia

Guinea Bissau

Guinea

Sierra Leone

PACIFIC OCEAN

Peru

Brazil

Bolivia

Paraguay

Chile

Uruguay

Argentina

ISLANDS OF THE PACIFIC

Northern Mariana Islands

Guam

Marshall Islands

PACIFIC OCEAN

Palau

Micronesia

Gilbert Islands

Nauru

Papua New Guinea

Solomon Islands

Kiribati

Tuvalu

Tokelau

Wallis and Futuna

Samoa

Vanuatu

Fiji

American Samoa

French Polynesia

New Caledonia

Tonga

Cook Islands

Pitcairn

Australia